AF247481

Also by Ted Gardner:

The Paper Dynasty

(and a few others
that no publisher
in his right mind
would touch).

Off The

WALL

THE NEWSPAPER COLUMNS OF TED GARDNER

ALLEN A. KNOLL, PUBLISHERS

Copyright © 1993
Allen A. Knoll, Publishers
777 Silver Spur Road
Palos Verdes, California 90274

Hey, it's all make-believe. Oh, maybe some of these celebrity names will ring a bell, but it's all a wild coincidence. Just remember, it's fiction through and through.

Most of these pieces first appeared in the Palos Verdes Peninsula *News* and Rolling Hills *Herald*, some in a slightly different form, depending on how meddlesome the editor was.

*A signed first edition was not
privately printed by the Franklin Library.*

First Edition

Publisher's Cataloging in Publicaion

Gardner, Theodore Roosevelt.
    Off the wall : the newspaper columns of Ted Gardner. -- 1st ed.
    p. cm.
    Includes index.
    Preassigned LCCN 93-77062
    ISBN 0-9627297-7-9

    I. Title

PS3357.A7146044 1993   814. '54
                                        QBI93-191

Dedication

I
should
like
to
dedicate
this
book
to
my
wife,
Ginny.

But
that
just
won't
be
possible.

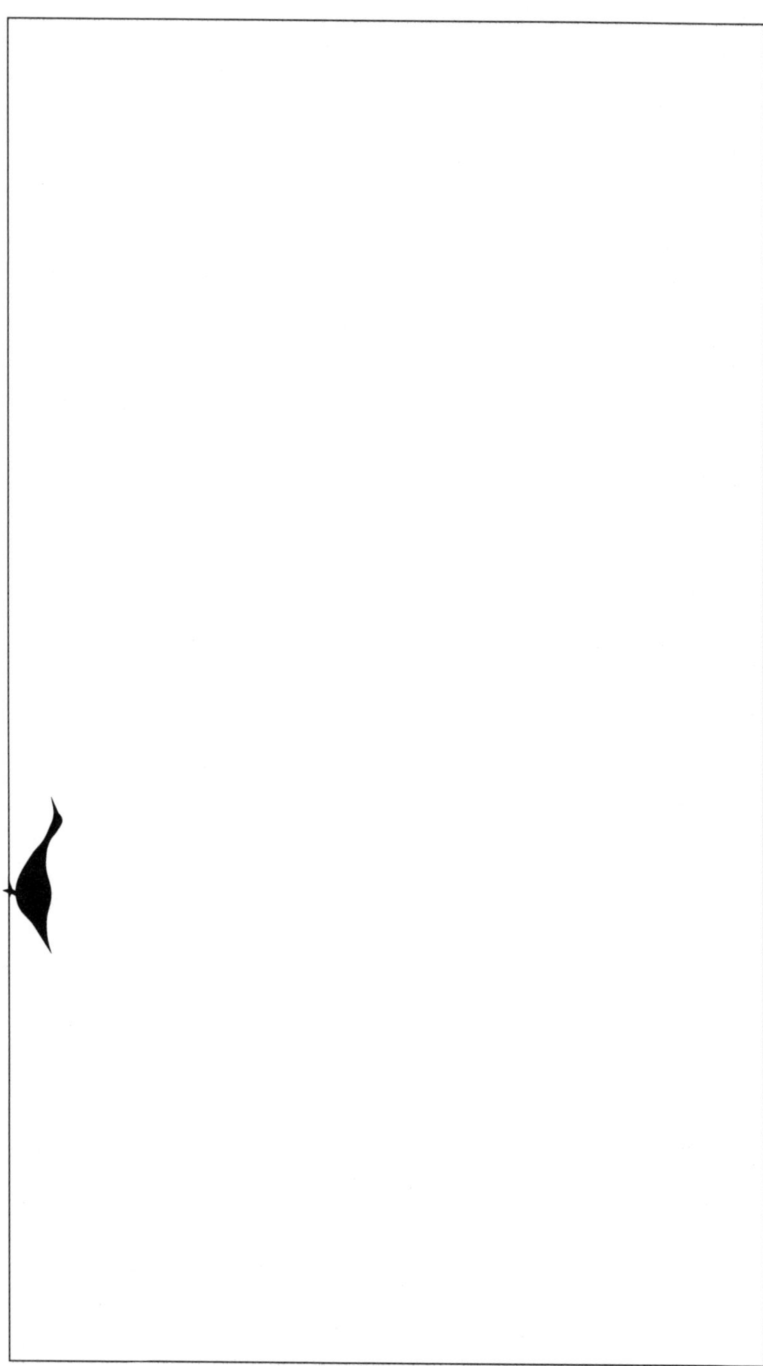

Forward march!

This book is real funny.

—Hester Honeyfunkle

(Hester has been, heretofore, backward)

 would like to thank the following institutions for their generous grants, enabling me to complete this book without having to work for a living: the Ford Foundation, the Rockefeller Foundation, the Mellon Foundation, the Guggenheim Foundation, the Corset Foundation and the Warring-Porridge Foundation.

Unfortunately none of them gave me a farthing.

Acknowledgments

The following people have put their noodles to a whole mess of these pieces in an effort to separate the wheat from the chaff. I would like to thank them now—even those I paid: Giulio Anfuso, Ruth Butler, Elaine Cappleman, Barbara Coe, Abby Gardner, Julia Gardner, Dianna Kinder and Mary Theresa McRae.

Even so, every now and then a little chaff slipped through.

Table of Contents

OFF THE

WALL

(In case you forgot.)

Boola Boola

Almost forty years after losing my battle with the Scholastic Aptitude Test, I take perverse pleasure in seeing the importance of these scores questioned.

Lux et Veritas, light and truth, are emblazoned on the Yale coat of arms. Of the many illuminating truths one suffers in a lifetime, perhaps none is as painful as when it becomes apparent your adolescent dream will not become a reality.

It never occurred to me that Yale might not be eager to have me wear their blue blazer with light and truth on my breast.

Paul Hindemith, the neoclassical German composer, was what attracted me to Yale. In my checkered career as a musician I had played the tuba. My favorite tuba part was in Hindemith's *Symphonic Metamorphosis on a Theme of Carl Maria Von Weber*.

I fancied myself a composer. I had written and directed our school's musical comedy, *That's for Sure*, as well as a symphony liberally employing the intervals of the octave and the fifth, some startling arrangements for band, chorus and our tiny high school orchestra. Hindemith and Yale were for me.

A visit to the campus and the ivy-covered brick Gothic buildings exhilarated me. In those hallowed halls I would surely meet the fellows who would offer me the job as music director of CBS. I would blend into the old boy network even before I was old.

I went home singing:

> Boola boola
> Boola boola
> Boola boola
> Eli Yale

the words presenting a young man of my intellect minimal challenge.

Definitely Yale material.

So confident was I of admission to Yale that I hadn't bothered to apply anywhere else.

Then the college entrance exam paper was put in front of me and I had to take my special pencil and blacken the appropriate circles. The *lux* faded in this moment of *veritas*. Those circles all looked alike to me.

Yale's dean of admissions was Alfred P. Noyes, Jr. His last name was a bizarre combination of the two words he needed as the tools of his trade. The message in the letter I got from him contained the first two letters of his surname, not the last three.

Realizing there must be some serious mistake, I called Yale's admissions office to request a personal audience with the dean. Of course they would be happy to oblige, but they did want to make it clear that the decision of the department of admissions was final and it might not be worth the four-hour trip.

Undaunted, I insisted. After all, I was a man (seventeen) who never left a stone unturned. That in itself should impress the dean. After all, what were old and impersonal scores next to a man with consummate drive and ambition? I drove north from my little town of Emmaus, Pennsylvania (Christ met Doubting Thomas on the road to Emmaus—Nazareth and Bethlehem are nearby), and went to confront Mr. Alfred P. Noyes, Jr.

On the four-hour drive I rehearsed my strategy. I would be polite and humble, but press my irrefutable qualifications: Senior Class President, lead in *Harvey* the class play, yearbook, newspaper, debate club, and all the music stuff. Maybe S.A.T.'s didn't measure all types of intelligence.

I would blame my S.A.T. deficiency on my small, slightly bucolic, high school, but I would be careful not to ask to take the test again, because the prospect terrified me. Never had I seen questions so foreign to my intellect.

I would wow him with my statesmanship, and he would say, "Well, perhaps we made a mistake, Mr. Gardner." He always called seventeen-year-olds "Mister." Alfred P. Noyes, Jr. was a Yalie himself. He knew how to talk to us future Yalies.

I would return home with a minimum prize of being

placed on the waiting list by a contrite and grateful Alfred P. Noyes, Jr.

Central casting could not have done better. If it was Jimmy Stewart for governor and Ronald Reagan for his best friend, it was Alfred P. Noyes, Jr. as dean of admissions, Yale University (*Lux et Veritas*). He wore proudly the blue blazer with the shiny brass buttons, and the Yale coat of arms over his heart. He had graying hair slicked back on his classical head, and he had the mien of a senator and the might of a king.

I bared my soul to Alfred P. Noyes, Jr. I told him how much it meant to me to go to Yale, to study with Paul Hindemith. I had been composing music for six years already, and I came from a small town where they were not sophisticated about things like the College Boards. He told me a lot of water would have to pass under the bridge before a greenhorn freshman got to Paul Hindemith. It was a liberal arts college, and the requirements were both numerous and stiff. It was a university where they put the emphasis on a rounded education, not a trade school where jobs were learned.

"I understand," I said. And I was sorry my scores were so low that Yale just couldn't deign to consider me, but were I given special dispensation, I was sure I could do the work.

Mr. Alfred P. Noyes, Jr. fixed me with his Ivy League eyes and said, in pear-shaped New England tones, "Mistah Gahdner, we have certain standards here. We have found out over the years who will succeed with our work load and who will not. We do not do favors to the latter by confusing them with the former."

And in that moment Alfred P. Noyes, Jr. (*Lux et Veritas*) found his soul suffused with all the sophistry and sovereignty of his calling. The light would soon fade from behind the leaded windows that let him look out on the grass he trod for countless semesters. As that light faded he was at one with the majesty of the paneled walls of his throne room where he could ply his truth, encouraging or discouraging the flower of youth.

Lux et Veritas indeed—with the emphasis on the latter.

I didn't give up. I summarized my argument one more time. "Mr. Noyes," I pumped out the earnestness as a wildcat pumping in a barren field, "I have always succeeded at whatever I set out to do. My ambition has no limits."

Then it came at me, like the final thrust of a freight train, not through the mouth of the Dean of Admissions, Yale University (*Lux et Veritas*) but through that exalted, imperial eye of a superior being:

"That may be very admirable, Mistah Gahdner, in other circumstances. But for our requirements I like to compare students to automobiles. While you cannot run a car with only a large powerful engine if you have no gas; neither can you run a car on all gas and no engine."

Lux et Veritas.

I went to USC. *Palmam Qui Meruit Ferat* (Let he bear the palm who merits it). Paul Hindemith left Yale that same year, no doubt in a huff over my rejection.

My younger brother went to Yale.

He had the engine.

I'll Take Cash

My mother is on the phone. She is telling me my law student nephew (my sister's son) is in need of a new car and has purchased one under the auspices of his grandparents (fifty percent of which team is my selfsame mother).

"Very nice," I say.

Some few days later my mother is again utilizing the Bell System to bring news of yet another automotive transaction.

It seems my brother's daughter has inadvertently totaled the family car, putting them in the market for a new one. My father happens to have a late model, low mileage Cadillac that the doctors prefer he doesn't drive.

Now my mother explains to me over some fiber optic network the nitty-gritty of the transaction.

"We decided to make these gifts to our children. It will save taxes later. You know I've always been a stickler for keeping my children even. So we gave them each this equal sum of money, deducting the value of the automobiles."

"Very nice."

"Now, of course we want to give you your fair share, but we didn't know how to do it."

"Just send cash," I said.

"I mean, since your brother and sister got cars for part of their share, we thought you might like to have my car."

"*Your* car?" I asked incredulously—"Your car is over seventeen years old."

"Those old cars are worth money sometimes," she sounded hurt. "What do they call that when a car increases in value?" she asked.

"A miracle," I said.

"No, there's a name for it," she said. "Classy or something."

"Classic," I said.

"That's it," she exclaimed. "A classic car."

"I hate to disillusion you, Momma Baby, but your nineteen seventy-two Cadillac is far from a classic car."

"Oh, I don't know about that."

"It's a battleship, without the lovely lines."

"It's a good car. It still runs well, you know that."

"It is a tank that gets two-point-eight miles to the gallon. That was okay when they made the thing because gas was twenty-five cents a gallon, but times have changed."

"It was like *new* when I got it," she said, sounding like Madman Muntz. "The man that owned it had just died—and all they had driven it was to the funeral and back."

"Yeah, but the funeral was in Texas."

"Well, I certainly wouldn't expect you to *drive* it. Not an important man like you." I could tell she was getting testy whenever she called me "important." "I'd expect you to keep it as an investment. The price of those old Cadillacs can only go up."

"Then you make the profit, okay? I'm not driving

that clunker three thousand miles from Pennsylvania to California on the hope that I live long enough to see a junker like that increase in value."

"Well you don't have to be ungrateful about it. If you don't want the car, what do you want?"

"Cash," I said.

Several months later I heard from my brother. He regaled me with the tale of his auto purchase from our parents, and of the purchase of the car for our sister's son. Then he said: "We understood that you didn't want the money."

"Who told you that?"

"Mother. We set up this gifting program for them, and we just figured you must be involved in a gifting program of your own."

"A gifting program?"

"You know, to avoid inheritance taxes."

"Inheritance taxes?" I asked. My brother, I should mention, is a judge in Pennsylvania, and has a somewhat more sophisticated grasp on these weighty matters than I do. "Isn't that something someone else pays after you're dead? I'm six years older than you are, are you going to think about dying in six years?"

"Hey, if you want the money, you'll get it."

"Great," I said. "Cash."

"Of course you know we got cars for most of our share," he said. "So what shall I tell Mother?"

"Cash," I said.

A day later, Mother is again utilizing the wizardry of Ma Bell:

"Ted, your brother tells me he gets the feeling you don't want the car."

"Trust his feelings."

She seemed at last resigned to another unfulfilled dream. "So if you don't want the car, how do you want your share?"

"Cash."

"You remember those candelabra you gave us for our twenty-fifth wedding anniversary?"

"Sure."

"They have certainly increased in value over the years. Silver is so expensive now, and we just don't have that many candlelit dinners anymore…"

Vive Les Femmes

I wish with all my heart that rebels would set fire to Disneyland.
—A French Intellectual
Anti-Disney Supplement
Le Figaro

France has dealt with more dangerous invasions than the arrival of a mouse.
—Robert Fitzpatrick
Euro Disney President

Bonjour. Allow me to introduce myself. I am the head of the expeditionary force located in Marne-la-Vallee, 20 *kilomètres* east of gay Paree. Object: To liberate the French *femmes* from this scourge on their countryside. *Merci beaucoup.* France has suffered too many *invasions* of their sacred homeland. Now comes *Monsieur et Mademoiselle Rat* and Donald *Canard.* It is the straw that broke the camel's back, *n'est-ce pas*?

We are the rebels. Rebel, *c'est moi.* We will teach them their lesson. Disneyland is not French. Disneyland is foreign.

Ma petite bande of mercenaries creep stealthily down *le Grand Boulevard.* We are all French intellectuals, but *le Général* is most intellectual. He is sitting out the operation in his Peugeot in the parking lot. *Le Général* must not sacrifice himself foolishly, for the troops would be in utter *chaos sans* their *capitaine.*

I am Jacques, the field commander. My only request of *mon capitaine* was to give me some men who are stout-hearted men, who will fight for the right they adore. Start me with ten who have stout hearts, and then you'll soon give me ten thousand more.

We are ten who *reconnaitre* at the *Chateau de* Sleepy Beauty. Jean Paul is our communications *directeur.* He will keep me in touch with our five field *rats* disguised as Mickey

Rat. At my signal, *"Brûle, bébé, brûle!"* they will make *crème brûlée* of the five lands of Disney: *Fantaisie, Demain, Frontière, Aventure* and *Pays de l'ours,* Bear Country to you dumbos. Disneyland becomes *fumée et cendre.*

Au revoir, cowboy, *au revoir,* Sleepy Beauty, *au revoir,* Donald *Canard.* Tomorrow you'll be *à l'orange,* Donald *Canard.*

Why? The French have given the world art *très joli, beaucoup du vin et du fromage, et les plus jolies femmes.* In return, America has sent us hot dogs, McDonald's *boeuf coupé,* and Disneyland.

Très fatigué. We will save our *femmes* from this anti-intellectual fate worse than *mort.*

When *la victoire* is ours, *cherchez la femme. Vive la France!*

Our dedicated band of mercenaries are out-manned and up against a four billion dollar *Bastille.* You can't even count that high in *francs.* But underneath our *chemises* beat stout hearts of intellectuals. *"Bonjour,* cowboy" leaves us cold.

It is twenty-three hundred thirty hours. The air is crisp but our *derrières* are dragging. "My Magic Kingdom for a cup of *thé,"* says one of my troops. *Très amusant.* Disneyland is <u>not</u> our cup of *thé.*

Chaos and *confusion* will *carpe diem. Au revoir,* Disneyland. *Très amusant.* Our brave *soldats* are deployed. All is in readiness. Let us be frank—we got a bad press for our wars. Too much collaboration, too little *résistance.* Not this time! They may be rich with *beaucoup des gendarmes,* but our spirits are *la victoire!*

It is one hundred hours. Jean Paul, our communications officer, has just reached me at my outpost behind the *Chateau* of Sleepy Beauty. The news is distressing.

It is not the Disney *gendarmes* who spoil the *consommé* but the very *femmes* we hoped to liberate from this anti-intellectual *faux pas.*

Les femmes are an *obstruction* on the battlefield. There is no *encouragement* of *"Brûle, bébé, brûle,"* but rather *incessant* laughter and smiles as *grosse* as the *Seine;* fawning and intimate *camaraderie* from *beaucoup des femmes* to our Mickey *Rats.*

A fine kettle of *poissons*!

One by one our brave *soldat rats* straggle back to camp, and on each arm is a *femme*. *Les femmes* are carrying the explosives! *Très formidable*! I am a broken man.

But what's this? *Merde*! An extra *femme* for *moi*! *Cherchez la femme*. Can one compromise the glory of *France* for *un petit chou*? What of our honor? What of *Liberte, egalite, fraternité*? My comrades have surrendered to *vin, femmes (oh la la) et chanson*! France is in the *consommé*!

Moi shall <u>not</u> *collaborer*. I shall join the *résistance*—*(les femmes* are *très jolies. Oh la la) après* tomorrow.

C'est la vie.

Her Secret Admirer

This was definitely not the first time I did it. So my wife should not have been at all surprised. For years I have been given to signing my name as someone else.

Psychiatrists might have some fun with this. They might say I was trying to escape my real identity. Oh, were it only that easy.

I might sign a Christmas card "Queen Elizabeth and Ted Gardner," or "Pope Theodore II." But, the point that must not be forgotten is this has never been secret from my wife. Her wedding ring from me is inscribed "Love from a friend." It should never become obsolete.

For Christmas I stumbled on and fell for roses-of-the-month, which I duly sent to her, signing the card "Your secret admirer."

I expected, naturally enough, with my long and honored history of pseudonyms, that when the first batch of roses showed up (complete with the introductory box of candy) Ginny would throw her arms around me, shower me with kisses, and be so generally touched with my thoughtfulness she would have trouble expressing her gratitude.

Something rather different transpired:

I came home from sweating and slaving to earn the price of the flowers—on the crest of twenty-odd years of marriage—and Ginny was quite excited all right.

"I got roses and candy from a secret admirer," she bubbled like the froth on any schoolgirl who had unexpectedly been invited to the prom by the quarterback.

"Who could that be?" I smiled, awaiting the credit.

"We don't know," she said, explaining that she and our daughters, two of them via prime-time telephone lines, had been wracking their brains to figure it out.

It was only a moment until I grasped the trouble my scheme was in. The affectionate appreciative response had already been forfeited. Surely she couldn't be serious. And yet, she seemed so ebullient I didn't have the heart to spoil it.

"So who do you think sent them?" I played along.

"We can't imagine," she said, her light eyelashes lashing about.

"Well, who have you considered?"

"So-and-so from the Garden," she said, using his real name, which I shall scrupulously avoid in this exposé to protect all the innocent blokes.

"Why?"

"Couldn't afford it."

"Hm." Obviously he wasn't sweating and slaving to buy her candy and flowers like someone I know.

"How about that guy who made eyes at you on the ship?" I fed the fire. "Vito, that Italian lover with the torrid eyes and extra belly." I don't feel I have to protect this cad from anyone. Vito is his real name. I mention it in case any of you should wind up on his ship, keep an eye on your wife.
"He was thinner than you," she corrected me, incorrectly. "I'm just so baffled by all this attention from a stranger."

"Maybe it's not a stranger. It might even be a relative," I offered.

"Nah. My brothers wouldn't spend the money."

"Your…" I strung it out, hoping to grab her attention to another relative.

"My father wouldn't call himself a secret admirer."

After ruminating over the vast array of fellows that doubtlessly admired her, including a few surprises for me, Ginny remained convinced she had a mysterious admirer.

I had also ordered the roses for our daughters, signing the card with the prosaic "Mom and Dad." But this was turning into so much fun, I called the roses-for-hire company and asked them to change "Mom and Dad" on the cards for our daughters to "Your secret admirer."

When our daughter called to say she got the same roses and candy and a funny card that said "Mom and Dad," I knew the game was up.

Not so. Ginny said it was another mystery; we didn't send them.

Now Ginny was sure, and our daughters agreed, the source of these bonbons and buds had to be a common one—a hypothesis I didn't dispute. But they were paying less and less attention to me and my contributions to solving the puzzle.

It was, Ginny decided, our daughter's boy friend. Poor guy, he could hardly afford it (sweat and slave, pal), but he just had the biggest heart of anyone Ginny knew.

The lad, when confronted, stoutly and convincingly denied it.

Though the rosy purveyors promised to keep my secret, our eldest daughter became assertive, and the home office spilled the beans.

"I don't believe it," Ginny said. No hugs, no kisses, no gurgling gratitude.

Just disappointment.

Next year I am sending myself a vile-smelling man's perfume. The card will say: "All my love—your secret admirer."

Let her squirm.

Bedtime For Boris

"...At the Lenin Mausoleum in Red Square the line is not so long as it is reputed to be; but not far away in Pushkin Square, in front of the largest and abruptly the most famous McDonald's on earth, a thick still river of patient humanity folds back and forth against itself and then undulates out along the edge of the square, around a corner and past the block-long Rossiya movie theater, around another corner and past the Bauhausy Izvestia building, and around still another corner past the statue of the poet, until it disappears behind the trees. It takes four hours to get to the hamburgers..."

—Hendrik Hertzberg
The New Republic

I had been to Russia only once before to squint at masterworks in the half-light of the Hermitage Museum in Leningrad née St. Petersburg before the Saints were kaput in that clime.

In those days museums were the *de rigueur* stopping points in a land noted for pogroms and repression. It was a time when Lenin's Tomb held the greatest fascination for the natives and visitors alike.

No more. My visit this time was not to some half-lit Goya or the waxy stiff of a revolutionary dictator, but to that great capitalistic crack in the Communist facade, the most famous McDonald's on earth.

I joined the still river of patient humanity just behind a Russian bear of a man who held in tow on a leash a bull mastiff sort of dog. It was an animal that looked poised to take your head off at the slightest provocation. Lyova, the master at the other end of the leash, matched his ferocity.

"Fine-looking dog," I said. "What's his name?"

"Boris."

"Nice name. Boris. Very Russian."

"*Da*. He is named for Boris Godunov the opera."

"What a good idea," I said. It is always a good idea to be friendly to strangers, no matter what your mother told you. Especially foreign strangers on their own soil.

"Wasn't my idea," he snorted. "Name came with his papers."

"Papers?"

He nodded the nod of the superior. "He has papers. You understand, he is a thoroughbred."

His companions groaned. They groaned whenever Lyova put on superior airs, which was most of the time. It was, after all, a classless society.

"Where they getting all this beef?" Lyova asked surveying the endless line of landsmen undulating around Pushkin Square. "We don't see this much beef in a year."

"Capitalism," one offered.

"*Da*," said another.

I asked a slight man with a cigarette dangling from his pinky lips why he was willing to stand in line for four hours for a hamburger.

"Hamburger?" he said in mild astonishment, "I thought it was shoes."

"No, it's hamburgers."

"Bourgeois," he said. "Where can I get shoes?"

"What are you waiting for?" I asked his companion, whose name was Vladimir.

"I never ask," he said. "The longer the line, the more desirable the payoff. I just look for the longest line and take what I get. But you say hamburgers?" he shook his head. "I don't know. I'm a vegetarian."

"Have you ever been to Lenin's Tomb?" I asked him.

"No, they got hamburgers?" he said, raising a startled eyebrow.

As we completed our third hour in line, one of Lyova's compatriots chided, "Getting a hamburger for Boris too?"

"Maybe," Lyova sniffed. "If it is any concern of yours. After all, the dog does have papers. That's more than I can say for you."

"Papers for what, going to the bathroom?" Maxim said in a saltier Russian vernacular. Everyone had a hearty laugh but Lyova.

As we drew nearer our destination, the golden arches swayed into view like a Volga boatman on holiday. Lyova reined in his dog Boris and gave him a loving pat behind the ears. The odor of searing animal flesh was folding back and forth among the queue. "Where are they getting all this beef?" Lyova whistled softly between his yellow-stained teeth. "We don't see this much beef in a year."

A glum functionary of the Soviet state, a relic of repression, marched up to Lyova as we undulated past the Bauhausy Izvestia building.

"Comrade," he said, "it is necessary to borrow your dog."

Lyova stiffened. "But comrade, it is perfectly legal to own a dog."

"Yes, yes," the officer answered impatiently. "He will be returned. It is an emergency matter."

"When will he be returned?"

"By the time you reach the counter. Don't worry."

"But perestroika?" Lyova let the question hang.

"Yes, even perestroika must bow occasionally to the needs of the state."

Lyova brooded for the next half hour, and no amount of gentle ribbing by his comrades could cheer him up.

As I had feared, by the time we hit the counter to place our orders there was no sign of the functionary *or* the dog.

There were only the familiar pricing signs on the board behind the uniformed clerks.

BIG MAC   70 Rubles

and underneath, a makeshift notice:

SPECIALTY TODAY
BIG BORIS 45 Rubles

Teddy Isn't 21, You Know

Mother's Day has always been a special day for me.

When I would try to goad my father into doing something for dear ole Ma, he would invariably say, "She's not *my* mother." So the responsibility fell on me.

One year I bought her a chess set. I played chess.

She didn't.

I suppose in my young mind I was eager to have her enjoy the game as much as I did. I also liked the particular chess set I bought her and would have been happy to receive it as a gift myself.

Fortunately, my mother allowed me to play with the little carved wooden pieces and the big board with the handsome red and black squares.

Another year, I made her a pin out of a hunk of wood splattered with sequins and the nicest royal blue shiny enamel paint. There was a safety pin glued on the back of it that was only partially visible when she wore it.

I was continually dumbfounded to see my mother leave the house to shop or go to a party, having apparently forgotten about the lovely pin.

Being a thoughtful son, I would run out to the car and yell, "Mother, you forgot your pin."

She would smile and thank me so profusely I began to feel I was performing a real service. It made me especially vigilant to see that she never left home without it.

When she decided I was old enough, she told me she would always pin the monstrosity to her dress and then, when she was out of sight, she would take it off.

One time she was preoccupied and forgot to take off the pin. She couldn't understand what her bridge club was laughing at.

I was about 35 when she told me. As I said, I think she thought I was old enough to take it. My wife thinks she may have underestimated me by a few years.

Mother was able to get back at me for these gifts.

After my freshman year at USC, I was back in Pennsylvania working on a road gang near Guthsville.

In some states this work is reserved for prison inmates. In Pennsylvania it is a political plum.

I took my lunch at the Guthsville Hotel. In back of the hotel was the famous Guthsville Playhouse.

There I saw, and was smitten by, an actress named Joyce Farris. Her father, I found out later, was Joe Farris, editor-in-chief of the International News Service.

She was gorgeous. She was 26 years old. I was 19.

Since I was terrified to ask her for a date, I left a note with the bartender.

After her gracious acceptance, I became preoccupied with convincing her I was almost her age, without actually lying.

I devised this scheme to make my summer employments sound like jobs of several years, bringing me just a shade shy of 24 years.

Joyce and I drove to a local club to swim and have lunch. I drove, of course, being old enough to have a driver's license.

By the time we were frolicking in the pool, I had planted the seed of my venerable adulthood in our conversation.

I looked up to see my mother appear on the scene.

If you have never experienced the unique sinking feeling of your mother appearing while you were trying to impress a date with your maturity, let me assure you it was, in spite of my great love for her, not a welcome sight.

She came to the edge of the pool. I tried to ignore her.

"Teddy!" she called. I dove under the water with a big splash to cover the sound of her voice.

But I could only hold my breath thirty seconds, and when I surfaced I was chagrined to see she had not taken the hint.

Joyce was smiling. "Your mother's here," she said.

"Hi, Mom," I said, giving her the fish eye in hopes she would take the hint and leave us alone.

"I just talked to Catherine," she said, referring to the

club manager. "She says it's all right for you to sign the check if Joyce wants a drink."

Then my mother turned to my 26-year-old date and got me back for a sequined wood pin, the chess set and every other slight, past and future.

"Teddy isn't 21, you know."

I don't remember much else about the date except that we went for a ride on the seesaw. It was Joyce's idea. I wonder if she thought that fitting entertainment for a boy my age.

Joyce and I then sat on the terrace, she with her gin and tonic, I with my tomato juice. She said, "I can have fun with anyone from 6 to 60."

She must have gauged me about 5.

It was the last time I saw Joyce Farris—but mothers are for ever.

Happy Mother's Day, Mom.

Let's call it even.

Beef Up
The Women

The call I had been waiting thirty years for finally came:

"I'd like to make you a small offer on your novel," said the senior editor of a New York publishing house.

While I was biting my cheek to keep from fainting, I asked, "How small?"

She told me. Small. Then she said something about wishing there was a stronger woman throughout the book.

"Well, it covers 132 years, she'd be a pretty old filly by the time it was all over."

"Well, we should beef up the women somehow. And it's too long. Look at it and let me know if you think you could get it down to 200,000."

Later, I called her to tell her I could cut to 200,000 words.

"Who is this?" she inquired as one who had been interrupted to no reasonable purpose.

"Ted Gardner. You offered to buy my book."

"What?" She was distressed. "That's impossible."

"Well, all I know is someone at this number with your name and a voice exactly like yours offered me blank dollars for my book."

"Are you the man who wrote me that nasty letter?"

"No, I spoke to you on the phone."

"No you didn't." She asked, "What's the title?"

"*The Paper Dynasty.*"

"Never heard of it. What's it about?"

"A newspaper dynasty, four generations."

"No. Wait a minute." I heard her rummage around her desk. "Oh, wait, here it is. Yes, I did indeed make you an offer."

I told her about the word count.

"Oh, we can't publish over 150,000."

"You said 200,000."

"Well, maybe since it's a saga."

I went to the cutting machine, and a month later I had cut to 199,700 words. And you still got the gist of the story.

"That's good," she said. "We're probably going to change the title."

I wrote her a whole string of silly titles with the clever purpose of making *The Paper Dynasty* sound better.

She still didn't like it. "Remember to beef up the women," she said.

"Don't some women find some men admirable?"

"Sure," she allowed, "but only women buy these books."

"I'd buy it," I said.

"You'd never find it," she said. "Our covers are all the same. We have a woman with her clothes falling off, a man naked from the waist up, a horse and a cactus." She paused. "Do you want to use your full name?"

"I don't care about that. You decide."

In our next conversation, a few weeks later, she said,

"We're going to have to put a woman's name on it. We always do."

Pause. "That's okay," I said.

"Oh, good," she said. "Some men don't like it. We thought about Theodora Roosevelt Gardner but thought it a little too historical."

Hysterical, I thought.

I signed my next letter to her "Teddi Gardner (Ms)" and we were spreading the word to look for Teddi at the drugstore. I was even doing a little preliminary dress shopping for my author(ess) book tour.

I didn't hear from her for three weeks. When I called to see if she was still employed, half expecting her to deny they ever offered to buy the book, she apologized and said it was on the top of her list.

"There's one thing I have to ask you," she asked. "Why do you have all this joke stationery?"

"I like to give a laugh now and then."

Silence. "We're very worried about it here."

The next day she called with the good news. They would publish my book. The contract followed. It was a lollapalooza.

In essence they owned all rights for twenty years. They could do anything to the book: shelve it, slash it, beef up the women, have someone else redo it and get the author credit. I would pay all the lawsuit judgments against them, and any settlements to any suers they asked me to.

I called. She had no heart for nit-picking the contract, she said.

"You neglected to insert the standard stipulation that the author poison his grandmother to get published."

There was a humorless pause. "Do you have a grandmother?"

"Well, no," I said.

"Then what are you worried about?"

I sent her my differences in a letter.

She replied in three generous pages, saying no dice. I borrowed a piece of stationery from my friend and mentor:

Felix Warring-Porridge, M.D.
Psychiatry
Practice Limited to
The Certifiably Bonkers

I returned the unsigned contracts with one word:

WOW

She responded:

Thanks for your letter. It's finally the right length for the book. Now if you could only beef up the women...

Knitting As A Spectator Sport

My wife is off on a knitting tour. You never heard of knitting tours, I bet. But if you are a world-class knitter like she is, maybe you have.

No, you don't knit on a knitting tour, and you don't learn to knit. It is assumed, I suppose, that if you fork over enough dough for a knitting tour, you already know how to knit. And not just in the knit one, purl two class either but, as I said, world-class.

What you do on a knitting tour is visit knitting mills in friendly foreign countries and watch other people knit. Knitting has finally become a spectator sport. It was not always so.

I once had a girl friend who was knitting a pair of socks. She said they were for me. They had beer mugs on the sides with fluffy white angora wool for the foam. Since I didn't drink beer I didn't think they were too appropriate, but I was so flattered to have something custom-knit for me, I didn't say anything.

Somehow that relationship fizzled. I think it was because I never got the socks. She probably thinks it was because I wouldn't drink a beer to legitimize all her hard work.

Anyway, I don't want to give the impression here I

married Ginny for her knitting. But early in the marriage I caught her red-handed, knitting socks. Socks without foamy mugs of beer on them. Whatever you want to say about Ginny, she knew I didn't drink beer.

"Are those for me?" I asked.

"Maybe," she said.

I'll admit it. I was inordinately excited at the prospect of someone knitting something for me. I fully realize a lot can happen between knit one and purl two. And to think that knitting has anything to do with any indication of affection is just nonsense.

I don't know what happened to those socks. Either they fell by the wayside or someone else got them. But you didn't hear a peep out of me about it. Not a mature macho man like me.

Ten, maybe fifteen, years later, Ginny got the knitting bug again. This time it was a full-fledged sweater—a crew-neck pullover FOR ME. And she let me pick the color. It was a glorious blue, I remember that much. I mean, that yarn was dyed with my eyes in mind.

And she finished it too. Maybe not right away—maybe it took a couple of seasons or so, but she finished it.

Only thing was, there must have been a terrible flaw in the directions, because it came out wider than it was long—just tailor-made for a guy who stood about four feet, eight, with a sixty-five inch waist and a basketball player's arms.

A daughter, amused by funky clothes, took the "sweater," and as far as I know may have even worn it. With stonewashed jeans it was probably a knockout.

The next sweater was a smashing success. The most beautiful greens, rusts and blues.

"Is that for me?" I asked eagerly after it started to take shape.

"No. I felt so sorry for our daughter who got that awful misshapen blue job, that I'm giving her this as a consolation."

"Wait a minute. That blue job, as you so cleverly call

it, was knit for me, as I recall."

"Mmm. So it was. But then, as I recall, you didn't want it, and you fobbed it off on the poor child."

"Hey, hold on. It didn't fit me, remember? I didn't notice you wearing it."

"Well, it didn't fit her either, but she took it."

"But, Ginny," I protested, "I didn't marry a girl for this very reason. She didn't follow through on the promise of a pair of knitted foamy beer socks."

"Oh, I'll knit you another sweater, don't worry."

And she bought the quintessential knit-kit, a cardigan pattern with 26 colors. They might have used more colors but they ran out of alphabet to number them.

That was several years ago. So far we have a sleeve and a quarter, I believe, but it certainly is stunning.

This year, completion had to be put off to take part in a knitting tour.

"Why don't you take the sweater with you on the knitting tour?" I asked. "You might be inspired to finish it."

"No room," she said, in a voice that would send the hardiest soul sweater shopping. And I have started the most casual shopping for sweaters that look hand-knit. If I find one, maybe someone will ask if my wife knit it.

Now, I am thinking of taking up knitting. I am able to complete simple jigsaw puzzles, so I ought to be able to knock out a sweater my size.

But first I think I should start small. Does anyone know where I can get a pattern for those cute foamy beer socks?

The Idol Is Idle

I suppose everyone who reads has a favorite writer.

The guy who gives me most laughs is Calvin Trillin. He writes in the *New Yorker*, and before his column was syndicated he wrote for *The Nation*, which he said was published for the entertainment of 1200 librarians and 8 unreconstructed old Trotskyites.

So when my wife, Ginny, announced he was speaking in Oakland to her Independent (very) Booksellers, there was nothing for it but to hightail to Oakland.

I visualized shaking his hand and telling him I was a columnist just like he (I would omit for the moment that I wrote in a local Saturday paper that was only read by those who didn't realize they could get it free on Thursday).

He would slap me on the back (or not) and say, "Gosh, Ted, it's good to meet a fellow writer. I sure hope you'll let me see some of your stuff. I wouldn't be surprised if the *New Yorker* would be very interested."

I think if you have read any Calvin Trillin, you will admit he comes across as that kind of folksy guy.

You can imagine my excitement in the big room of the Oakland Hyatt when my wife wangled me a seat right next to Calvin Trillin.

Well, not at the same table, but we were back to back. I was within eavesdropping distance.

I had expected Mr. Trillin to be kind of a fatty, what with all his talk about his passion for Kansas City ribs—and how he didn't weigh as much as his wife thought because, in calculating his true weight, he always allowed 14 pounds for clothes.

Imagine my surprise, then, to be seated behind this guy, my age, who looked like he had jogged himself to a frazzle. The long thin strands at the back of his balding head (the view from my vantage point) looked like they had been immersed in the guacamole dip.

Unhappily, try as I might—pushing my chair back to almost touch his—I couldn't hear a blessed word, he was so soft-spoken.

I was able to notice he didn't eat his chicken. I mean, if I could eat my chicken and he had this great reputation of being a human garbage pail, and here he was anorexic almost, there was an image crisis.

His speech was hysterically funny. He had impeccable timing.

He and I were, I noticed, almost identically dressed. A blue blazer, gray slacks, blue shirt and tie—his red, mine blue. We had an awful lot in common. I could see at a glance he would take to me like a duck to eggnog, and in no time we would be pen pals.

I was the first to congratulate him on a riotous speech.

"I think you are the funniest man in America," I said.

"Thank you," he smiled.

"And I have impeccable taste," I winked, "as you can see by my clothes," I said, waving between our similar outfits.

"Oh," he said.

For some reason he didn't ask if I was a writer. Probably jet lag, or the post-performance blues. I didn't push it. He was autographing books the following day, so I would have another opportunity.

The next morning, I hung around the autographing table where they were giving his books away to book dealers—a compilation of his best columns called *If You Can't Say Something Nice*.

He has this great signature. He drops the dot of the last "i" behind Trillin, like it had fallen off and rolled away.

When I got my chance to speak to my idol, I said, "I'm a fellow mudslinger." (He had referred to himself as a mudslinger in his speech.)

"Oh."

"I write a column like yours, but not as brilliant."

Smile.

"I also wrote a four-generation novel—the kind of book you said was awful."

"Hm."

"I see you are in good shape. Funny, I expected you to be fat, what with all the eating—do you ride your bicycle?"

"Sometimes."

"I mean, your clothes are supposed to weigh 14 pounds."

"Something like that."

"I noticed you didn't even eat your chicken last night."

"No."

Believe it or not, he never asked to see my work, let alone offer it to the *New Yorker* for publication. Afraid of competition, no doubt.

But what the heck, writers are shy. What other motivation could there be for someone to choose a line of work where it is just you and a typewriter?

Oh, a couple of them like Norman Mailer and Jimmy Breslin may make believe they aren't shy, but it's just a cover-up.

If you happen to hear of Robert Penn Warren speaking somewhere, please let me know.

I have a book he would just adore.

Take Your Choice: Two Commandments Or A Rolls Royce

My daughter Esmeralda (not her real name) has just graduated from a local college that has the reputation of being a rich-persons' school, and it is a reputation that the administration has heretofore been at no apparent pains to disabuse.

One of the charming manifestations of this image is a poster sold on campus. It shows a shiny new Rolls Royce with a license plate saying:

THANX SC

A well-scrubbed couple of the Aryan strain not too far removed from their student years, are hovering over it with delighted propriety.

Next to it is a decade-old or so Honda, much the worse for wear, with the license plate:

UCLA MD

The scruffy bearded hippie standing by it looks dazed.

In this spirit, I made my way to the graduation exercises dressed up like a junk bond dealer in my pinstripe suit. It was the one I wore to my own college graduation on the same campus, some years before.

I am very fortunate in my physique, in that no belt is required to hold up my pants.

Well, I should have known when I didn't see any Rolls Royces around the place that it was not the USC they promised my daughter and me. Not to mention my wife, who never turned a nickel with her Masters in Library Science. Well, I mean, how could you?

The huge crowd gave me an uneasy feeling—like when I heard Esmeralda's classes in this elite private school had many hundreds of students in them. One of her classes, I figured, grossed the school $185,000 for one semester, which I calculate is just about enough to buy a new Rolls Royce.

As if that weren't enough, they started right in lowering everyone's expectations with the speeches.

First the valedictorian quoted Ralph Waldo Emerson to the effect that if you affect just one life, your life has been a success.

Then the main speaker closed his speech with the identical minimalist sentiment. Doc Michael I. Sovern is the President of Columbia University, the only other college in the country besides SC to smile favorably on my application.

Serendipity.

His address struck me as a heavy portion of lowered expectations. The education may cost as much as the cockpit furniture in a B-52 bomber, but don't look for any direct hits.

As long as you affect one life—even your own kid's—you've done your bit. He never mentioned the Rolls.

And—(this is my favorite): Just try to keep two of the ten commandments. *Any* two.

Oh brother, I thought, that's it? That's all you need nowadays to get a Rolls Royce? Two commandments. Any two? A snap.

Then I ruminated over those moral laws to see how many I could remember.

The first six were easy. (With help I got to eight.)

I had to check the Bible for the other two. Honor the Sabbath, and not taking the name of God in vain.

Though the challenge was certainly not hurled at me, an old graddy, but at the new crop, which two could I really say I kept?

1. *Thou shalt not kill.* Kill what? People? I had no trouble with that, but it didn't say people. I've killed a lot of insects in my time, and have directly benefitted from the killing of chickens, fish, cattle, etc.

2. *Thou shalt not steal.* Candy bars from my uncle's gas station when I was 8. Too late to erase that one.

3. *Remember the Sabbath day and keep it holy. Six days shalt thou labor.* Well, I've labored on the seventh, there is just no getting around it. Of course, so have ministers, but this test is just as tough for them.

4. *Honor thy father and thy mother.* There is some deficient history here, and I have fallen short of perfection—just ask them.

5. *Thou shalt not covet thy neighbor's house.* (OK.) *Thou shalt not covet thy neighbor's wife.* (This, I am afraid, very much depends on thy neighbor's wife, and I have had some neighbors with wives who anyone in their right mind would covet, so that one is out.)

6. *Thou shalt not take the name of the Lord God in vain.* I did have an aunt many years ago who could hit her thumb with a hammer and say "Oh pshaw," but they don't make them like they used to.

7. *Thou shalt not make unto thee any graven image...*I

think I'm home free on this one, though I did have an associate once that considered photographs graven images.

8. *Thou shalt not bear false witness against thy neighbor.* I'll take this one. Unless it might shut up a <u>barking</u> <u>dog</u>.

9. *Thou shalt have no other gods before me.* Well, if we're talking God gods, okay. But chocolate ice cream? A toss-up.

10. *Thou shalt not commit adultery.* Do you think I could keep my options open on this one?

Do I get my two or not? It depends how strict you want to be.

Good luck to the Class of '89 with *your* two commandments.

For myself—I'm shopping for a Rolls.

Get Rich Quick

I used to work with a guy named Jack Parker, who was forever looking for a scheme to get rich quick.

One day it was garbanzo beans, another raising chinchillas for pelts.

One morning he stood at my desk and said, "Bought a bitch." I could see he was proud. "Five hundred bucks."

"What's got into you?" I protested, "Finley's secretary is trying to give them away."

"Not English setters with papers. I'm going to breed her. I've really got it made this time. They get two hundred bucks a throw for the pups, and the guy I bought her from just had a litter of thirteen."

A week later he said, "She's breeding tonight." He told me his wife was so excited about his forthcoming affluence, she went out and bought a new living room suite on time.

The first bout resulted in a false pregnancy. Vet fee: twenty dollars. After the second two hundred dollar mating he was all smiles. "She's digging holes in my grass." He couldn't contain his elation. "She wouldn't dig that many nests unless she had a belly full of pups."

But nothing happened. He had the dog injected to induce labor, and she dug more holes. He said, "It's getting frustrating, but tonight I've got an appointment for some super injection."

"For you or the dog?"

"Very funny."

Jack missed work the next two days. On the third day he sat morosely clipping his fingernails. He looked up at me and said, "The whole yard is completely shot. The bitch is digging nests like they're going out of style. I worked six months making a lawn out of that jungle. That's what I got for the twenty-five buck super shot."

"Caesarean," he said the next day. "The only way to get them out, the vet says. I'll be glad to get it over with and I'll still make a bundle."

We got a little office pool on how many pups she'd have. Four to fifteen was the span.

Saturday I drove to Jack's small house in the Valley. His usually cheerful wife, Jill, opened the door looking bedraggled and despondent. I saw the brand-new furniture had been torn to shreds. No sign of Jack. We sat on what was left of the twelve hundred dollar sectional couch.

"What happened?"

"The vet," she said, "doped up the dog for the Caesarean. Jack brought her home and put her to bed. The vet explained it on the phone this morning. The dog can't reason like a human, and when she comes out of it she is afraid, she wants her pups, and while we slept she simply started digging more nests in the living room furniture."

"So how big was the litter?"

That was when she broke into hysterical sobs. "One," she cried, "and so scrawny he's in an incubator in the doggie hospital, and we're spending money like Beverly Hills millionaires. Our loss to date is over twenty-five hundred."

The next week an ad appeared in the company paper: "English setter, female, best offer."

Within a week, Jack arrived at work with a big stack of glossy color brochures with figures scrawled all over them.

"Hey…" he boomed, "any of you guys know anything about fish and chips?"

Tom And Jane Make A Baby

From the lifestyles of the rich and famous—courtesy of Tom Hayden and his *Reunion: A Memoir* (Random House, $22.50):

…(Jane Fonda and I) must have appeared like a remake of Beauty and the Beast, *but…we happily came to know each other that summer.*

Not the least of the pleasures was getting to know her daughter, Vanessa, then 3, who was born at the time of Chicago, 1968, and had lived at the Blue Fairyland Day-care Center in Berkeley just after I left the city…; it seemed that Vanessa and I had been just missing each other at these key moments of our lives. The first night that Jane and I made love, Vanessa marched out of her bedroom, a 3-year-old inspector, and stared at me. I stared back, smiling; here I was starting over in yet another relationship with a young child not my own…

Then on a spring day in a New York hotel room, fresh from a trip to Vietnam, where she had seen women having children in the face of death, Jane was moved to create life as her answer to numb alienation. With a slight sigh, she stood behind me, naked, and whispered, "I want to have a child with you." With a tearful smile, I said yes.

Jane and I Stand
On a Möbius Band

If you think they had it bad in the foxholes and trenches of sweltering hot and humid Vietnam, you should have been in that New York hotel room.

It was 92 degrees outside. Inside, the air conditioning was busted and I mean it like to melted me into a disgusting puddle, right there on that moth-eaten carpet.

I was on the top floor and the sun was bombing that bargain-basement asphalt roof without mercy. It was 110 Fahrenheit if it was a day.

Next door, babies were crying in the face of certain death from the stinking hot enemy.

I know Jane could have put me up in a suite at the

Waldorf, but you had to live without air conditioning when your country was at war. It wasn't that unusual. I don't want any credit for it.

The mosquitoes were as big as baked potatoes, and their buzzing was more frightening than any enemy aircraft strafing the villages of the South.

My Jane (of exercise fame) was hobnobbing with our friends in Hanoi. There the simple agrarian souls pleaded to be left in peace to have their babies with the face of death turned south.

Well, sir, I sat in that stinking apartment waiting for Jane to come home from jogging the Ho Chi Minh Trail to maintain her reproductive system in a healthy state of repair. The beast doesn't move when he awaits the beauty.

I'll never forget that key moment of my life—when I heard her footsteps on the rotting wood stairs as she climbed the five flights of cockroach-occupied territory—coming home at last to her lover.

I knew it was Jane because the footfalls on the stairs were so light they could only have been made by bare feet, and Jane loved to go barefoot. Next to naked it was her favorite thing.

When I heard the door start to open, I purposely turned my back to it. If it was the Vietcong, I didn't want to offer any tacky resistance.

To my surprise Jane was not only barefoot, but naked too, and with that slight sigh only an Academy Award-winning actress could bring off without a big guffaw from everybody, she made her statement:

"I want to have a child with you." My first thought was she was talking about some new gourmet veal dish. God knows I was hungry enough sitting there waiting for ever for Her Highness to get her you-know-what back from Nam.

I honestly can't tell you how I knew she was naked, since she was behind me and I don't profess to have eyes in the back of my head. But naked she was, as I was able to verify when I turned around.

(I, on the other hand, the modest member of the

Chicago Seven, had thrown on my uniform duds: stonewashed jeans and a T-shirt emblazoned with a vulgar gesture and an appropriate profanity.)

"What will Vanessa say?" was my first question.

"Don't worry about Vanessa. She's at the Blue Fairyland, happy as a clam. Roger, her daddy, sends her bon-bons every year for her birthday."

"He certainly is a loving and supportive parent," I said, examining my naked Jane for Vietnam battle scars.

I smiled. Slightly. "Now what's this about a child?"

"I want to make a baby," she sighed slightly.

I took a deep breath. "Out of what?" I asked.

"Well, not out of the dust of the ground," she laughed slightly.

"But why do you want another baby?" I asked, slightly perplexed.

"I have seen so many women having children in the face of death that I am moved to create life as my answer to numb alienation."

"I see," I said, having seen only slightly. But by then I was in no position to argue. With a tearful smile I said, "Yes."

Where Is Your Gratitude?

Dear Daughter Melora:

Well, it is official.

I just got back from the doctor, and I had a pulled tendon, dislocated shoulder, tennis elbow and jogger's knee during our tennis match. He says it is a miracle I was able to stay on my feet, let alone take six games from you, what with the intense pain I must have been in. He said if my opponent had been more formidable, I never would have won six games.

When I told him you only weighed 100 pounds, he frowned and said no wonder I was able to beat you six zip, the condition I was in.

You will forgive me for not telling him you did take a few lousy games. I'm sure you will understand I have my reputation to think of.

Tennis, we all know, has long been recognized as a metaphor for life.

A lesser man would have thrown in the sponge the second the old shoulder separated from its socket. But not your father, a man known and respected for his athletic prowess, as well as his nerves of steel.

I did explain you were my daughter visiting from the frozen North, and I didn't think it would be at all hospitable to welch out on our match.

I also explained how tennis was practically your whole life since you played day in and day out, and so it should be no surprise that you can hit the ball over the net occasionally. Of course, he knows I never play except when you come to visit—and then only out of my well-bred sense of chivalry.

Oh, I didn't mention you have a grueling 40-hour-a-week job. And maybe I did exaggerate just a smidgen how much you played.

I told him how important winning seemed to be to you and how, as a doting father, I naturally eased up my dynamite serve when playing with you, and how I might relax a bit when your feeble serves plop at my feet.

He was a very understanding doctor, but he annoyingly persisted in asking how many games you won.

I'm sure you understand I didn't go to a psychiatrist by choice. My mental state is just fine, thank you. My pain was just so intense I mistook the door of this shrinker for my orthopod man. A perfectly natural mistake. And he seemed so hungry for business I didn't see how I could leave without hurting his feelings.

But he was helpful in many ways. For instance, he said it is perfectly normal for a loving father to let up when playing tennis with his daughter. He wants to encourage self-esteem in her—to instill the feeling of winning in one who might not ever get to beat a father of superior strength, judgment, coordination and timing.

I'm sure you remember the excessive bounce the new

tennis balls had—the reason so many of my hits went so long. The stronger player is bound to suffer with the more resilient tennis ball.

Actually, I was a little surprised at the vehemence of some of your shots, considering the physical handicap I was enduring for your sake.

I am sure you recognized how stoically I was carrying my pain, since I didn't complain at all while we were playing. You might even think I am making this up now as an excuse for letting you take a few more games than usual.

Do you remember when I taught you to play tennis? Hour after selfless hour I patiently lobbed the ball over the net so you could take your awkward, heart-rending swing at it. Everybody said I was a model father.

Well, in case you don't remember it, I'm reminding you so that next time you will think twice before trying to humiliate me on the courts.

Some people might feel you were a tad ungrateful to play so hard against your own father who had a debilitating handicap, who was the one responsible for teaching you to hold a racquet in the first place.

But I want you to know I don't hold it against you. I mean, how often can you do so well against a man who would be a top-ranked player if there was any justice in the world?

Carpe diem, they say—and boy did you *carpe diem*!

So maybe you did beat me eight games to six, you ungrateful little snip.

Just don't you think I'll ever forget it.

Love,
Your Dad

Join The Club

In my mail, yesterday, came the most exciting letter.

It was from the President of the United States, Ronald Reagan, on his personal monarch stationery. It had a wonderful soaring gold eagle in a circle, and "Ronald Reagan, Washington, D.C." in Old English type, underneath.

It's a cinch it was from the President, personally, because I know Nancy would have gone for a plainer, more tailored typeface.

Whenever she turns her back, he's off on his own.

He personally signed in blue ink. The ink was of such high quality, it didn't smudge when I wet it. I was impressed. I once saw Ron and Nancy from a distance at some luncheon at the Music Center. My wife and Nancy went to the same college, which offered the excuse for the luncheon. And, Ron and I belonged to the same club: The Book-of-the-Month.

But, we weren't what you would call close. Not, until now.

I do remember him smiling at me at that luncheon, and I think I smiled back. But, I didn't realize I had made such an indelible impression on him. I mean, he was the governor then, and he must have had a lot of other things on his mind.

I admit I was flattered to get this personal letter from him.

"Dear Mr. Gardner," it began. He could, of course, have called me "Ted," and a lesser man would have. It was just another subtle sign of the warm feelings I inspired.

In the first paragraph, Ron says he is "delighted" to tell me I was nominated for the Republican Senatorial Inner Circle by Senator Pete Wilson." My heart sank. I have never even seen Senator Pete Wilson, let alone had him smile at me. Probably Ron put him up to it.

I was relieved to see I was "accepted for membership."

I was a mite disappointed there was no mention of my acceptance being unanimous. The letters I get regularly from Congressman Guy Vander Jagt of Michigan, and the

GOP National Committee, all say my acceptance into these exclusive clubs is always unanimous. For those clubs, they send me gold membership cards and filigreed certificates, all suitable for framing.

The second last paragraph of the letter from Ron, however, made me feel good all over again.

Last year, it said, there were only thirty-one hundred in the whole world in this elite Inner Circle: familiar neighbors like John Connally, Gene Autry, Ted Turner, J.W. Marriott and others. Ron says he knows I will enjoy meeting them. How thoughtful he is! Actually, I'm not all that crazy about meeting people. Perhaps I did smile at him at the Music Center, but did he misread it as some gregarious bent on my part?

It was his last paragraph that was the clincher.

"As usual," it said, "Nancy and I will do our part to personally thank the Inner Circle in the fall, and we look forward to seeing you at that time."

He signed his letter "Ronald Reagan." He could have written just "Ron," and I would have known who he was, what with his name in the newspapers so often, not to mention our warm friendship dating back to the Music Center.

He's a great self-effacing guy, isn't he? Particularly to remember me all these years, and to invite me to Washington personally. No wonder he's so popular. That wonderful letter came yesterday. Today, I even got my handwritten "formal invitation." It contained sobering news:

"Inner Circle members contribute an annual membership of $1,000," it said.

You see, Ron always did think very highly of me.

Shoes Or Toilet Paper?

I have a talent. Some people might say I was inordinately proud of it. I say it is nothing to be ashamed of.

My talent is for standing in lines.

You may not rank it with musical genius, chess prodigy, scientific acumen, but you can't deny it is a bona fide talent.

I was not born with this talent; far from it. I used to be a terrible line-stander. Short-tempered, irritable and impatient, always impatient. And pessimistic. It was part of the package that if I stood in a line, I was sure I wouldn't get in to see whatever I was standing in line for. I hated the prospect of wasting time, as much as I hated wasting time.

In my youth, after our most popular war, I stood four hours to walk through the "Freedom Train," parked at the railroad station in Allentown, Pennsylvania. As I look back, it is a mystery to me why they were pumping our patriotism when it was already at an all-time high. I'm not even sure what I saw—a good copy of the Declaration of Independence with those wonderful signatures is all I can recall. But I've never forgotten the four-hour wait in the line. Nor have I stopped talking about it.

Standing in line is an art. I last plied my line-standing art at the Santa Barbara Film Festival. It was a triumph of patience, good nature, gregarious good cheer and good clean fun. It was also a study in logistical wisdom.

No longer do I worry about not getting in to a show. Standing in line is sufficient for me.

I eavesdrop and hear a lot of deadly conversation. Whenever anyone has anything really interesting to say, they drop their decibels like someone pulling the plug on the Grateful Dead.

Sometimes I read a book. But it has to be paperback. It isn't chic to lug around hardback books to stand in line.

In my more intense youth I spoke to no one. If someone spoke to me, I grumbled with my head down and it never failed to sever all communication. But in my mellow years I have even been known on occasion to initiate the conversation.

On the evening I am now chronicling, a film called *Earth Girls Are Easy* was playing at the Victoria Theater on guess what street.

Since the tickets are sold to the show 15-20 minutes before each performance, and the performances run back to back, there is an art to assuring you will get a seat for the popular later performances.

I am about to disclose my secret with the understanding that it remain just between us, for, obviously, if everyone practiced my ploy, it would ruin it.

I sit in the last row for the first performance. Then as the music begins to build during what is obviously the final scene, I vault over the seat, tear through the door and join the line of the folks who are waiting (who did not go to the earlier performance). On this night, the line was already around the corner. But by the time the whole audience sauntered out, the line was around the block, coming close to touching on the beginning. Of course, there are people who must come out and go back in before us: Series pass-holders, VIPs, special guests. But I was first among the peons. I will leave it to you to decide if this subsidiary talent is a minor one or an indifferent one.

On this night, I think I spent as much time in lines as I did in the movies, for you line up to buy your ticket, then 45 minutes later when you have it, you spend more time in line until they decide the stars are converging congenially and they let you into the theater.

There you wait until those who do not share your line-enhancing talents come into the theater and line up for popcorn and bonbons.

A case in point to illustrate the separation of the line-standing artist from your run-of-the-mill line-stander:

A bus stopped at the corner light next to our humongous line. A young lad stood up in the bus, lowered the window and said: "Hey, what are you standing in line for?"

The humdrum line-standers said nothing.

The artless line-standers said, "A movie."

But the consummate artist at line-standing, yours truly, said, "Shoes or toilet paper, we aren't sure which."

At the risk of detracting from my art by explaining it, I'll risk it. If you are a line-standing artist yourself, you don't need the explanation and can skip the next paragraph.

My line, "Shoes or toilet paper," is from the movie *Moscow on the Hudson*. Any artist would realize that, and by deductive reasoning discover we were standing in line for a movie. If, on the other hand, he got off the bus expecting to see *Moscow on the Hudson*, he was in for a disappointment.

I will be teaching a course in "The Art of Standing in Line" on alternate Tuesdays. Watch the Rolling Hills *Herald* for details.

Clutter Control

Clutter Control Group Forming

A "Clutter Control" group is now forming to provide a supportive environment to explore, understand and begin to control personal clutter with others who share similar struggles and feelings.
Some of the areas to be covered will include storing and collecting items, letting go of clutter, feeling out of control with the mess, deciding what to keep or discard and understanding the need for clutter.

—From the Palos Verdes
Peninsula *News*

Hello, I'd like to speak to someone about the Clutter Control group—yes...you can? Oh, thank you.

I've got this wife, see, who is what you might call a clutter bug. I mean, you can hardly move around here sometimes, it gets so bad. Yes, well your course looks real good, but I was wondering is it something like Alcoholics Anonymous? Do you have to stand up and share your struggles and feelings with others?...

No, it's not for me, it's for my wife. Oh, Lord, books, empty boxes, book carts. She has a book business and it's just all over the house. I can hardly get from room to room. But I don't think I'd want to embarrass her or anything, like, you know, having to stand up before a crowd and say, 'I'm a mess,' or something. Well, I don't mean she'd deny it or anything. I just want to know how gentle you could be with her. Yeah...but when you say understand clutter and share similar struggles and feelings with others, doesn't that sort of, you know, reinforce the mess mentality? I mean, if you have a bunch of women get together and they discover they are *all* messy, it might lead them to believe if so many others are messy, it might be all right.

Oh, okay, sorry, women *or* men. Yeah, yeah, I just thought...Okay, you don't have to shout, I realize men can be messy too—sure—Sorry. I am *not* a sexist pig. Yeah, yeah, okay—So do you have to attend all the sessions for it to be effective? I mean, the one on understanding the need for clutter, could that be skipped? That seems like a real reinforcer to me. We don't want her to understand the need for clutter, we want her to overcome it.

Yeah, sure, but what if it doesn't? I mean, what if she comes home from your seminar all smiles, saying, 'I understand the need for clutter. That was the best thing you ever did for me, sending me to that class. Now that I understand the need for clutter, I'm more at home with it and I don't ever have to feel it's a needless thing. There is a genuine *need* for clutter, so why don't you go to the class and understand the need yourself and stop your endless complaining about it?'

Well sure, but I don't *want* to come to the class, the

problem is hers, not mine, and if all you do is teach, 'Hey, it's hunky-dory to be messy. Cleanliness isn't next to Godliness after all, it's more like next to psychotic dementia or something,' well, I mean, who needs that?

Look, we are talking about a woman who never throws away a magazine. We have magazines from forty years ago, and we get about thirty a month. She never took a note on a scrap of paper that she doesn't have warrened somewhere to this day. Yeah, chronic. That's what I'm trying to tell you. The stuff just piles up all over the house. There are hundreds of boxes of newspaper clippings she couldn't look at if she lived another hundred years. You remember the guy in San Diego or somewhere who suffocated when all his books fell on him? That's my wife. That's why I'm calling you; I don't want that to happen to her. I mean, we have bookshelves in the bedroom loaded to the ceiling, and it could happen to *me*.

Excuse me a minute, yes, Ginny?—Well move it.

Oh, nothing, just my wife complaining about my bicycle in the garage. Can't get her car in, she says—Petty— So I guess I'll have to run now—hold on again, will ya? Yes? Well I'm reading them—just pick them up if you can't walk through…Oh, I don't know, it's on my desk someplace, but I got so much junk here I can't put my finger on it. I'm on the phone, I'll find it in a minute…Well, okay, it might take an hour to wade through this stuff…

Thanks for holding. Well, so long and thanks for the info. I'll try to send her…Oh, no, *I* don't need it.

The Best Seat In London

With the dollar sinking to another all-time low, it was the most inauspicious moment to travel to London, so we took it.

What is London without a concert? I saw an intriguing one in the listings: Simon Rattle and the Birmingham Symphony Orchestra and Chorus.

When I got to the Royal Albert Hall, several semi-savory looking gentlemen bounded toward me.

"You looking for tickets for tonight?" one of them asked, looking like a heavyweight wrestler, lately out of training.

"Yeees," I answered, reluctantly, always a little suspicious of these hucksters, yet not entirely immune to the prospect of a bargain.

"Where do you want to be?" he asked.

"Right in the orchestra."

He looked at me quizzically. "Here, I got a map," he said, pulling a brochure from his pocket. "Show me."

I pointed to seats behind the orchestra. He winced.

"You can't see anything there," he said.

"I don't care about seeing, I want to hear."

He looked again, as if to see if I were trying to put him on.

"I've been here before," I explained, in case he thought from my accent I might be an unsophisticated tourist, "and it's a dead hall. You can't hear anything unless you are practically in the orchestra."

"Can't hear anything?" He nodded, not so much in understanding as in acceptance that this turkey was not going to be an easy sale.

Over the loudspeaker came the following warning: "Attention all patrons. Do not buy tickets from people standing in front of the hall. You may not be able to get into the performance."

The wrestler waved a ticket at me and it was computer printed. I couldn't make anything out on it.

"Where's the seat?" I asked.

He pointed to a position very similar to my last seat in the hall—"No thanks," I said, trying to get away from him because they were repeating the warnings about not buying from the crooks out front. "That's about where I was before and you can't hear—no resonance."

He huddled with a guy who looked like his trainer. Their expressions told me I had expressed a legitimate concern and they were willing to deal with it.

"Can't hear?" his buddy said. "Here, how about this one?" And he handed my personal salesman another computer ticket.

"Oh boy—here's one," my man said. "Door four," and he pointed to door four on the other side of the hall—exactly opposite of the first offer.

"But that's no different," I said.

"Yes it is," he insisted. "Look, here, it's right up where you want to be."

"No," I said. "I want to be closer to the stage. Door one. That's door four."

"But that's only the door you go in, not where you sit."

"Let me go inside and see how close it is. Oh, by the way, how much do you want for it?"

"Fifty pounds," he said, without flinching. As I have noted, the almighty dollar was almighty puny abroad and his fifty pounds was close to one hundred dollars after you get through paying the usurious exchange commission.

"Fifty pounds?" I said. "You're kidding."

"No. What did you expect to pay?" he asked.

"No more than eighteen pounds."

Then a light seemed to go on in his head. "Say, mate," he inquired, "what do you think you are going to tonight?"

"A concert," I said. "Simon Rattle and the Birmingham Symphony."

"Not tonight," he said. "This is a prizefight—for the heavyweight championship of Britain."

"Yeah? Where's the concert then?"

"Royal Festival Hall, South Bank." He smiled, showing the teeth that had survived with him. "I thought it a little odd you only wanted to hear it, mate."

I ran for a cab. What with the traffic and all, I arrived to a sign posted on the box office. "This performance sold out."

But the woman behind the till had a few left.

"But it's just about to start," she said.

I paid through the nose and ran. When I found my door upstairs, the concert had begun and I was given the intelligence that I would stay out for the first twenty-two-minute movement, then I could go in and STAND in the back for the remainder of the first half of the program.

I should have gone to the prizefight. I might have had a seat.

Sex On
The Beach

The Peninsula News *regrets that the following wrong article inadvertently appeared last week under the heading:*

City Halts Illicit Beach Sex
By Anne LaJeunesse
News Staff Writer

Abalone Cove area visitors who have reportedly used the beach's foliage to screen both heterosexual and homosexual activity will have to find some other haven because the city is currently trimming trees to diminish the privacy that once made the area an attractive trysting spot.

The City of Rancho Palos Verdes recently gained ownership of the beach property as the result of the Horan landslide lawsuit settlement and decided to trim foliage in response to several complaints voiced at a recent Abalone Cove Task Force meeting.

To thwart any sexual activity in the beach area near Portuguese Point, the city staff was ordered to trim off lower tree branches and cut bushes back so that they reach a height no greater than two feet…

We apologize to our readers for any inconvenience or shock to the sensibilities this may have caused.
With your indulgence we will reprint the correct article now.

City Halts Illicit Beach Sex
By Anna Younger
News Staff Writer

After Rancho Palos Verdes (the City of) gained ownership of the Abalone Cove beach property, as a result of the Horan landslide lawsuit settlement, an unidentified staffer noticed the area was tailor-made for illicit sex, thanks largely to the secluded nature of the beach, as well as the crowded conditions in City Hall.

An anonymous source, high in local government circles, insists that the crowded conditions at City Hall had absolutely nothing to do with the acquisition of the heretofore nude beach.

"It was simply a fringe benefit," he said anonymously, noting that illicit sex at City Hall was becoming next to impossible without a substantial audience.

The high shrubbery surrounding the Abalone Cove site made the area an attractive trysting spot. And, it was just a short stroll from City Hall. Bored staffers could take their lunches there and reportedly use the beach's foliage to screen both heterosexual and homosexual activity.

Suddenly, what has become a dependable lifestyle for some of the city staff, is threatened.

Some of the older members of the staff (viz. decrepit), in a fit of jealousy at younger members' increasingly long lunch hours, have conspired to thwart any sexual activity in the beach area near Portuguese Point. The point being that staff productivity had been sagging as a result of these lunch dates.

However, participants at the beach claim the opposite. "Staff morale has never been higher," Joan Airos, Director of Landslide Settlements, said for attribution.

"Especially after lunch."

The old fogies counter that morale may well be higher after lunch, but productivity is squandered on the beach, as many staffers never make it back to City Hall.

Members of the City Council, who are said to lunch elsewhere, could not be reached for comment.

Not that anyone tried to reach them.

Hector Snethkamp, group leader of the Abalone Cove Bring-Smut-Back-Into-the-Home Task Force, says:

"I got nothing against this kinda stuff, don't get me wrong. But my house is overlooking this beach and I want the trees cut down to the ground."

"To thwart any sexual activity on the beach?" I asked.

"No, so I can see what's going on."

"Why the two foot height limit on the shrubbery?" the Task Force's *force majeure* was asked.

"It will screen the illicit sex from the little kiddies who should be protected at all costs, yet it won't block the views of the rest of us."

To straighten out this mess, the following memo was distributed to all departments at City Hall:

To: All Staff Members

From: Arbiter of Moral Rectitude

It has come to our attention that the City has been using the Abalone Cove Beach property for illicit purposes of a sexual nature. As a result, the foliage has been trampled and will now barely grow two feet. The new view this has afforded the neighbors has severely limited their productivity at lunchtime, to say nothing of ours.

Consequently, we must henceforth and immediately halt all illicit beach sex.

Impressing The Old Man

TAOS, NM: Of all the mating dances performed by various earthly species, perhaps the most bizarre is that carried on by Homo sapiens.

I am having an opportunity to observe this peculiar dance up close.

It is to a particular phase of this mating dance that I address myself today: It is the subject of my proposed doctoral dissertation in behavioral psychology (working title): "The Complex Symbiosis Between the Father of the Female and the Female's Suitor in the Homo Sapiens Mating Dance."

My three daughters, Hortense, Esmeralda and Jambalaya (not their real names), are assembled in the land of enchantment, Taos, New Mexico; the home of D.H. Lawrence, whose philosophy of life is succinctly expressed in his best-known novel, *Lady Chatterley's Significant Other*.

You may have observed that from time to time when I mention my daughters, I do not use their real names. This is not, as some suggest, because I can't remember their real names. It is because of the burdens imposed on the children of the famous by a fickle society that I am protecting their privacy. You can just imagine how difficult it would be for them if everytime they flashed a credit card people would say, "Geez, I read about you in the paper—That father of yours is some fabulous writer." It is a proven fact that kids of famous fathers suffer with secondhand celebrity. It is for this reason that I deliberately avoided becoming famous until they were all adults.

Assembled in Taos with our three daughters are three presentable lads dancing the mating dance. You can tell from the gleams in their eyes they are eager to impress the father of the family.

I remember well this aspect of my own youthful mating dance. I had taken a young SC woman home to Pennsylvania. I leaked the answers to my father's test to her. I told her he was very partial to being addressed as "Judge," having spent some twelve months in that appointed capacity.

Alas, she continually called him "Mister Gardner." After she left, my father said, "She's a nice girl," (pause) "but she isn't very bright, is she?"

When Ginny came along (her real name, remember) primed with this intelligence, out shot her hand, "Good to see you, Judge."

His verdict? "She has real class."

So what do my daughters leak about me? The lads can't call me "Judge." But my test is simple. I give the suitors each a box of Father Gardner's Candies, and all they have to do is say, "That's the best candy I ever had in my life." They may, of course, put it in their own words, as long as "best in my life" is in there somewhere.

When one completes his fulsome praise, I think quite adequately, I hear one of our daughters whisper, "Best you had in your life."

"Best I ever had in my life," he says.

Very intelligent lad, he is.

The girls request I try to behave like a normal father. But several things conspire against it. First, the snow gods turn their back on me for most of the trip, so I can't strap on my brand-new cross-country skis. The swains, being champion downhill skiers, have phony snow manufactured for their pleasure, but we sloggers are not similarly coddled. When I find a place to ski only 38 miles away, some inhospitable New Mexico policeman helps me celebrate the New Year with a $78 speeding ticket.

Being in a state that pollutes its air with the waves of radar is not conducive to being a normal father.

Then the coup de grace, I get a hacking, tubercular cough, so that everytime I respond to some pleasantry I explode like a series of land mines. I impress them like any sniveling tubercular weakling. But how do the lads measure up?

Well, the first one gives me a beautiful onyx chess set which works okay for a while, but then my pieces begin to malfunction and the suitor beats the pants off me. Bad judgment on his part.

The second buys me the world's most difficult jigsaw puzzle. It has the same picture on both sides, only 90 degrees off. And the pieces are cut the same, so you never know which side is up. I sweat over it daily for eight hours while he is having fun skiing, and tell him, when he returns to check my progress, that I have only glanced at it for five or ten minutes. Then he proceeds to sit down for five or ten minutes and virtually do the whole thing. Bad judgment on his part.

Swain number three brings fudge his mother made, and it is better than Father Gardner's Candies!

Wretched judgment.

Well, at least I still have my cough. No one can take that away from me.

And by the way, if you happen to bump into me on the Peninsula, call me "Judge," will you?

Intellectual Pretensions

Some of my harsher critics have been suggesting my writing should take a more intellectual bent. Some have gone so far as to taunt me with the suggestion that I show my mettle with a reader's guide on how to get the most out of Homer's *Iliad*.

And why not? It is a book, I am not ashamed to say, I have just finished (in a manner of speaking).

I *have* always aspired to be a Peninsula intellectual. I can hardly be blamed if things didn't pan out that way.

First, my credentials:

In the Navy I was given a speed-reading course. Since I was learning to fly (rather slowly), they wanted to speed up my reading for some reason. Perhaps because the new jets flew so fast I would not, at my reading speed, be able to read the landing instructions before landing the airplane.

I began the course with a reading speed of 350 words

per minute with 90 percent comprehension. In two short weeks I had increased my speed 1000 words a minute—with zero comprehension.

The instructor suggested I read easier stuff.

For the *Iliad* I brought my speed down to about 250 words per minute. My comprehension was still zero.

However, ability to give advice should not, I have long observed in practice, be limited to those with expertise in the subject.

The first question you should settle is should you get a book with big type or little type?

With big type, you turn the pages faster and oftener and you build up momentum. With small type, you have fewer pages to turn and there is less between you and the end of the book, giving you more hope than momentum.

The next decision is paperback vs. hardback. I strongly suggest the hardback—the heavier the better. The *Iliad* is a weighty book and not to be taken lightly. If your friends see you with a paperback in your hand, they will most likely conclude you are reading a trashy romance, no matter how much effort you make to show the title.

Surveys show that you are 8.5 times more likely to have a friend or stranger ask what you are reading if the book is hardcover.

The heady feeling you will get when you say, "Oh, just Homer's *Iliad*," will be well worth the extra cost of the book.

While it is certainly advisable to be seen in public reading the *Iliad*, the methods I am going to give you for getting through the book must be reserved for strict privacy.

If you begin reading as you would an ordinary book, you may find, early on, the going a trifle sluggish.

My advice is skip the introduction. It is probably only some English professor showing how much he knows. If it doesn't confuse you, it will give you hopeless feelings of inferiority.

So plunge right into the book. Scan the page until your eyes catch on something that suggests the slaughter of a human being.

Words to look for are: spear, javelin, sword, lance, arrows, darts. Where they appear, there is sure to be blood, and consequently the meat and main thrust of the work.

Never go back. You will find if you missed it the first time, you should count your blessings.

The Trojan band is mentioned, which just points up the wealth of information the *Iliad* contains. Little did I realize USC had a football team 3,000 years ago, let alone a band.

Whatever you do, *use* the intelligence you have gleaned from the book in conversation. Maybe you are in the stands at a Peninsula Little League game. You should casually say to your neighbor, "That was a particularly nasty javelin to the breast of old Nestor's son, wouldn't you say?"

You don't want to wade through a tome like that without reaping some rewards.

You aren't liable to get many laughs from the *Iliad*. If you find yourself smiling now and again, it will not be because the author intended you to be happy.

One final note. If you read the *Iliad* in the original Greek, this advice may not be for you.

Requiem
For A Genius

From time to time momentous documents are uncovered which shed further light on the early history of mankind.

The Dead Sea Scrolls and the Q Documents are but a few of these historical finds. And now an astonishing revelation in the world of music, which is being capriciously referred to as "The Amazing WAM-O Papers," after Wolfgang Amadeus Mozart's very own initials.

The discovery, as well as this subsequent reporting, was made possible by a grant from the Warring-Porridge Foundation, Felix Warring-Porridge, Executive Secretary. It is being revealed here in celebration of Mozart's 132nd birthday, next Wednesday, January 27.

The motion picture *Amadeus*, as well as the stage play before it, focused the world's attention on Mozart's writing of his *Requiem Mass* in the most outlandishly contrived fashion.

It is too bad the following was not discovered in time for Peter Shaffer, the author, to check his facts.

The newly-discovered document goes a long way toward pointing up the real inner workings of the mind of a genius.

The transcription of the historical conversation between Wolfgang Amadeus Mozart and an unidentified interviewer dated 1791 was unearthed in Salzburg, Austria, in a recent excavation to provide ample free parking to visitors for the Mozart Geburtshaus.

INTERVIEWER: Well, Wolfgang, how does it feel to have completed *The Magic Flute*?

WAM: It feels real good, Art.

INTERVIEWER: There were some rumors that your father, Leopold, wasn't too keen on the work.

WAM: My father never heard the work. He's dead.

INTERVIEWER: Oh, I'm sorry to hear that. I didn't know.

WAM: That's all right, he's been gone fourteen years now.

INTERVIEWER: Well, there's a rumor he wouldn't have liked the work had he heard it. And speaking of rumors, there are some rumors that your father didn't, well, should we say, approve of your wife.

WAM: Well, Constanza wasn't too crazy about him either.

INTERVIEWER: Wolfgang, what can we tell the folks is in the works?

WAM: A couple more kids, I hope, if I can get these symphonies out of the way so I can get to see Constanza before she poops out for the night.

INTERVIEWER: No, no, I mean musically.

WAM: Oh, sorry. Well, I've written over six hundred

works, you know. Every kind you can think of. Symphonies, string quartets, piano concertos, clarinet concertos, operas, Masses, horn concertos, violin sonatas, concertos, piano sonatas, fantasias, fugues. I mean, you name it, I've done it.

INTERVIEWER: Is there nothing left then?

WAM: Yes there is. I think before I die I'd like to write a Requiem.

INTERVIEWER: Wolfie, we've got to pause here for a few minutes to hear from the people who are making this fascinating moment in history possible.

WAM: Sure.

INTERVIEWER: You'll probably write a symphony during the commercial.

WAM: In the old days, yes—now it could be two.

PITCHMAN: Hi, folks, Maxie Blumme, Salzburg's most reliable used-harpsichord dealer, is featuring one-owner harpsichords with only a minimum of broken strings at prices you simply cannot afford to pass up.

We have Ruckers, Hitchcocks, Blanchets, Shudis, and many more. Some of them dusted by the household help of the great and near-great.

Stop in today. We will not be undersold. But hurry, supplies are limited, and in fairness to our many friends and customers we will limit our sales to one harpsichord per customer. Back to you, Art.

INTERVIEWER: Well, we're back here with the delightful young genius Wolfgang Amadeus Mozart, and I just wondered, Wolfie, have you ever gotten a used harpsichord from Maxie Blumme?

WAM: Junk, Art, real junk. Don't go near the place with a ten-foot staff. I mean, half the strings are busted, and the other half are out of tune. The keys are sticky. I don't think they've ever dusted one of them.

INTERVIEWER: (coughs) Ah, yes. Before our sponsor break we were talking about death music, I believe, and Wolfie was saying he figured it would be appropriate to write a Requiem before he died. Is that right?

WAM: Yes, Art, that's right.

INTERVIEWER: Why is that, Wolfie? What is it that motivates you to write death music before you die?

WAM: I haven't figured out how to do it afterwards.

INTERVIEWER: And the rest, ladies and gentlemen, is history.

Hanging Paper As Art

"Your Majesty, what have you done to the checking account?" My distaff, Ginny, was addressing me with a distressing lack of human understanding. In better moods she calls me "Your Royal Highness."

"Not enough, apparently," I said, injecting a touch of drollery.

It started with a call from our daughter Esmeralda (not her real name—I thought if I used a pseudonym for her, she wouldn't know which daughter I was referring to).

"All my checks are bouncing," Ginny lamented.

"Yeah, so I heard," I said, trying to offer some synthetic sympathy for her plight.

"Well, what are you going to do about it?"

"You just can't get a decent bank nowadays," I explained.

"What's the bank got to do with it?" she asked naively. "It's *your* fault, not the bank's."

"You'd think with all those accountants and computers they'd be able to do a little adding and subtracting for us and they'd know when we were running a little short."

"Oh my—"

"And why not?" I bristled at her response. "They are sitting there playing with our money and we haven't the foggiest notion what they are doing with it. They're just soreheads."

"Soreheads?" She wasn't sympathetic.

"You bet. They're mad when we spend a little of our own money—so they can't go fooling with it. So out of spite they don't tell us when we get a little low."

"In this case I believe we were trying to spend *their* money."

"Nit-picking," I said. "They use our money all the time. Why shouldn't we use some of theirs once in a while?"

"The neighbor submitted her little check twice for Girl Scout cookies, for God's sakes, and it bounced twice."

"Heh, heh, heh," I couldn't help chuckling.

"You think it's funny? It's not *your* check."

I responded with a little ditty I composed on the spot:

> *"Kite a check and fly it, high, high, high*
> *You're a deadbeat now, until the day you die."*

It was a paraphrase of a sorority song of our daughter Jambalaya—also not her real name.

> *"Find a kite and fly it, high, high, high*
> *You're a Theta now, until the day you die,"*

is how the original goes. I just love sorority songs.

> *"Kappa, Kappa, Kappa Gamma*
> *I'm so happy that I am a*
> *Kappa, Kappa, Kappa Gamma."*

But I digress. We hung a little paper on Jambalaya, too.

"It's nice to hear from the kids once in a while," I offered.

"You mean you deliberately let me bounce a dozen checks just for the phone calls?"

"Maybe you shouldn't write so many."

"Oooo!"

"Doesn't it stand to reason if you had only written half as many checks, only half as many would have bounced?"

"You're a laugh a minute," she said.

Women don't understand high finance.

For over 25 years I kept a check register, dutifully recording deposits and withdrawals, and at the end of each month heroically balancing the checkbook whenever it was humanly possible.

In that time, the only error the bank made that I could detect was in our favor. Is it any wonder that I decided to turn the bookkeeping over to them?

Now we have a bunch of daughters with whom I am occasionally engaged in hard-nosed business transactions. Let it be understood right now that I am *not* a pushover for women, and my children do *not* have me wrapped around their little fingers. In these "transactions," I am definitely in the driver's seat.

Of course that may be diminished somewhat when some two-bit bank has the temerity to send one of our checks back to them with the tactless message "Not Sufficient Funds" garishly stamped all over it.

They say money isn't everything, but it does keep you in touch with your children. And children, being rather less experienced than their parents, sometimes have trouble understanding the great American banking system.

Why else would a daughter say to her father, "No one else bounces checks on me." She lacks a basic understanding of our monetary system. Why should it be otherwise? They don't teach it in the schools.

"Maybe if you had the energy to keep a check register," Ginny said, "you would have realized what havoc tuition checks can wreak on a bank account."

I smiled a smile of barely-disguised condescension.

Ginny will never understand high finance.

Call Me Amadeus

I am a very modest, unassuming person by all accounts. Uncompetitive.

I do not experience the petty jealousies so many of my fellows seem to feel at the slightest provocation.

Something has recently occurred, however, that would push any reasonable man beyond the breaking point.

This newspaper has taken to putting a table of contents on the front page. It is a very handy reference for what can be found within the paper.

By itself, this is a laudable practice.

What I am forced to point out is that my name is listed alphabetically, flying in the face of venerable tradition, based on my first name.

Now any literate person should know that the alphabetization of names occurs throughout history with the last name first. Imagine the chaos if encyclopedias listed their entries by first names.

Listing me with the "T's" instead of the "G's" puts me between sports and want ads. One rung down from religion, and right across from legal notices.

I am sure any fair-minded person would not find it petty that I point out that Ann Rutkosky appears before the crime roundup on the very top of the Thursday list. Whereas, I am second to last in the Saturday list.

You might think this discrepancy is of little importance. You couldn't be more mistaken.

As Tevye observed in that wonderful Broadway musical *Fiddler on the Roof,* it was tradition that kept their balance in the face of terrible adversity. They even sang a song about their glorious traditions.

"Right on," I say. Traditions don't have to be big things, they can be little-often-taken-for-granted facts of everyday life.

Like alphabetization.

I have already received several letters addressing

themselves to this very ticklish point. One of them being:

Dear Sir:

I take exception with the Peninsula News *and their place-ment of your name in the alphabetical listing of the table of con-tents.*

Rather than list alphabetically, I am recommending the articles and sections be listed in order of merit, as sort of a guide to what is worth reading and what isn't.

I suggest you change your first name to Zeke.

Name withheld on request.

I received several other suggestions, but they don't measure up to my standards of fairness.

All my arguments have fallen on my esteemed editor's deafest ears. I just want him to know that if it weren't for his dogged intransigence, it would not have become necessary for me to take my case to the public.

I have explained to this editor that no one looks beyond sports in the index, ergo, no one would ever see my name.

And if they did see my name, reading from left to right as we are carefully taught in Occidental societies, my billing reads, "Legal Notices, Ted Gardner."

This suggestion that I am a bankrupt or eviction deadbeat in itself is sufficient cause for libel action, and many of my friends are encouraging me to file suit.

Another acquaintance pointed out that should someone read beyond sports, what they would read would be, "Ted Gardner, Want Ads," and would naturally think, "Oh, he's out of work again!"

In the Navy I was known as Gardner, T.R. I would have no argument using that in the table of contents because Gardner, T.R. would put me significantly ahead of Rutkosky, Ann. It would be a reasonable listing based on solid alphabetical tradition, and not fly in the face of custom as this curious arrangement does.

My patient and forgiving nature persuades me to

make a final offer, based on sound logic.

Instead of using Ted, dear Editor, I will change this nickname to my given name, Theodore. Theodore means "gift of God" in Greek. In Latin, "gift of God" translates to Amadeus.

The solution is simple. Without changing my name, I can henceforth be known as Amadeus Gardner. It's not a change of name, really. It's just a different translation.

That would put me comfortably above the crime roundup, at the head of the list.

And should Ann Rutkosky and Amadeus Gardner ever appear in the same issue, you know who would be first.

If you happen to run into my editor about the Peninsula, please tell him Amadeus says "Hello."

He'll know who you mean.

Hands Off My Organs

Dear Friends at the Department of Motor Vehicles (DMV):

A quandary is what I am in. I recently had the good fortune to have my driver's license renewed by you good people. I aced the test, only missing one—you know, the one about what happens to you if you refuse to take the breath test if the *gendarmes* suspect you might be a little tipsy. Since I don't booze myself, I haven't paid much attention to those punishments.

Okay, that's neither here nor there. The thing I'm writing about is definitely not to brag about my test score. And it isn't to complain about the funny picture you stuck on my new license, though God only knows where you got it. It certainly wasn't the one that nice lady took—the one who said to look at the red dot. Because I know for a fact that in that picture I was debonair, world-wise, in a pinch I'd be up for a Cary Grant role with Audrey Hepburn or some-body. I was well-groomed and had one of those all-knowing smiles on my face that said, "Sure, go ahead and take my picture, but we both know it won't capture my soul."

All well and good, but where did you find the picture of that long-haired simp you substituted for my picture? I know how those kids who were mixed up at birth must feel. Because that is definitely not the picture of me that came out of that camera when the nice lady told me to watch the red dot.

Maybe watching the red dot throws you off a little, I don't know. You ought to do some scientific studies on the thing so you could get better pictures—because it is well known happy drivers are safer drivers. But shucks, I'm not writing to complain about my picture, I'm writing because of my quandary. And if you don't know what quandary means, you can look it up. And if you look like that picture you stuck on my new driver's license, chances are you won't know what quandary means.

So anyway, here's the thing: What is this little red card you sent along with my license? You know, the one with the little punch-out dot that says:

Donor

And the dot is, you guessed it—red! Then it says:

Pursuant to the Uniform Anatomical Gift Act. I hereby elect upon my death the following option(s):

> A __ To donate any organs or parts
> B __ To donate a pacemaker (date implanted________)
> C __ To donate parts or organs listed ______________
> D __ To not donate any organs, parts or pacemaker.

Well now, I just don't see through all this ambiguity. "I hereby elect upon my death," but as far as I know I'm not dying. And if I were, I don't know how much electin' I'd be doing, considering the shape I'd be in.

Now I know it is more blessed to give than to receive and all that, but when you start fiddling with my pancreas and all that internal stuff, it gives me pause. Actually, the willies is what it gives me.

I mean, has anybody looked into the implications of this thing? A cop stops you and the first thing he does is ask for your license, right? Now he turns it over to see if you are a heroic donor, or a welcher. No matter how legitimate your concerns about the far-reaching effect of someone fiddling with your pancreas. And who says you are dead anyway? Mistakes have been made.

It used to be you could just politely ignore this donor business. No more. Now it says if you *don't* want to donate, "fill out this card and attach it to the back of your license..."

But what will the cop think? If there is a chance to save my life, will he look at my license, then abandon me as some pancreatic welcher? Or will he be more likely to give me a ticket, just because I have legitimate concerns about my liver?

It's definitely a deprivation of my civil rights and *clearly* unlawful discrimination against a coward.

And what if I *don't* fill it out and attach it to my license? Does that give you license to grab my spleen?

So after giving careful consideration to your request, I am reluctantly checking number D.

"To not donate any organs,..." under which I am writing:

"But you are welcome to my piano."

The 5 Minute Blessing

The call came on Valentine's Day. Clarence Darrow (not his real name) was calling from an airport in Cleveland.

Clarence is otherwise known as a suitor of our daughter Hortense (not her real name), and when my wife of some decades said he desired my presence on the phone, I said, "Tell him he has the wrong number." I was cleverly thinking he had meant to call Hortense in Northern California and had mistakenly dialed us.

Not so.

In a becalmed voice that he summoned from God knows where, he said, "I want to m—— your daughter and I'm calling to ask your blessing."

Unfortunately, I didn't catch the fourth word of the recitation when he said it, so I was just as confused as when I came to the phone. By the time he finished the spiel, though, I was on the right track. "Wow," I said. "Gee, I never expected to be asked that."

"We're old-fashioned in Cleveland," he said.

"The East has more tradition," my aforementioned wife Ginny said on the other line. Ginny is her real name. I tried a pseudonym, but she is just too well-known. There was unmistakable excitement in her voice.

I was cautious.

Now the lad, of course, was eminently suitable, but the surprise threw me off my feed. There is a delicate balance between being cordial and anxious. On the one hand, you aspire to see your daughters unionized, but you must be careful not to water her stock by appearing overanxious. On the other hand, you don't want to discourage any reasonable possibility, and this chap was a more-than-reasonable possibility.

And, then too, there's the obligation one has in such circumstances, an obligation honed on reputation, to say something witty.

Nothing witty came to mind. It was just as well, because it wouldn't do to ruin the moment with some misunderstood sarcasm.

"Well, ah, how long do I have to decide?" I asked, in a tone clearly calculated as suave, conservative, wary, and yet not disinterested.

"Seven or eight months," he said generously. That was nice, but misleading. It developed he was to make the proposal that evening in San Francisco, so it behooved any blessings to be proffered before that. To wit: now, while he was on the phone in the Cleveland airport awaiting his severely delayed plane.

While I was fumbling for something brilliant to say, something witty, perhaps—erudite, Clarence said, "Excuse me, I think my plane is being called. I'll be right back."

I took his absence as an opportunity to discuss our obligation under the circumstances with the real Ginny, who was on the telephone extension.

"What do we say?" I asked her.

"Say yes," she said.

"Just like that? I mean, shouldn't we be careful not to

appear too anxious?"

"Well, what are you going to say otherwise? 'I'll think about it'? He's on his way to California to propose, he needs an answer now."

"But it's such short notice. I mean, he could have called yesterday. Now we have to make a snap decision while he waits for a plane that is taking off at any moment."

"You don't have any doubts, do you?" Ginny said. "Not that it would matter one way or the other if you did."

"Well—he's a good catch, all right, but..."

"But what?"

"Do you think...I don't mean this personally, you understand, but more as a general thing—I mean, do you think he praises my columns enough?"

"Oh my..."

"Oh, don't take it the wrong way. You know I don't require slavering outlandish praise..."

"Not much," she said. "All he has to say every week is that it's the best thing he ever read."

Clarence was back on the phone, speaking in his sublimely modulated voice, as though he hadn't a fear in the world. It was something I would just have to accept: I was singularly unable to inspire fear in anyone. I can't imagine my asking Ginny's father for his blessing. What if he had said no?

"My plane is leaving," Clarence said.

"Oh...well..." I was frankly flustered at being pressured so subtly. "Well, yes, I guess, go ahead."

"Thanks," he said, and was gone into the wild blue yonder, or black yonder, I suppose, because it was after sundown.

When he hung up Ginny said, "Good for you."

"What do you mean?"

"You gave your blessing."

"Huh? I wasn't given any time to think. Do you suppose he planned that on purpose? I mean, why call us five minutes before takeoff if he wanted us to have time to consider?"

"Oh, it's sweet," she said. "*You* didn't do it. Anyway, you already said yes, so stop stewing about it."

"Yes? I said yes?" I said. "I said yes he could catch the plane."

Santa Invades Biosphere Two Too

He parked the reindeer and sleigh in the parking lot near the steel-and-glass structure outside Oracle, Arizona. He had circled the 3-acre monolith a half-dozen times looking for some chink in the armor, some opening that he could breach, but, finding none, he made his way across the parking lot to a uniformed security guard.

The guard's eyes were full of the old jaundice as they perused the red suit with the fluffy white trim, encumbered as it was with ashes and soot.

"Can I help you?" came the cliché sally. The literal translation was, "Buzz off, bozo."

"I've got to get some gifts in there."

"I'm sorry, that won't be possible. The Biosphere II is sealed, it cannot be penetrated for two years. Nothing in, nothing out."

"Well, some provisions should have been made for Santa Claus. You can't have a viable environment that has not made provision for a visit from Saint Nick around the winter solstice."

"That may be, but that's just the way Mr. Bass wanted it."

"Mr. Bass?"

"He's the honcho ponied up the hundred-fifty mil for this here habitat. We got 3,800 species of plants and animals and 5 different ecosystems—We got a desert, a savanna, a rain forest, a marsh, even an ocean with a coral reef."

"But no provisions for Santa Claus?"

"No, sir."

"There ought to at least be a chimney."

"No chimney."

"Not even a doggy door?"

The security guard clamped his lips and added a stern switch of his head. "Nothing," he said. "Now I have to ask you to move your sleigh, it's blocking traffic."

"But I'm Santa Claus, and it's Christmas Eve!"

"I don't care who you are, jelly belly, get your reindeer

outta my parking lot."

"Come on, there's got to be some way for the spirit of Christmas to penetrate this shell."

The guard shrugged his shoulders. "No can do," he said smugly. "Face it, man. The whole thing doesn't wash. Reindeer don't fly. It's a fantasy."

"Really?"

"The laws of physics, man. I mean, there is just no possibility," the guard was banishing all doubts. "You'd be better off spending your time at Weight Watchers."

"You think so?" Santa was starting to look glum.

"Besides, Santa Claus is for kids, and we got only adults in the Biosphere II. You don't expect grown persons to believe in Santa Claus, do you?"

"Why not?"

"Well there *isn't* any Santa Claus, for starters," the guard said.

"So," Jelly Belly said, "if I told you I had a new car for you—you wouldn't believe it?"

"A new car?" he gulped. "For me?" He stole a quick glance at the 15-year-old heap he called his "Transportation."

"Not if you don't believe."

The guard frowned. "What—just for the sake of argument—would happen if I, ah, that is if I, ah, could become a, ah, believer?"

"Can you get me in the Biosphere II?"

"I wouldn't know how to go about it."

"How about a tunnel?"

"Take a lot of time," the guard said, "screw up the ecosystems." His eyebrows tangled in ponderous thought. "Let me see the car."

"No can do—"

"A Ford—a Chevy?"

"A Rolls."

"Cut it out."

"This is Christmas, isn't it?"

"Yeahss…"

"And I'm Santa Claus…?"

"Ah…I…ah…guess."
"And you believe in Santa Claus?"
"I do?"
"Even though you aren't a kid anymore?"
"Hmm—A *Rolls*?"
"A new Rolls Royce."
"For *me*?"
"For you."
"Let's start digging."

Unopened Toothpicks And Blue Chips

Two seasons late, I have gotten the spring-cleaning bug. I am cleaning out the middle drawer in my desk at home.

No great task, you say. No big deal.

Being of limited size, it has become the repository for small items, items it would seem foolish to store in larger drawers. For instance, I have just found two Blue Chip Stamps. Not two sheets, or two books, but two Blue Chip Stamps. You may remember them as the incentive gas stations gave you to buy their gas. Everybody gave them. I got two.

A penny saved is a penny earned.

There are Boy Scout merit badge cards: Machinery (I don't know a stroke from a bore), Pathfinding (I still get lost going around the block) and Bookbinding are among the most unlikely.

Also numerous unopened toothpicks, one from Air France and one that says, "Enjoy life—eat out more often." And, presumably, pick your teeth afterwards.

I just uncovered twenty-three 13-cent postage stamps from the 1976 bicentennial. Will they still stick? There are one-,two- and three-centers, twenty-two cents, a Eugene O'Neill dollar stamp, and a six-cent F.D. Roosevelt stamp lifted from some uncancelled envelope. The guy at the local post office used to say it was a very difficult stamp to work with around here because people were always spitting on the wrong side.

My old stamp collection includes one from the Peninsula Car Care Center, circa 1980, awarded to me for a car wash. Only nine more to go and I get a free wash.

Buttons that have mysteriously separated themselves from garments, long abandoned.

There are several keys to unknown locks, and the two-dollar bill my daughter Jambalaya (not her real name) gave me for safekeeping when she was just little. Nails, dead batteries of every description, Father Gardner's Candy inserts, e.g.:

Better if used before
April 1, 1967.

A 1983 letter from Stanley Ellin of Brooklyn, N.Y., thanking me for my praise of one of his books. Frequent flyer stickers from an airline called PSA—not one used.

A $5 check written in 1982 to SPCA for a skunk trap.

Sterling silver teething ring I chomped on as a tot. My mother thought I should have it. (You can see why *she* has clean drawers.) Where would *you* put it?

A group picture taken in kindergarten. There were 15 of us, and I hope you will not find it unseemly if I say I looked rather rakish, in a leather pilot's cap, galoshes and a tweed scarf tied outside the coat at a, yes, rakish angle.

Terribly British.

A five-year calendar, very handy since I only look in the drawer every five years or so.

I notice a number of the business cards in my drawer are from people who are dead. I call that loyalty.

As I dig deeper, I notice my business card collection is heavy on art galleries, piano tuners and barbers. Eyes, ears and vanity?

A pencil note from my wife: "I took your last $5— yuk!"

Why did I keep that?

A wild collection of matches. About seventeen packs all told. I don't smoke, but I guess I didn't want to rule out arson, either.

A note from one daughter complaining about money spent on another daughter, and my rapier-keen rebuttal tearing her argument to shreds. I have always been at the top of my form when debating a twelve-year-old.

The car dealer's key tag for a 1972 Audi 100LS, seventeen years in the drawer. "Worst car ever made," another Audi dealer told me when I was trying to unload it. "And you're getting that from an Audi dealer," he reassured me.

I am three fourths of the way through the job and, frankly, bogging down. Without much trouble I have thrown away the expendables; i.e. the two Blue Chip Stamps, snips of ribbon, the frequent flyer stickers (when there is an incentive for the infrequent flyer I will be interested).

But now that the drawer is three-fourths empty, I am beleaguered by two dilemmas:

(1) Where am I going to put this junk I can't bring myself to throw away, and (2) Assuming I can find another place for the above-mentioned junk, what am I going to put in the empty drawer?

The cleaning had become so all-consuming that I hadn't even considered this larger reality:

There simply isn't anything else I'd rather put in the drawer.

So where did I put those two Blue Chip Stamps? I know they're here somewhere.

The Fertilizer Perspective

One word has changed my life. That word is "fertilizer." The charming and engaging motion picture *Dead Poets Society* put me onto it.

In the picture, Robin Williams has refined the part he played in *Good Morning, Vietnam* to a high art. Still the outsider with his commanding officers, still beloved by his troops, still the maverick, Williams, a teacher, leads his students, at the acute acne stage of their lives, out into the corridor. There he shows them pictures of graduates, long dead, and tells them they are now fertilizing daisies. They should, therefore, he says, get the most out of life (*"carpe diem"*), seize the day.

And why, indeed, not?

Of course you know what happens to mavericks in real life. It happened to Robin Williams in *Good Morning, Vietnam*, it happened to him in *Dead Poets Society*, and if he doesn't watch his step, it will happen to him in the great outdoors.

Fertilizer.

The movie, as I have said, was charming, with one exception. Just as I finished saying to myself, "Isn't this great? Here's one movie without a gun or a hint of violence or graphic sex," a gun appears. Though we don't see it go off, we see the smoke (which could only have come from a dry ice machine, it hung in the air so long), and we find out it did the deed guns are made for, which is to say, killing.

More fertilizer.

I was disappointed at that point in the film, and hard pressed to find any relevance to the act so jarring and out of character in this warm, fuzzy movie where dramatic impact was constantly achieved with laudable economy.

But now, some weeks later, I suddenly see the connection. The basic theme of the film was "All life becomes fertilizer," and the gun made fertilizer.

This new Fertilizer Perspective has changed my life.

It's like the Australian saying, "Rooster today, feather duster tomorrow." But "Fertilizer" has more economy, brevity, more bite, and it has kind of a roguish smell to it.

I am, however, forced to admit, though the Fertilizer Perspective has changed my life, others have not been so fortunate.

My wife, for one. She refuses to acknowledge the great impact this simple concept could have on the world. It's therefore my duty to convince her.

For instance, when she gets it in her head that the grass might be getting a trifle long and maybe, just maybe you understand, the appearance of the place might benefit from a little mowing thereof, I smile to myself and say:

"Fertilizer."

"What's that supposed to mean?" she asks.

"It is not supposed to mean anything. It is a universal truth. We are all on our merry way to becoming fertilizer."

"That's nice," she says, "but the grass needs mowing, not fertilizing."

"But doesn't that throw a new slant on mowing the lawn and mundane chores of that ilk?"

"No," she says. "You want the grass to go to seed like you have?"

"Perspective, Ginny," I say. "You've got to have a perspective about these things. What you've always been short on is vision."

"*Au contraire*," she says, flaunting her French in an effort to camouflage her German heritage. "I have vision in spades, and that's why I can see how hellish long the grass is getting."

"Fertilizer," I say again. Children learn by rote, why can't she?

"Manure," she counters.

"It's not the same. Look at it this way," I try again. "Not only are we on our way to the bone-mill where we will be ground by some higher being into nitrogen, phosphorus and potassium, but once rendered into that state, what will we be used for?"

"Oh brother," she suffers with a certain dignity.

"Fertilizer," I say, "to make the grass grow even faster. And if that happens, it will need mowing even oftener."

"Look," she says, "I will be in a more receptive frame of mind to listen to your claptrap philosophy after you mow the lawn."

"Mowing the lawn kills part of the grass. It turns to fertilizer too. You can't win this game. The dead grass mulches and fertilizes the lawn creating new and greener grass, so that the grass will always be greener on the other side," I say. "Whatever we do in life, we are all destined to become fertilizer—so why worry about anything? You know, I'm beginning to feel a little like fertilizer already."

"Is that what I smell?" she says.

For The Deployment Of Local Submarines

If you want to avoid, evade or just defer your taxes, the man to turn to locally is Rolling Hills resident Dr. Artimus Cryer.

I called Dr. Cryer for an appointment to get advice on evading the new Rancho Palos Verdes Utility Tax.

"I live just off Flying Triangle in Rolling Hills," Dr. Cryer explained on the phone. "I used to live on Flying Triangle, but the earth slipped."

We met the next day in his expanding front yard.

"I spend as little time in the house as possible," the doctor apologized. "I get so seasick."

"You certainly have a beautiful big front lawn," I complimented him.

"Gets bigger every day," he said. My first question was about the Curve for which Dr. Cryer is so famous. "What inspired the first Cryer Curve?"

"Heartburn," the doctor said. "I had eaten too much pastrami at the Appetizer and I just grabbed a napkin to stifle a belch. It came out of nowhere. I wrote the curve on the napkin—right on the spot."

"And the rest is history," I said. "Can you explain the Cryer Curve?"

"It's deceptively simple," he said.

He took a napkin from his pocket and told me there was such a demand for his Cryer Curve that he bought napkins by the case.

He drew an upside-down U and put it in front of my face as though I were chronically nearsighted.

"The more taxes people pay, the angrier they get," he said, his chest heaving with well-deserved pride. "The converse is also true."

"Was it this curve that brought you to the attention of the intellectuals surrounding Ronald Reagan when he was Governor of California?"

"Yes, it was."

"Were you in Reagan's kitchen cabinet?"

"Heavens no," his mouth dropped in shock. "I was always allowed in the living room."

"Did you go to Washington?"

"No. I was invited, of course, but I opted to stay in Rolling Hills to keep an eye on my Flying Triangle house."

"Is that when you formed your tax partnership, Cryer, Mea, River?"

"Yes. We do oil, real estate, farming and miscellaneous evasions."

"Have you ever considered running for public office, Dr. Cryer?"

"I toyed with the Senate, but I decided it would split the already tiny Rolling Hills vote to have both a Laffer and a Cryer on the same ticket."

"How would you evade a utility tax?" I inquired.

He slapped his bald forehead. "The taxers are getting so sneaky." He fought to clear some phlegm from his throat. "I am digging my own well, and setting up my own generator. I am buying a wood-burning stove, planting a lot of fast-growing trees and subscribing to the Sunday Los Angeles

Times. There is enough fuel in one edition alone to keep me warm for a week."

"And finally," he said, stopping for breath, "I am advocating war."

"War?" I gasped. "With whom?"

"Rolling Hills Estates. They are getting all the sales tax revenue, while Rancho Palos Verdes has all the customers." Dr. Cryer proudly punched the air with his forefinger. "I have personally volunteered to lead a submarine task force off the coast of Abalone Cove."

I begged him for other ideas. "Dig up the streets. There's nothing wrong with dirt roads—the city simply wastes money." Dr. Cryer was turning red. "City Hall's another big expense. Let them meet in somebody's house."

A light froth was forming at the corners of his mouth.

"Say, Dr. Cryer," I asked, "why are you so wrought-up about this Rancho Palos Verdes utility tax? Your house is in Rolling Hills?"

"That was yesterday," an agitated gasp gurgled in his throat. "Today, the ground really slipped."

"So?"

"Now I live in Rancho Palos Verdes."

Theodopholis Gardeniski To Succeed Andre Previn

Mr. Ernest Fleischmann
Executive Director
Los Angeles Philharmonic

Dear Ern,

You probably don't remember me, but I was the guy who smiled at you at the Hollywood Bowl a couple seasons ago. I'm not sure you smiled back, but you were pretty busy in your box with all the high-powered communications stuff so I didn't want to bother you introducing myself.

Now I could kick myself for being so thoughtful.

I see by the papers Andre Previn is kissing you all good-bye—so the search is on, once again, for a principal conductor for the Los Angeles Philharmonic. You sure have had some luck, haven't you? No sooner do you hire someone than they get ants in their pants and take off. I guess the sunny skies in old Los Angeles makes them lazy. You don't find that problem in the Northern climes. During the concert season it's too cold to go outside and do anything fun—so they stay put.

I sympathize with your plight, all right, but I am not writing you just to sympathize.

No, sir! I am writing with a solution to your problem.

I see you are quoted in the papers, Ern, saying, "There is too little time in the day to beat around the bush," and, Ern, I couldn't have said it better myself.

So here's my deal, no beating around the bush:

As you probably know, yours truly is a prominent Southland conductor, having been toiling in those vineyards for nine years with the internationally famous South Coast Choral Society.

If you could promise me that I wouldn't have to sign an exclusive contract with you, I would consider the appointment as Music Director of the Los Angeles Philharmonic. Of course, I couldn't dream of giving up the Choral Society for the Los Angeles Philharmonic, but what the heck, Previn was schlepping all over the world when he was in charge, so you shouldn't get out of joint if I kept on with the South Coast Choral Society.

Now I don't expect you to hire me without a sample of my work (I'm not that naive).

But it just so happens we are giving the *Verdi Requiem* tomorrow right here in Rancho Palos Verdes, so you wouldn't have to drive very far. Heck, I hear you have to fly all over the world to find conductors, and here I am right in your backyard.

And here I am directing an orchestra and chorus, the whole bit—and the admission is free. Not that we wouldn't gladly send you a couple comps even if we did charge admission.

I just figure it's the perfect opportunity for you to get to know my work. We can talk salary later. I see Previn got a half mil a year, and, I can say up front, that would satisfy me.

I am realistic enough to realize I have one small handicap, but it is nothing that a half-decent public relations firm couldn't gloss over.

I was born in this country and have a fairly Anglo-Saxon name.

I know you are a broad-minded man and wouldn't dream of holding that against me, but I also realize you have to please the audiences and we are, God bless us, enamored of the foreign flavors when it comes to music.

It is said Leo Stokes was born in merrie old England. But he knew how to get ahead in the U.S. So he started calling himself Leopold Stokowski, and passed the word he was born in Poland of solid Polish ancestry, and then adopted a Hungarian accent.

How does Theodopholis Gardeniski strike you, Ern? It's just a thought, and, as always, I am open to suggestions.

You know, Fleischmann has a nice ring to it. What does it mean anyway? Flesh man? A man of flesh? Butcher?

Anyway, I guess that's academic because it is apparently spoken for by a man of considerable stature in musical affairs (that means you, Ern).

I can do a nice German accent if that's okay with you. You know all those Germanic composers, Bach, Beethoven, Schubert, Mozart, Haydn, and Giuseppi Verdi (4 o'clock tomorrow, Ern), I'd fit right in—my wife is Pennsylvania Dutch, you see, so I get to hear a lot of that guttural stuff.

But if Eastern Europe is your bag, Ern, I could pick it up easy.

Also in my favor—something you should consider about my credentials—is I used to work at MGM with Andre Previn. I was in an office just down the hall from him, and I expect he will give you a glowing reference. So you see, our backgrounds are virtually identical. Well, maybe he had a couple more wives, but I'm talking music.

Of course, come to think of it, I'm not exactly sure Andre ever smiled back either—but why don't you bring him along to our concert, Ern (tomorrow 4 p.m.—*Verdi Requiem*—on the house), and refresh his memory.

Well, so long for now…I'll see you tomorrow. Be sure and bring Andre and drop in afterwards to say hello.

Ted Gardner
Music Director, Artistic Director,
Conductor, South Coast Choral Society

Was Charlemagne Pennsylvania Dutch?

Here comes my mother-in-law to gripe and moan about a perfectly innocuous line in one of these humble-pie pieces.

It was about my filling Andre Previn's shoes at the L.A. Philharmonic, where I said my wife was Pennsylvania Dutch so I was good at that guttural stuff so sought after in U.S. music circles.

My mother-in-law is full of praise for her son-in-law's more insignificant abilities. Carving a turkey, for example. With a necktie spattered with turkey grease, the drumsticks skimming the floor like flat rocks on a pond, I heard her exclaim, "Doesn't Ted carve well?"

We've always had a good relationship. The rumor that I don't want her to visit more than a day at a time is simply unfounded. It's just that I can't seem to fit her bed in the broom closet.

"Ginny is not Pennsylvania Dutch," my mother-in-law insists. "She goes back to Charlemagne—and Robert Bruce."

"Yeah, yeah," I riposte, "and the family came over on the Mayflower."

"Right."

"I don't know how that old ship ever stayed afloat with all the people who were supposed to be on it."

"Well the very idea of you writing that Ginny was Pennsylvania Dutch is an affront."

For years, Ginny (my mother-in-law's daughter) and her mother told everyone, "Ted is Pennsylvania Dutch, you know." I thought nothing of it.

Then one day a mutual friend made the harmless statement that Ginny had more of a Dutch accent than I did. Ginny was outraged.

But why? I wondered. "All these years you've been calling me Pennsylvania Dutch. You mean it was an insult?"

Apparently, that was exactly what she meant. Here is the letter I got from the grande dame:

Dear Son-in-Law:

You know you are my favorite son-in-law and I enjoy your Peninsula *News* columns very much. I cut them out for friends. Aunt Jane even read one aloud to her literary group. You remember, it was the one that made some sense.

However, I must register a complaint about something. In one of your articles, you said my daughter was Pennsylvania Dutch, which we both know is a peasant German stock that migrated from the Palatinate in Germany to Pennsylvania some years after my ancestors came over on the Mayflower.

We were New England thrifty with hardly enough to eat, while your people had seven sweets and seven sours at every meal.

Ginny is not, and never has been, descended from Germans. She is descended from Scottish kings and English noblemen. And what's more, I think you know it and therefore should print a retraction in the newspaper.

Grandmère

(This "Grandmère" affectation is because she has a daughter-in-law who is French. We have been toadying to the French for centuries.)

The trouble may have all started with this genealogy that Ginny's grandfather commissioned.

It takes the family back to Charlemagne, that great bloodletter. And William the Conqueror was in there too. And Robert Bruce.

It's a fat book because nobody sired more illegitimate kids than Charlemagne, and it ties Ginny in with everybody who was anybody, anywhere, anytime; and by extension affects our three children, Hortense, Esmeralda and Jambalaya (not their real names. I don't know why I can't remember their real names).

Dear Grandmère:

I'm so glad I'm still your favorite son-in-law, and my pride is not diminished just because I'm your only son-in-law. But, why do you seem somewhat skittish about having your German background exposed?

Ginny has just relocated the genealogy under a basket of winter laundry in her library, giving me a rare opportunity to reexamine the lineage. I notice in addition to the 7-generation gap under Robert Bruce, there is a 10-generation gap in the main line. William the Conqueror seems to have been appended with adhesive tape and doesn't match up with any of the exotic names. Maybe that means, while he wasn't related, he might have conquered some of the women? The Mayflower seems connected to a step-grandmother—out of the bloodline. I also found a king of Germany. Face it, your daughter's thick German accent couldn't be cut with a bull-dozer blade or hidden under a regiment of Charlemagnes (who I understand might have been a little Dutchy himself). But what's to be ashamed of? Think of Bach, Beethoven, Brahms, Daimler and Benz.

Affectionately,
Your British Son-in-Law

Dear Least Favorite Son-in-Law:
    Achtung!

Grossmutter

Taking The Pay Out Of Payroll

Recently I wrote a letter to the Peninsula *News* payroll department. I tactfully asked why my paychecks had stopped coming.

What follows is a sampling of responses and counter responses:

*   *   *

Dear Ted:

Thank you for your good letter.

Gracious, does anyone get paid for having so much fun? But seriously, we are looking into your problem.

No, I'm sorry you can't come and see us, as we no longer have a phone extension since Clem made all those calls to his girlfriend in Azusa.

We are working on paying on the merit system, so the checks, if any, might not be in any regular amounts.

I really got a kick out of your last column and I was all set to write you a check, but the boss says we can't write anything under a dollar.

I hope you understand.

Yours truly,
Hester Honeyfunkle
Head of Payroll

*   *   *

Dear Hester:

Your letter was so amusing; I recommend you write for the paper. But don't give up your present job, not if you get a steady check.

My patience is waning.

Sincerely,
Amadeus Gardner

*   *   *

Dear Amadeus:

There seems to be some computer confusion here. You were once listed as Ted Gardner and once as Amadeus. This conflict seems to be a mutually canceling signal to our computer. Please bear with us.

Very truly yours,
Hester

*   *   *

Dear Hester:

But the checks stopped long before I became known as Amadeus.

Sincerely,
Amadeus

*   *   *

Dear Amadeus:

A concerted effort is being made to find your payroll records. But in the move from our nice big office with the picture window on Silver Spur to the new office in the old broom closet, a lot of our records have been mislaid.

It is a devious effort to downgrade the importance of payroll, and you are just one of the victims.

Your patience will be appreciated.

Sincerely,
Hester

*   *   *

Dear Hester:

I'm out of patience.

Sincerely,
Just one of the victims

*   *   *

Dear Victim:

I have good news for you. A voucher has just been approved by the powers-to-be to pay you in newspaper copies, a practice not uncommon for writers of your stature.

Sincerely,
Hester

*   *   *

Hester dear:

What would I do with all those newspapers?

Sincerely,
Ted

*   *   *

Dear Ted:

You won't get that many.

But to answer your question, you could always sell vanity copies to the people who get their pictures in the paper. Of course, we sell them too, but you could take them to their homes and get the jump on us. If you don't want to do that, you can sell them to the recycling center.

Yours truly,
Hester Honeyfunkle

*   *   *

Dear Hester:

Thanks for the newspapers. I started going door-to-door to sell the papers as you suggested, but I found out Reid Bundy, our esteemed editor, had been there before me selling them for five cents off the cover price.

Then I took them to the recycling center and got 3 cents for the lot. I understand a bunch of writers from the PV *News* were down there with stacks of papers and it drove the price down. I didn't get enough to pay the gas to make the trip.

I see you have enough money to paint your building, so how come you can't pay me?

Sincerely,
Desperate

*   *   *

Dear Desperate:

Thank you for your letter.

Funny you should mention repainting the building. It is causing havoc in our payroll department. Half the staff was out sick from the fumes, and those of us who remained couldn't take our eyes off the cute guys on the ladders.

Patience is its own reward.

Hastily,
Hester

*   *   *

Dear Hester:

Wasn't that Reid Bundy I saw painting the building?

Sincerely,
Impatient

*   *   *

Dear Sincerely Impatient:

Mr. Bundy categorically denies any part in painting the Peninsula *News*. He would deny it personally, but he's up to his elbows in turpentine.

Some of us here feel you might be getting a little pushy. Some writers always think they are better than anyone else in the real world. Well, let me tell you something: the business end of the newspaper is where it's at.

You have nagged us so long we are enclosing a check.

Sincerely,
Hester

*   *   *

To Whom It May Concern:

Thank you very much for finally sending me a check.

I am a little confused, however, since it is only for $0.00 and is unsigned.

I would appreciate your earliest attention to this matter.

Sincerely,
Your Fretful Columnist

*   *   *

Dear Frightful Columnist:

We are sorry for the error.

Unfortunately Hester Honeyfunkle, who drew the check, is engaged in repainting our building. I can't see her from this windowless broom closet, but on my way in this morning she was holding the ladder for Reid Bundy.

Thank you for your patience.

Sincerely,
Whom It May Concern

* * *

Should Education Interfere With Football?

The front page of the New York *Times* brings shocking news—the high school students in Texas have to pass all their courses to participate in extracurricular activities—not only sports but music and hog calling.

To get the story, I hotfoot it down to a little town halfway between Houston and the Hereafter—a place called Cheesecake, Texas. I chose Cheesecake because of their active athletic program: 80% of their football team went on to play college ball. A few of them could even write their names.

Of those college players, all but those who were killed in action went on to the pros, and 72% of those earned more money than the President of the United States, without ever having to endure a single press conference.

Coach Bellbottom sits with his feet up on his desk. On the wall are 8x10 glossies of some of his prize protégés: "Killer Whale," "The Meat Grinder," and his illegal backfield, "Slaughterhouse Five."

"Coach," I say. "How is the new law going to affect your football program here at Cheesecake?"

"Miserable, boy, I'm miserable. We can't even field enough cheerleaders to get the blood circulating on the bench. Why, I got 167 studs on my squad, and yesterday I had only 9 at practice."

"Maybe you can recruit a couple band members."

"What band members? Nobody left but the drum major and a piccolo player, and she's a girl—things is rough, boy."

"Sounds that way," I sympathize. "You feel the rule is unreasonable?"

"Certainly it's unreasonable. Them politicians don't realize we're keeping the dimwits off'n the streets. Now I spec's they'll be into drugs 'n alcohol."

"Won't they be studying to qualify for the team again?"

"Nah—what for? Only readin' they need's read X's an' O's to follow the play diagrams."

"What about math?"

"Only math they need's to see there's enough zeros on the pro contract. I tell you, boy. This country is in a real bind."

"Why's that?"

"The way they's overemphasizing academics all'va sudden. Oh I wouldn't mind they tried it in some namby-pamby state like South Dakota, but Texas, boy?—I tell you they're destroying the American way of life."

"You don't think your players should have to pass their courses?"

"Let's be realistic, boy. As I tell my boys, I got nothin' against education, long's it don't interfere with football none."

"So what are you going to do?" I ask.

"Best I can—I'm recruiting from the student body who can pass their courses. What good's it do me to have a linebacker who can separate a potful o' kneecaps of a Satiday if'n he's out for the season cause'a some history teacher's got a hang-up 'bout sports?"

"So, can you build a team?"

"Gonna give it the ole college try," coach Bellbottom says scratching his red hairs at the back of his neck. "Come on along—I got my first practice with the new team. It's going to be the finest team in the state, far's grade-point average goes."

We go out on the field. I look at the team and decide there is something peculiar about it.

"But," I finally realize, "they're all girls."

"At least I know I'll have 'em suited up at starting time," the coach smiles. "Mightn't be such a bad law after all."

To Lose Is To Win

My dear wife has found herself in something of a mess. It is nothing she can't extricate herself from for a consideration of $2,500 or so, but she was hoping to do it cheaper.

Some weeks ago she read an impassioned letter in this paper calling for volunteers to run for library board. It seems they had more vacancies than they had candidates. The correspondent feared ennui would result in county takeover of our unique, independent library district.

Ginny jumped into the fray before she had time to ask the basic questions, like when the board meeting was.

After she got herself on the ballot, she found out the meetings were on the same night as another of her activities where she has been on the board of directors for 10 years or so.

The nice registrar of voters patiently explained the facts of life to Ginny: To get off the ballot requires a lawyer to file in the Superior Court a charming document known as a Writ of Mandamus.

After calling several lawyers to find one with the expertise for this maneuver, the low bidder on Crenshaw told Ginny that for a $2,500 fee he would take her case, but 90% of these petitions fail to find sympathy in court.

Getting on the ballot is free.

Getting off the ballot costs $2,500.

Ginny decided to stay on the ballot.

Though women may be (notice I say may be, I am

not conceding the point outright) brighter, stronger and better adjusted than men, sometimes they affect a charming helplessness.

Ever mindful of the temporal nature of this defenselessness, I took it on myself to extricate Ginny from the mire of political embarrassment.

Soon after taking her 20 petition names to the registrar, my opportunity came in the mail in the form of a glossy brochure entitled "Winning the Race."

Inside was a darling picture captioned "Political Entrepreneur" showing a young man trying to look like Oliver Wendell Holmes before his moustache amounted to much.

His glasses were held out at chin level. It was an impressive pose.

I scanned the brochure and, remembering something about equal and opposite reactions, I wondered if the entrepreneurs could show you how to lose an election.

I called:

"Winning the Race," a feminine voice said, "good afternoon."

"I'd like to speak to a political entrepreneur, please."

"I'm sorry, all our entrepreneurs are in the field at the moment. May a lesser mortal help you?"

She had such a warm voice I unloaded the whole tale of woe on her. When I finished, she ran down the list of products available, from the "Winning the Race" textbook for $49.95, to the Power Package at $197.50 for the book, tapes, newsletter and video.

"But we want to lose!" I reemphasized.

There was a silence at the other end of the line. Then she said, "Can you hold a minute?"

I started to protest, but she was gone.

In a moment she was back on the line. "Is this the loser?" she inquired.

I bit my tongue. "Hopefully," I said, without a lot of hope.

"Sure," the swami assured me, "we can show you

how to lose an election." The fee she mentioned was modest by Writ of Mandamus standards.

"You can't do it the obvious way by advertising in the Peninsula *News* and saying, 'Don't vote for Virginia T. Gardner for library board,' because people will think it's a good joke and decide the library board could use a few laughs; or when they get in the voting booth all they will remember is the cute ad and not what it said, and, whammo, they'll poke the little hole right behind her name. Or the other possibility is they will think someone is running a negative campaign against her, and vote for her in a sympathetic backlash."

"So what can she do?"

She put me on hold again. "Offend people," she said when she came back. "Advertise she's for book burning to the Left, and pornography to the Right. Make telephone calls promising, if elected, to work day and night for a special library tax on every person of voting age."

"That's it?"

"That should do it. Oh, one other thing. Hold, please."

Finally I realized I was talking to an answering service.

She returned to say, "You'll want to give a victory party at a local restaurant. We have a $97 package for the perfect victory party. Books, tapes, hats and noisemakers."

"But she doesn't want to win."

"If she loses, it'll be a victory."

So, you are all invited to Ginny's election night victory party.

But only if she loses.

Come To Your Census

Director
Census Bureau

Dear Sir or Madam as the case may be:

I just want to alert you to the fact that my wife got to your census form before I did. So don't count on the information about me being accurate in any way, shape or form. In fact, I am sending this epistle so you can correct the various misstatements she has made about me. Just to keep your records straight.

Before I get to that, let me compliment you on a job well done in making up that super-comprehensive survey with all that valuable information. My wife was happy to devote a couple days of her time to filling it out, and we are just so encouraged to know that hundreds of millions of our fellow citizens also will take the time and care to accurately give you what you want. I'm sure that will make your statistics all the more reliable. I mean, just imagine the incredible value of knowing exactly how many people in this great land of ours have a physical or mental condition that causes difficulty in going to shop.

Of course, my wife has oodles of time to fill out forms like your wonderful compendium of valuable information, since she works somewhat less than the exaggerated hours she has given you—and I work significantly more. I mean, if you believe her notes and comments about how much work I do, for example, you are going to get some distorted picture of reality.

So, with your intelligence, I would like you to get the following changes to my form when you get it from my wife:

Now, I don't know if you are a man or a woman because there isn't one of those warm and encouraging personal notes like we get on the front of the income tax forms. But I am betting you are a man, and if you are, it will give you some insight into my wife's character to point out that she has listed herself as Person 1 in the household and you-know-who as Person 2.

It will put her answers in perspective.

I must say, I had been largely unaware of her peculiar sense of humor, heretofore. But when she lists me, under number 13, ancestry or ethnic origin, as "Nazi," and herself as "Vedy British," she not only has us mixed up, but betrays herself as something of a hysteric where origins are concerned.

And this comedic hysteria is, I'm sure, responsible for her answer to "H21. What were the real estate taxes on THIS property last year?" So when she says, "Taxes are for little people," I hope you will have a little laugh out of her little joke and not get it into your head to share her witticism with any federal prosecutors.

You say the answers are confidential, and I'm going to have to trust you for that. But I give you fair warning—if we find ourselves hauled in front of some tax judge, I'll know you broke your word. Let it be perfectly understood, I am as happy to pay my taxes as the next fellow.

I notice the questions on your form sometimes take an anxious, even pleading, tone. Like: "31a...did this person work, *even for a few days*, at a paid job or in a business or farm?" Now, even though you provided those cute little circles for a yes or no answer, my spouse saw fit to write in, "Don't I wish." I ask you only to take it with a grain of salt and in the wonderful, humorous vein it was surely intended.

Under "Occupation" I would have listed so many things, had I gotten to the form first. My wife's description of me as "Deadbeat" seems a gross exaggeration.

Where it asks for age, she has put her age for mine. Since this makes me a bit younger, I don't mind if you leave it as it is. Actually, I'm a couple years older, and you can change it if you want. I'll leave it entirely up to you.

Now, number 33 is another kettle of fish entirely. You know, the one about how much money do you make? I'm sure you have your reasons for asking this, because it's fun to know how many rich guys there are out there, and if I had gotten to the form first, I'd surely have made a stab at an accurate answer. I don't mean to belabor the point, but when you have spouses grabbing these forms first, you take your chances with the accuracy of your results. Like when my wife answers the "How much money do you make?" question with, "Not nearly enough," you see what I'm getting at.

So thanks again for giving us the opportunity to share all that fun information with you. It helped us kill a slow Saturday (and Sunday, and part of Monday). I'm glad to know it only was supposed to take 43 minutes to fill out, and I'm sure if I had gotten to it first, I would have broken even your record time. So anyway, I just wanted to set the record straight, and I would appreciate it if you made the changes I noted above.

Please don't hesitate to call me if I can clarify anything that could be of value to you, as I am only too happy to stand up and be counted, anytime at all.

Really.

Sincerely yours,
Person 2

T.S.
T.S.

T.S. Eliot, that old windbag, wrote just fifty-four poems. That is after some prominent works like those cute lyrics for *Cats* are deducted.

I have written more than fifty-four poems.

Cynthia Ozick, an exceptionally bright woman, has relieved herself of an incisive review in the *New Yorker* of the great T.S. (His friends called him Tom, so he didn't hear that often.) The occasion was yet another biography without benefit of cooperation from the heirs and assigns of the great T.S.

T.S. was apparently rather rough on his wife. After he skedaddled, she would follow him around and he would ignore her. He had her institutionalized for a time, but somehow she got out.

I have never even dreamed of institutionalizing my

wife, though the reverse may be true.

T.S., it must be grudgingly admitted, got off some good lines:

> *"This is the way the world ends*
> *Not with a bang but a whimper."*

> *"Bustopher Jones is not skin and bones—*
> *In fact he's remarkably fat."*

I've gotten off some good lines myself:

> *The end of the world*
> *Will not go unher'l'd*
> *There won't be so much noise*
> *More a slow slipping of poise.*

> *Though it's not a sin*
> *To be remarkably thin*
> *I once knew a cat*
> *That*
> *Was really very fat.*

More than one critic has noticed a remarkable kinship between the work of T.S. Eliot and my own poetry.

Without bragging, I really feel it is fair to say that, given his breaks, I might be in T.S. Eliot's position today. I don't mean dead, necessarily, I mean famewise.

I mean for example, take his famous poem (one of fifty-four, remember) "The Love Song of J. Alfred Prufrock."

It opens thusly:

> *"Let us go then, you and I,*
> *When the evening is spread out against the sky*
> *Like a patient etherized upon a table;*
> *Let us go, through certain half-deserted streets,*
> *The muttering retreats*
> *Of restless nights in one-night cheap hotels*
> *And sawdust restaurants with oyster-shells:*
> *. . .*
> *Oh, do not ask, 'What is it?'*
> *Let us go and make our visit.*
> *In the room the women come and go*

Talking of Michelangelo."

There is a lot more of the same. The thing that amazes me is how similar this is to a work of my own: "J. Allen Klinker Sings His Heart Out of Love."

Whatya say we hit the trail?
Ya know when it's dark as hail
Like some stiff at the morgue.
Let's take a shortcut through the alley
So as not to run into Officer O'Malley.
Hotels run by an unemployed swami
And sawdust restaurants that smell of salami.

If you have any questions, just don't ask.
Inquiries interfere with my important task.

In the room the ladies trot
Talking of some Hottentot.

Some thoughtful people have observed that some of T.S.'s work is a bit on the obscure side. I have never been accused of the sin of obscurity, except in the fame/obscurity dichotomy.

In fact, I have written a poem on that very subject:

You may be more famous than I, T.S.
But that doesn't mean my poetry's any less
Than yours. You know everything isn't fame
Not when you got guys like me in the game.

Guys who with any kind of luck
Write verse like water off a duck.
Guys who wouldn't sell out for fame
By substituting initials for their full name.

So you may be more famous, T.S.
And you may let the boys on Savile Row dress
You. But with fifty-four poems, more
Or less, there's a lot in store

Competition-wise. Oh, it's cute, your Cat *piece*
And the stuff about the cat that's obese

And the whimpering world not banging,
But I gotta tell you, I'm getting the hanging

Of your stuff
And enough
's enough!

The Love Song of Old Prufrock
Far be it for me to mock,
But, geez, that song's as much about love
As terminal athlete's feet on a dove.

Isn't it amazing, a guy like you with fifty-four
Poems can be so famous when guys like me with more

Are teetering on the brink of obscurity?
In life there's just no justice in security.

And what's this I hear about your prejudice?
Your stuff may be good but it's no Porgy and Bess.
So if I were you, I'd look to my laurels
And mind my manners and my morals.

Cause you may be more famous, T.S.,
But some of your stuff's a real mess.
The meaning of your poems we can't guess,
But as you'd say, T.S., That's just T.S.

$48,700 Bricks

I have always been fascinated by contemporary art. I always wondered if the artist was really serious about those graffiti-like squiggles (Cy Twombly—$418,000) or those juvenile smudges on canvas—Willem de Kooning cleaned his paint brush on newspaper, signed it, and it sold for $15,100.

My favorite is the pile of 120 bricks carefully piled two deep on the floor, 4 across and 15 long. The bricks, arranged by artist Carl Andre, sold at a Sotheby auction this year for $48,700. That's just under $406 for each 30 cent brick. Who bought it? Why? Imagine the thrill of being the first to discover that a few rows of buff-colored bricks on the floor is art.

Or the ability to see this as art when the uneducated scoff—and bidding in that august Sotheby Hall—bidding the bricks up to $48,700—it must have been a spirited contest.

Where did the bidding start? At the retail value of the bricks separately (about $36)? Or at the intrinsic value of them laid end-to-end by Carl Andre? Or does he just number them and you set them in place yourself? 4x15, two rows high. That may be the genius of it. I have seen 4x8, but this is daring.

Imagine the excitement in the neighborhood when the delivery truck pulls up and unloads your priceless work of art. The envy is written all over the faces of your neighbors. You try to appear blasé, but your heart is beating too wildly. For while anyone can buy 120 bricks, not anyone can pay $48,700 for them.

I have just bought 120 bricks for under $40, and laid them on my living room floor. That translates to roughly $50,000 worth of art.

Pablo Picasso, in an interview with Giovanni Papini over 30 years ago, said:

"The rich, the professional idlers, desire only the peculiar, the sensational, the eccentric, the scandalous, in today's art. And I, myself, since the advent of cubism, have fed these fellows what they wanted, and satisfied the critics with all the ridiculous ideas that have passed through my head. The less they understood the more they admired me!

"Through amusing myself with all these farces I became celebrated, and very rapidly…Today, as you know, I am rich. But when I am alone, I do not have the effrontery to consider myself an artist at all…

"…I am only a public clown, a mountebank. I have understood my time, and have exploited the imbecility, the vanity, the greed of my contemporaries.

"It is a bitter confession, more painful than it may seem; but at least, and at last, does have the merit of being honest."

Prices for his Picasso's "farces" continue to climb.

There is a story about a man paying $100,000 for a simple, primitive line drawing of Picasso's. He took it to the artist for authentication. Picasso studied the work, a puzzled frown on his forehead.

"Tell me," he said. "What did you pay for this?"

The buyer told him. "A hundred thousand dollars."

Without hesitation, Picasso said, "It's mine."

I got a letter from a San Francisco art gallery saying the wonderful thing about the featured unfathomable artist was the artlessness of it all. The brave stance of one who said, "I don't have to be good."

I once saw a docent at the Whitney Museum in New York point to Jasper Johns' 7th grade rendition of the American Flag and say the museum paid a million dollars for it so the Germans wouldn't get it.

Covetousness *Über alles*.

What a shame, we could have made a dent in the balance of payments all those Volkswagens have made so unfavorable.

The docent then pointed to Claes Oldenburg's stuffed vinyl toilet and said he, like so many other modern artists, is showing us the beauty of everyday objects that we take for granted.

It all reminds me of the tulip mania, when several centuries ago covetousness had reached epidemic proportions and tulip bulbs sold for a million dollars (when that was real money).

My wife, Ginny, does not share my unique appreciation of valuable art. She has requested I move my $50,000 pile of bricks outside.

"Would you have a priceless Matisse outside?" I ask.

But she is not listening. She has already stubbed her toe twice on my bricks, and she obviously doesn't dig their unique beauty.

She also has no understanding of the priceless inflation hedge this offers. The $50,000 bricks will surely appreciate in value…especially as I become better known as an artist to be reckoned with.

Any day now I am expecting to go over $100,000 for the bricks. The Tate Gallery in London paid about $75,000 for a similar pile of bricks. I have seen them there, and if I do say so myself, I like my bricks better.

And if they don't sell right away, I will console myself with the cost breakdown of my $50,000 work of art: Bricks, $40.00; Artistic genius, $49,960.

I may even spend another $40 and buy 120 more bricks and sell the piles for $50,000 each.

All I need is a buyer.

The Brain Is Mainly In The Drain

It is with a mixture of solace and sorrow that we announce that Ted Gardner's brain is on vacation.

Mr. Gardner, who ordinarily submits something more or less comprehensible for this space on a more or less weekly basis, is not on vacation himself—just his brain.

It is a moot question whether or not the aforementioned brain has in recent times functioned at a sufficiently effective level to warrant a vacation. Very few signs of any significant stress have been sighted by our staff brain-stress observers.

Mr. Gardner wishes it to be known that while his brain is on its off, so to speak, the rest of him is functioning normally (for a man of his age). He is still able to brush his teeth, comb his hair, pick lint and comprehend any movie made after 1959.

This brain vacation, says our columnist, is not to be confused with writer's block, since the entire brain is blocked, not just that tiny portion that performs his writing function.

He wishes to allay all fears that have been making the rumor circuit that he is brain dead. Other parts of him could be considered "dead," but not his brain. Though there exists a substantial body of opinion that claims this particular brain was never notably alive.

Actually, with his brain on vacation, Mr. Gardner is not as different as you might expect. Oh, we find him more personable and interesting, but other than that it seems like business as usual from those quarters: The usual griping about what we pay him, as well as the outlandish attempts to promote his novel.

Some wags have suggested the incongruity of a single part of the body (no matter, in this case, how insignificant) shutting down, while other parts continued to carry on. If, however, the level of function of this "carrying on" were fully understood, it might not be so difficult to understand.

On further consideration, perhaps vacation is too strong a characterization for the state his brain finds itself in. It is not on a trip, but rather in a state of pause, hiatus, or simply out of order (though a case can certainly be made that there wasn't a lot of order there in the first place).

We will avoid, at this juncture, the temptation to take cheap shots like, "What brain?" "You mean there *was* a brain working in that head all this time and we didn't know it?" or, "Brain? You could have fooled me."

No, in fairness to our Saturday columnist, it must be said that regardless of the content of some of his columns, we only suspected that his brain had atrophied once or twice (a month).

While Mr. Gardner may have been the first known person to send his brain on vacation while the rest of him stayed home, he is not the first to attempt it. Many people try to send their brains on vacation while the rest of them watches television.

Exactly where his brain is spending this holiday is not known. The thing is simply too tiny to track.

There are many advantages of scuttling the brain off on vacation while the rest of you stays home. Accommodations and air fares are much cheaper, since the brain weighs so little and takes minimal space. There is virtually no impact on the water and sewer systems. And the part that stays home has the potential for accomplishing many feats that too much rationalization from a meddlesome brain might hinder. Conversations with the distaff come to mind. You might even be moved, without your brain, to seek employment as a postal worker or in politics. But that is, of course, a brainless digression.

Naturally we have considered the danger of the precedent this brain vacation might set. Everybody's brain might decide it was due a vacation. On further consideration our fears proved groundless. Certain brains are susceptible to sabbaticals, most are not. The normal brain, astounding machine that it is, continues to function, day in and day out, without interruption for frivolous reasons. Only rarely does the unusual brain come along—one that switches itself off from time to time. Gardner possesses such a brain.

Obviously there are many disadvantages as well to sending your brain on vacation. Unfortunately, in Gardner's case, we can't think of any.

—The Editors

Books You May Have Missed

"Books You May Have Missed" is a one-shot feature in this month's *American Spectator*. It features *The History and Social Influence of the Potato*, published by Cambridge University Press in 1985.

It is a capital idea and, if I may say so, long overdue for this paper. I am submitting an idea along these lines for the Peninsula *News* and Rolling Hills *Herald*. I am sending it directly to the *News* typists to escape the predictable scorn of a certain Executive Editor who has, alas, in the past, shown a certain want of farsightedness vis-à-vis my higher-plane intellectual endeavors.

Simply stated, once a week we could run little reviews of overlooked books—capsulizing them to whet the appetite of potential readers.

Stubble Mulching in the Great Plains, H. Hopkins; WPA Press, 1934. Long a favorite of this reviewer, this Depression classic tells all you need to know about mulching with stubble. Copious footnotes and illustrations slightly marred by the artist's obvious lack of understanding of the nature of stubble, mulching and the Great Plains. Suitable for beginning farmers of all ages.

The Potato as Auto, N. Edselford; Fourwheeler Press, 1987. Traces the origins of the automotive potato back to the word go. Amusing anecdotes about how the wheels kept popping off the earliest models. Why hungry, malnourished engineers ate some of their best early efforts. Recommended for all potato lovers, potatophobics and couch potatoes.

The Lima Bean as Metaphor, Gay Stritus; Legume Press, 1957. A mildly-amusing account of metaphorical limas of every stripe. Will broaden your understanding of bean culture and is guaranteed to quicken your pulse and provide sophisticated bon mots for cocktail parties.

Manual of Pig Farming, O. L. McDonald; S. L. Ops Press, illustrated, 1912. All you ever wanted to know about pig farming is contained in this neat little booklet, splendidly illustrated by Sweden's leading pig artist, August Sower. The chapter on the care and feeding of these beautiful animals is especially engaging and should send all but the hardest hearts scurrying to the nearest pig farm to make their selections for breeding. A male and female in any combination is considered best.

Ersatz Fats, Elmo Weisenheimer; Die Yet Press, 1981. For the calorie-conscious—the substitution of many low-calorie everyday items for fats, including, but not limited to, rubber bands, horseshoes, carburetors and shaving cream.

Decorative Rutabagas, Their Uses and Misconceptions, Heartland University Press, 1898. Straightens out all the misconceptions you have doubtlessly harbored about the decorative applications of all parts of the oft-beleaguered rutabaga—the skin, pulp and seeds—in such obvious applications as wallpaper and wart remover. Paperback.

Edible Hardware, U. L. Givens; Dandelion Press, 1965. Don't throw out your old screws, nuts, bolts, coat hangers; creative and legendary chef U.L. Givens gives helpful hints for the preparation and cooking of nuts and bolts (not to be confused with Mr. Given's earlier work, *The Nuts and Bolts of Cooking,* a far more pedestrian effort). Appendix on succulent sauces of every stripe (not to be confused with *Sauces on Appendix*, an inferior earlier...

Epic Poetry of the Mau Maus, T. Wolfe; Flackcatcher Press, 2 pages, 1969. The origin and social history of the intelligentsia caste of the Mau Mau tribe. Leading authors discussed in detail and excerpts from tedious epic poems of the tribe mercifully omitted. The author's view is that where Mau Mau epic poems are concerned, the less said, the better.

Mating Quirks of the Equatorial Tse-tse Fly, Bugme Gently; Equator Press, 1784. A division of General Motors, revised impression; 27 pages. Scandalous vignettes and astonishing adulterous patterns of the equatorial tse-tse fly never before (or since) revealed. Appendix on bizarre parallels to human behavior.

Little Known Vignettes From the Boer War, A Reed Bundie; Action Press. Did you know, for instance, that the Boer war was not fought over boars, or any swine for that matter. Exactly why it was fought is still to be determined, and this amazing book tells you why!

(Editor's choice: *How to Dispense with Boorish Writers*, Rolling Hills Herald Press, 1989.)

Look Who's Not Losing A Daughter

By the time you read this I shall be gliding down the aisle in a ceremony of matrimony. I am not taking a second wife. I am not renewing any vows. My trip on this occasion is to the accompaniment of my daughter Hortense (not her real name).

Hortense is marrying a lawyer, Oliver Wendell Darrow (not his real name—but he really *is* a lawyer). Here are the lawyers in my family: father, sister, brother, father-in-law, brother-in-law—my only nephew will graduate from law school this year, and now a son-in-law. My mother even wanted to go to law school in the 1920's, but the establishment lawyers talked her out of it. "No place for a woman."

Here are the non-lawyers in my family: me. Oh, you may think I was the only one in the family who never amounted to anything, but you don't need a law degree to write for the PV Peninsula *News*.

I knew right away, when the engagement was announced (on Valentine's Day), that I would be expected to trot down the aisle with the bride. While I don't generally approve of this meat market approach to the male sex, I realize that the attention might be somewhat deflected by the bride.

My other duties were hazy. Did you have any idea, for instance, that as the father-of-the-bride I would be expected to pay for the whole thing? This caused me quite a bit of consternation until I struck an agreement with my wife, Ginny (her real name, take it or leave it). She would sign the checks out of our joint account without telling me how much they were for, and I wouldn't tell her there was no money in the account.

Then, a few days ago, I was told by the bride-to-be that etiquette books had been consulted and I was to give a toast.

"Toast?" I inquired. "Ginny does the toast in our family.

I only scrape it."

"Very funny," Hortense said.

"But I don't even drink—what am I toasting?"

"You just thank the guests for coming."

"That's a toast? I raise an empty glass and say, 'Thanks for coming'?"

"You don't need the glass."

"Yeah, but wait a minute. I'm paying for the thing, shouldn't they thank *me* for having *them*?"

"Well, they send me gifts," she said.

"You mean, if we had hot dogs and sauerkraut, buffet-style, at the reception as I wanted, you'd do less well gift-wise than if we tie on the feed bag in grand style and give them chicken à la King in silver bowls?"

"They don't know when they buy the gifts if it's hot dogs or chicken—it's just the tradition."

"Oh—I see. Tradition. Okay, what's the tradition on the father-of-the-bride (FOB) walking down the aisle with the bride? Why not the MOB (mother-of-the-bride) or one of the SOBs (sisters-of-the-bride)?

"Thanks for asking," Hortense responded gratefully. "I just happen to know how that quaint custom began. It was sometime back in the Middle Ages. The father-of-the-bride had always been something of an embarrassment. He usually drank too much and generally made a fool of himself. Some bride got the bright idea to carry him down the aisle because he had passed out from strong spirits. This also gave the bride an opportunity to show her in-laws how strong she was and, *ergo*, what a good catch the groom had made."

"What about the toast, how did that begin?" I asked this surprising font of wedding lore.

"Same way," she said. "The father was so drunk it seemed natural for him to say something at the reception— waving his glass unsteadily as he did so."

"You have any idea why the fathers-of-the-bride had to get so drunk? Do you think it had anything to do with the staggering cost of giving a daughter away? Why, in those days it wasn't enough to throw a reception with hot dogs and sauerkraut, you had to have a dowry—and that usually took the form of hard cash."

"And the tougher sell the daughter, the more cash it took for the dowry," she said.

"So I'm getting off cheap?" I asked.

"Cheap," she said.

"And you're getting off easy," I hastened to add. "You won't have to carry me down the aisle, I'll just be leaning a little."

"Because you are broken-up at losing a daughter?" she asked.

"No," I said, "I'm not losing a daughter, I'm losing a tax deduction."

Mint Julep Solicits Fatty Fox

As I remember, it was in the bleak December when this sore-head ex-client put a couple neat bullet holes through our frosted glass door.

The gold leaf used to say, "Fatty Fox, Shamus." Now it said, simply, "Fatty Fox, Sham."

Fatty and I were out. He was eating. I was furniture shopping with a blind date, so all they got was a couple lousy letters which didn't contribute much to the literature of the genre anyway.

I was buffing my nails with my new electric nail buffer, when in walks this statuesque blonde without knocking.

There was no knocking her, either. She was as cool as a mint julep that went easy on the mint, and woman enough to turn a teetotaler into a hard-drinking man.

As she slithered into the chair across from my desk, I shielded my eyes. I shan't describe her microskirt. Some things are better left to the imagination.

Our little office was hot as eggs frying on all burners

at high noon on the equator. Perspiration began frosting our Mint Julep.

The glands of her thoracic cavity heaved with her sibilant breath.

"Fatty Fox, I presume?" she said. Her voice was a low rumbling hum, like a sterling silver leaf blower with stripped gears.

"Archie Bunkhousen," I said. "You are?"

"Jessy Julep. My friends call me Mint." She threw a wink my way, letting me know in no uncertain terms she hoped we would soon be friendly.

"Where's Fatty?" she asked, being used to service from the top.

"On the roof," I said, tossing my curls toward the bulkhead.

"Working with his orchids, no doubt," she said as though it were a foregone conclusion.

"No, the air conditioning is on the fritz."

She pouted. "The school board told me not to settle for anyone but Fatty Fox."

"Fatty's the thinker. I do the scut work."

"I beg your pardon. Do I look like a scut to you?"

"I don't think so, but then thinking is Fatty's department."

Her lungs fell two stories at the news, an action I noted with a polite, if passing, interest.

"Missing Palos Verdes school checks," she said through gleaming Cheshire chiclet choppers. "I want you to find them."

"Two thou a day and expenses," I responded like a compact disc with a laser off its beam.

She looked surprised. "You a lawyer?"

"A lot of people mistake me for one," I spoke through a Virginia Slim that parted my teeth like a beached oyster.

"Hard-boiled?" she asked.

"Sunny-side up, if you don't mind," I retorted. I couldn't take my eyes off her sunny side. She did things to me my mother never mentioned in mixed company.

"Sure is hot in here," she said, fanning herself with

her blue suede purse.

"The air conditioning is on the fritz," I reminded her.

"You seem rather inscrutable this morning," she noted. "By any chance, are you Chinese?"

"More people mistake me for a lawyer."

She threw a sultry smile at me that hit me between the eyes like the Amtrak out of Chicago with that windy city's contingent of Costa Nostra aboard on their way to the Catskills for the yearly confab.

"The checks are turning up in Gardena card clubs," she purred like a feline version of Mae West after a year holed up in a dive with a Jane Fonda aerobics tape. "I want you to nail the culprit."

"You play poker?" I asked.

"Five-card stud," she said. "Love it. Will you take my case?"

"I'll have to consult with Fatty. We'll need a five grand retainer, just to keep things friendly, Mint," I winked at her. She was turning a lovely shade of lavender. It clashed with the blue purse in her lap that she opened, pawing through the contents.

Suddenly the heat got too much for her and she fanned herself with the open purse and a bunch of checks fell on the floor. Being gallant (and for *no* other reason), I swooped down to the floor to retrieve them for her.

Mint Julep gave a stifled cry, just at the moment I saw the scattered checks were from the Palos Verdes Unified School District.

Ms. Julep really *was* a mint.

Gathering up the checks, I spied, quite by accident, a tiny tattoo of a royal flush high on her thigh. The microskirt had ridden up to expose it.

I had caught the culprit completely independent of Fatty Fox's legendary genius, but I was blushing like crazy.

She tried to make a run for it, but at that propitious moment Fatty Fox filled the doorway and Mint Julep wasn't going anywhere.

"The compressor went out on the sucker," he said.

Jack Nicholson Is Real Busy

This is the inside story of the love life of Jack Nicholson.

My daughter Hortense (not her real name) has a good friend whom I shall call Griselda, and, for the sake of reasons which shall become obvious, Griselda is not her real name. Not even close.

Griselda lives and works in Hollywood, California, U.S.A. She works in the movie industry that substitutes celluloid images for real life. She works for a company that makes what is known in the trade as trailers—the short previews of coming attractions that make you (1) impatient to see the feature you came for, and (2) promise yourself you will avoid the previewed movie at all costs, for the preview telescopes and super-charges all the violence in the feature at such a frenetic pace, with such ear-splitting sound, that you are halfway through the feature film before you begin to regain your composure.

And now for our featured presentation:

Jack Nicholson, it will be remembered, sired two offspring in 1989, one month or so apart, without the slightest benefit of clerical dispensation, during which, we are given to understand, he was domiciled with a third, more celebrated, woman.

It was during this period that our Jack tried to pick up our Griselda.

Here's how it happened:

Griselda was driving her compact car down Hollywood Boulevard toward a luncheon destination. She noticed this guy in a blue Mercedes 560 coupe roadster following rather closely, and when she checked her rearview mirror, here was this joker smiling at her as though she were an Eastwick Witch or something.

At the next light, he pulled into the lane next to her and signaled for her to roll down her window. She complied, and instantly recognized the grin beneath the sunglasses.

"So," he said, "where ya goin'?"

"To lunch," Griselda answered with her own shy but firm smile. It should be pointed out at this juncture that Griselda is devastatingly beautiful, and, before you jump to label me a sexist pig, I hasten to add she is intelligent, competent and personable in the extreme. So you'd like her even if she were a man, and homely, capisce?

The light changed and they mushed on down the Boulevard to the next light. The window was still down. Jack pulls next to her, leaving a two-car gap—with his four-star grin.

"You're a very beautiful woman," he said.

"Thank you," she must have blushed.

"What's your name?"

She told him her real name.

"That's a pretty name. I have a daughter named that."

No one knows just how many offspring of the great Mr. N. are floating around, but probably enough so sharing someone's name is not all that remarkable.

"So call me up sometime, I'll take you to lunch." And he named the studio where he could be reached.

The light changed, traffic intervened, she turned off the Boulevard.

Griselda, it should be noted, was not a child of Hollywood or a Valley girl, but rather the product of a Northern California environment of erudition and refinement. She hadn't been at all sheltered, but how many young women have been exposed to the seduction of the stars? She was legitimately unnerved.

Griselda sought advice on whether to call Mr. N. or not. She had surveyed several contemporaries as well as her mother by the time she called Hortense.

"Oh, no way," Hortense said as the story unfolded.

"Hortense!" Griselda exclaimed, "you're the only one who told me not to call him. Even my mother thinks I should."

Mr. Nicholson wasn't available, so Griselda left her name and number.

She received a call at her place of employ the next day from a voice of caution and protection—it was also the voice of a female. Somewhat schoolmarmish. She inquired into the nature of the call.

"I'm calling at his request," Griselda said, beginning to wish she hadn't called at all.

"Oh, I'm sorry," the schoolmarm brightened some, "you must understand, whenever a woman calls here for Mr. Nicholson we have to screen the calls. I'll give him your message."

Jack called. Griselda was out. But her stock was rising with her employer. They had just done one of Jack's trailers, and as the boss said when he heard the proposition, "How can it hurt?" She called Jack back. Finally they connected.

Griselda heard papers shuffling, and she decided Jack Nicholson was consulting some notes before he said, "I can't resist a girl with glasses."

Griselda wondered if all the girls he tried to pick up that week had glasses, or he had written somewhere "Griselda—glasses." There is nothing like the personal touch.

"So..." he drawled, "would you like to go to a preview with me sometime?"

"That sounds like fun," she said.

There was a pause. Then, "I gotta tell you something," he said. "I'm *real* busy."

Griselda still hasn't heard from Jack, but it's only been a month.

So when my daughter called me to tell me Griselda was leaving her job because she was passed over for a promotion in favor of a male with a quarter of her experience and a tenth of her intelligence, and when she explained how this would throw Griselda into some rather tight financial straits, I had the solution.

"Tell her to marry Jack," I said. "Her financial worries will be over."

"There's only one problem," Hortense said. "He's *real* busy."

Pale(ozoic) Blue Denim

Here is the story as I remember writing it. That is, before it was stolen from my desk by a sinister subversive.

My daughter Jambalaya (not her real name) has asked for anonymity in this piece. So I am calling her Jambalaya (not her real name—not even close—and don't bother looking her up in the phone book, she's not even listed).

She is having a time trying to get a new denim jacket to fade to look like an old denim jacket. The rich blue jacket is laying in the back yard on some rocks the Paleozoic era coughed up. The rocks are pale white in the sunlight and the denim, lying on them, looks even deeper blue, she complains.

"But those rocks might have been blue 550 million years ago," I offer, soundly. "It takes a long time to get the color out of rocks. I don't see how you can expect instant bleaching of denim."

"Can you think of any way to do it quicker?" she asks. I am always flattered to be asked questions by my legitimate children. But I am, I confess, more flattered when I can approximate an answer.

The question the children most often ask is, "What can I do? I'm bored."

I suggest, "Write a symphony." But that admonition falls on deaf ears.

That's okay, I say. Beethoven was deaf.

Instead, Jambalaya sings a song with the enchanting words, "Psycho killer, *qu'est-ce que c'est?*"

Beethoven should be glad he's deaf.

"How can I make this look old quicker?" she asks again.

"Bleach?" I ask, naively as it turns out, for her noise is turned up.

"But that makes uneven fading," she says. That, I should have realized, had already been considered.

"What do you know about stonewashing?" she asks.

"Nothing," I have to admit. I hang in there. Soon

there will be a question I can answer.

"Could I put a stone in the washing machine with the jacket?"

At last a question I can answer unequivocally. "No."

"Why not?"

Another one I can handle. "Because I don't want the washing machine smashed up with rocks."

I search her face—I'm not sure she sees the wisdom of that judgment.

"Maybe I could just hit the jacket with a rock a couple of times," she suggests.

I respond with arching eyebrows. "I have an idea," I say at last.

"What?" She is eager for a solution.

"Wear it new and start a new fad: Blue Denim, you could call it."

"Oh, Dad," she says, "no."

"Why not? Someone has to begin these style trends. Why not you?"

She sighs. "I'm almost 18 and you're 100," she says with a characteristic want of accuracy. She will be 18 in only 11 $^1/_2$ months. I will be 100 in a somewhat longer time.

It is an impossible generation gulch.

That's pretty much the opus as I remember it. I was going to fatten it a bit with a digression about another daughter, named Hortense (not her real name), who shouted in ear-piercing agony from the bathroom, "Help me!"

Rushing in like Lochinvar the friendly paramedic, I discovered what she needed help with was nothing more life-threatening than her hair. Getting it to stay in place, as I recall.

Men, I admit, are slow to pick up on these crucial matters.

Who was it—Mencken?—who said no one ever went broke catering to the vanity of women.

Men, of course, are above all vanity. Very few have pierced ears, buy lipstick, or dress any differently than they did 50 years ago. Ask my wife. She says my suits all look 50 years old.

Jambalaya sees the article on my rolltop desk, and reading it, says, "You can't send this in, they'll laugh you out of the place."

I wave her off. "Don't worry," I say, "there's not enough meat in it anyway. I'd need twice as much to fill a column."

"You could talk to kids and find out if anybody ever put a rock in a washing machine," she suggests. "You might discover that was the origin of rock music."

She is so entertaining.

"Naw," I say—"it's too thin."

"Didn't Barbara Paley say you couldn't be too rich or too thin?"

"Maybe," I say. "But she was both. This denim piece is not too rich, just too thin."

Today I fish around on my desk for the blue denim piece and it is nowhere to be found. Jambalaya, that devious little sweetie pie, just decided to give herself the ultimate protection. She trashed my masterwork.

This poor imitation is written from poorer memory under cover of darkness with a silent pen.

But I still think there's not enough meat in it—so I've decided against submitting it to the Peninsula *News*.

Jambalaya will be so pleased.

Wedtech And Me

At my alma mater, USC, there stands a statue endearingly known as Tommy Trojan. Symbolic of the college, Tommy is muscular, wrapped only in loincloth and sandals. His sword is drawn against ignorance.

Some claim that constitutes self-immolation.

When I arrived from bucolic Pennsylvania, I was force-fed curious statistics: e.g. "Two thirds of the judges in Los Angeles County are SC graduates."

In those days there was, of course, no prediction of the number of Trojans who would be indicted for malfeasance, governmentwise.

Since then, a few illustrious public servants, it must be confessed, served a little time in the slammer. I like to think the education they received at SC helped them pass the time.

All these fellows were older than I. At last I am in a position to name-drop. At last one of my very own classmates is, as we used to say sitting at the feet of Tommy Trojan, in deep doo-doo.

He has been in the news for a year or so, and they haven't been stingy with pictures of him. But he seemed to have shrunk to only a nose and ears, so I didn't recognize ole Bob Wallach until I saw the huge cover story in the *New York Times Magazine*. There he was in living color, and a light went on between my ears.

Wedtech, it was called. It was a New York minority company, and Bob put in a good word for them with his good pal Ed Meese 3, and Wedtech was so grateful, they paid attorney Wallach a million 3 in legal fees.

Good lawyers aren't cheap. The bad ones aren't shy about charging, either.

Bob said he helped Wedtech and he helped Ed Meese because he loved his country and he loved Ed Meese. The million 3 was coincidental.

Retiring to my SC yearbooks, called—perhaps in keeping with the Tommy Trojan, Troy shtick—the El Rodeo, I found him.

There he was where I should have been, pictured with his balled fist on his waist, the other arm outstretched on a waist-high pillar, some Corinthian pastiche, no doubt.

He wore a V-neck sweater, white shirt open at the neck, corduroy jacket with just the right amount of savoir-faire. On his lips a million three hundred thousand dollar smile (in 1988 dollars). His eyes, full of vision, were cast far off—far into the future, perhaps—a time when SC would seem small potatoes to him, a time of greatness, a time of coziness with the inner councils of big government.

Behind Bob Wallach in that picture stood the Doheny Library. An omen, perhaps? Teapot Dome Doheny, as some of us affectionately referred to him (at the feet of the aforementioned Tommy Trojan). Mr. Doheny got in his doo-doo while he was only helping his friends in government.

We were given to understand that a couple of holy institutions, Loyola among them, politely rejected the tainted largesse of the Dohenys until SC, in a fit of pragmatism, embraced it.

So there was Bob Wallach standing where I should have stood: Sophomore Class President.

Only a few votes had separated us, as I recall. He got something like 900 some, and I got a shade under 12.

Now with Meese 3 giving up the ghost, I thought it must be getting lonely for old Bob Wallach, being friendless, so to speak, governmentwise.

By golly, I thought, what are old friends for if not to lend a helping hand in time of need?

So I called my old foe and was shortstopped by a nasal functionary who insulated His Nibs from the riffraff.

I intimated I was part of the old boy network, but it didn't cut anything, icewise.

If Mother Meese brought Ed and Bob sandwiches in law school, Bob and Ted were on the same ballot at SC. You realize that makes the Attorney General and me practically cousins.

"What is the nature of your call?" the factotum asked with that polite disdain that separated the winning candidates for soph pres from the losers.

"I'm calling as an old friend to offer my help to Bob Wallach, to show him I hold no grudge because he narrowly beat me for sophomore class president at USC; even though the size of his win and recent events might suggest electioneering fraud, I'm not that kind of guy."

"What kind of help are you offering?" he wanted to know. You could cut the suspicion in his voice with a kind thought.

"Altruistic."

"Why?"

"Because Bob and I go way back. Because I love Bob Wallach and I love my country, in no particular order. A small honorarium in the low to mid seven figures would also be appreciated."

"What?"

"Oh, don't get the idea the money is important to me," I assured him. "I'll admit I naturally mentioned it in passing, but you will notice I mentioned it last, long after my love of country and of Bob himself."

Before he hung up the phone profane words escaped his lips, giving me to understand he didn't believe my professed altruism.

I wonder why?

Premarital Snoop

Is it possible your spouse hired a private detective to check on you before you were married?

The San Francisco *Chronicle* has just run an article indicating the practice is on the rise.

I was surprised to discover in our own yellow pages, under Spouse Snooping, a Sally Snopes who specializes in "Premarital Investigations."

I called Sally Snopes the Shameless Shamus right here in Malaga Cove and I got an earful.

"You'd better come down here," she said. "My business is entirely confidential."

Her office was tucked away on the second story of a

quaint old building in the Malaga Cove Plaza between a bunch of banks and real estate offices.

The bronze plaque on her door read succinctly,"Sh!" Inside, a stoutish woman with a telephone at each ear sat behind a scarred desk of the early Akron period. Her hair was washed out and in want of another bleach job, but her smile was as big as all outdoors as she waved her hand in my direction.

On the walls were 8x10 glossy photos of the Peninsula's prestigious couples, all lovingly inscribed to Sally the Shamus in overflowing gratitude for a job well done.

Some were familiar to me. One smallish one bothered me. I kept trying to place it through my entire meeting with the Shameless Shamus.

"I'll get back to you," Sally said into both phones simultaneously, and hung them up.

Sally stood up to greet me. "You're looking at Sally Snopes the Shameless Shamus," she announced shamelessly with a pert pucker of her petulant lips—and there was nothing else pert about our Sally, who weighed in a tad over a well-fed Clydesdale.

"How did this all begin?" I asked.

"In the old days, parents investigated the background and the financial condition of prospective mates and arranged marriages accordingly."

Sally sat, putting her meaty elbows on the vintage desk.

"With the growing impersonality of life, the services of a private detective became imperative."

Sally was wearing an orange button with black letters. It said, "Ask about our weekend special."

I did.

"For $99.95, I run a quick background check, look at a few pictures of the subject and try to size him or her up."

"You can do that by looking at a picture?"

"You bet," she said. "People fall into certain types. For instance, men are philanderers, drunks, wife-beaters and gamblers."

"Any redeeming qualities?"

Sally turned her nose up to ponder. "Haven't found

any yet," she said. "Of course, I've only been at it 32 years."

"Is your business at all seasonal?"

"Oh my, yes. I pick up going into June. The brides month, you know. I am a little off at Christmas, not that people get married less often at Christmas; it's just that trust seems to run a bit higher then."

"What sort of things do you check on?"

"I put recording devices in bedrooms…"

"Infidelity?"

"Naw, that's old hat. I put my bugs in to record snoring levels."

"Anything else?" I asked.

"Messy housekeeping." Her eyebrows arched at the seriousness of it all. "There are so many legitimate areas of vital concern for men. Areas too sensitive for them to probe on their own."

"Can you give me an example?"

"Can his bride-to-be match a pair of socks?"

"He couldn't ask her that himself?"

"People used to speak to each other—but now things are so hectic."

"What about your own marriage, Sally?"

Sally Snopes the Shameless Shamus turned stone cold. Her eyes clouded over like a June fog. "Don't talk to me about that creep—he's a low-down traitor to the profession."

"He's a traitor, you say?"

Sally nodded. She was in another, unpleasant world.

"Charlie defected to a computer dating service."

"He found romance through a computer?"

"Not through. With! The computer doesn't snore or litter—so he's snuggled up in an apartment on Ravenspur—just Charlie and his computer."

When I left, I got a closer look at the familiar picture on Sally's wall.

There was an inscription in a recognizable hand. "Thanks a million for all your help. You may be surprised to hear I've decided to marry him anyway."

It was a 26-year-old picture of my wife.

Uncle Barney Is Single And Available

My Uncle Barney is threatening to visit me. My mother warned me he would write to put the touch on me for a touch of hospitality.

Uncle Barney is a wit. Some think only half—but his jokes you wouldn't tell in church. Nor would you hear them there—unless Uncle Barney stumbled in by mistake.

Today the dreaded notice lay in my mailbox like a time-bomb threatening to blow the sanctity of my home to kingdom come:

Dear Teddy,

A line to let you know that my presence will be felt in the vicinity (in Reno at Uncle Clinton's) after the 2nd of June. Now this was meant to be a warning, and if you are on a trip, extend your trip for another 30 days...and you will have no remorse in having missed me.

Now that we are over the preliminaries of relativity, feel free to express your preference to having me climb over your threshold for a two or three visit, years that is, and feel free...to extend it for another three years or more. If this sounds confusing, you should be here.

My marital status is: single but available. Retired and having a roving eye. The field has never been too large for me, and if you have any widows out there looking for a kook, tie them down and I will try to keep up tradition.

Better close, as my tendency is to oversell myself and usually I am the one to be disappointed. So I will enclose a ten dollar bill to cover any cost you might encounter trying to reach me.

Give my love to your progeny, and try not to build me up too big as it is tiring living up to what I already have created.

All my love,
Your Uncle Barney

P.S. I am sorry I forgot to put the ten spot in, but I thought of it after the letter was sealed.

Dear Uncle Barney:

Not only didn't we get the ten dollars you forgot to put in your letter, we didn't get the letter itself.

Let me get this straight, Uncle Barney. You are dumping on Uncle Clinty for a whole month, then you plan to come here and do the same?

Let me tell you, there is nothing to do here in Palos Verdes since Marineland closed. It's a ghost town. The only real fun things are the City Council meetings, and they are only twice a month. If there were any sidewalks to begin with, they would roll them up at 8 p.m.—if there were any "they" here to do it.

All the widows are dead, and even those that aren't would wish they were if they met you.

On the other hand, Reno is fun. Nightspots, gambling, fishing. It has everything. All the widows are in Reno. If you can't catch one there, you are wasting your time here. Maybe Uncle Clint would like to have you for two months. He is your brother after all.

As for seeing us, we look about the same.

So other than to eat us out of house and home, what would be your purpose?

Nobody here wants to hear the Fokker/Messerschmitt story or the sweater joke. I mean, this is a hotbed of conservative refinement.

Our travel agent is working around the clock to find a trip for us when you plan to be here. Your letting us know your dates as soon as they are firm would help us expedite this.

Please be assured of our good opinion of you, Uncle B, without all the self praise. We just think distance lends a kind of enchantment. Like someone once put on a sampler:

> HOUSE GUESTS
> AND DEAD FISH
> START TO SMELL
> AFTER 3 DAYS

However, if you must come, I am including our unlisted phone number. I would respectfully submit several ground rules for the visit:

1. Come and go under cover of darkness.

2. If someone should drop in, go out back to putter in the yard. If anyone speaks to you, say you are the gardener—preferably in Pennsylvania Dutch.

3. Practice sleeping standing up, as we are unable to fit the mattress horizontally in the furnace room.

Yours in trepidation,
Teddy

P.S. Sorry I forgot to put in the unlisted phone number. I thought of it after the letter was sealed.

Dear Teddy:

I'm looking forward to seeing you too.

Sorry I will not be able to stay with you for more than six months as I promised my parole officer I'd be home for Christmas.

And remember not to build me up too big.

Liberty, Equality, Sorority

While I was at USC, I once asked thirteen girls to a fraternity formal dance before I got one to say yes.

In commemoration of my final success, I was going to present a plaque to the frat house with the names and dates of my turn-downs.

But by the time number thirteen said yes, I had forgotten some of those middle rejections.

My early inquiries were to sorority girls.

The young woman who acquiesced was not a sorority girl.

When all else fails, lower your standards.

I may not have been considered a prize catch by those

USC sorority sisters, but one thing that sets me off from my fellow graddies is my enviable ability to hold a grudge for over thirty years.

It's not that I'm a procrastinator, my opportunity was just a long time in coming. It came thanks to Jesse Unruh, that redoubtable politician with the face of a beagle in the early stages of a nuclear meltdown, and the United States Supreme Court.

As the leader of the Assembly, Jesse did his bit to make all kinds of discrimination illegal in California.

A woman wanted to join the Rotary Club (there is no accounting for taste). Rotary headquarters nixed it, and the U.S. Supreme Court, by a vote of seven to zip, nixed the Rotary Club.

No more keeping the girls from the boys, and vice versa, for verily I say unto you, what is sauce for the goose is sauce for you-know-who.

I welcome demolishing the barriers of sex discrimination. I had always rather preferred women to men. And I welcome the court-sanctioned opportunity to join their ranks.

What I really wanted to join was a college sorority.

I called Double Delta Pi at my alma mammy and inquired how I might sign up for rushing.

"For your daughter?" the cheerful member on the line said. I could tell she was statuesque and sophisticated.

"No, for me. My daughter will probably join a fraternity preparatory to her membership in the Rotary Club."

"You're kidding," the young bubbling voice carried charm over advanced fiber optics.

"No—the Supreme Court is on my side."

"Well, we don't take just anybody," she stammered her way out of a tough spot. "I mean, you have to go here to college for openers."

"I'll register."

"Well, ah…then, ah—you'd have to live in the house with all the girls."

"Beautiful," I said.

She didn't think so.

"But the girls would have to vote on you," she said in a singsong that clearly spelled D-I-S-C-R-I-M-I-N-A-T-I-O-N.

"That's okay. If the girls vote nay, I'll get the Supreme Court to vote. It will be nine zip for sure."

"But"—she was clearly worried now—"I'm afraid we couldn't offer you a bid under any circumstances."

"Oh, I don't need a bed, I'll just bring my sleeping bag."

"Our girls are all young ladies," she assured me. "We don't pledge any sleepy bags."

"Hold on just a minute, sweetheart," I said. "Are you trying to discriminate against me just because I'm male?"

"Gosh no," she hastened to assure me. "Why, how would I know what you are? I mean, I've never even seen you."

"Okay, for the record, I'm a man. Now what have you got to say for yourself?"

"I'm not," was all she could come up with. After a long pause, she stammered, "I mean, we have formal things where all the girls wear gowns."

"Listen, honey," I said, asserting my constitutional rights, "I'll get a gown. You aren't trying to put me off, are you?"

She tittered. "How would you look in a formal ball gown?" she asked.

"Flat-chested."

She thought that was awfully funny, and said with a feminine finality, "I'm sorry, sir, we just don't pledge any guys at Double Delta, and I don't care what the Supreme Court says."

There was a deadly click, and that devastating dial tone in my ear.

In this age of absolute equality, the little filly hung up on me.

I'm taking Double Delta Pi to the Supreme Court for discrimination. Just as soon as I can find a lawyer to take the case for a contingency fee.

The Defilading Derriere

Concert Review
by T. Hyperbole Stone

*As Zukovsky's perfor-
mance progressed, the ever-
increasig (sic) proximity of her
posterior to the first violinist's bow
made concentration on the music
more and more difficult. Odds
were given, bets were made, there
was money to be won or lost. Alas,
the violinist evaded Zukovsky's
defilading derrier(sic)...*

—Peninsula *News*

You can imagine my shock when my bookie called me on a recent Sunday night and asked if I didn't want to get in on the action.

"What action?" I asked. My mind, frankly, was not on wagering.

"Zukovsky's defilading derriere."

"What does 'defilading' mean?"

"To arrange troops so the terrain will protect them, especially from enfilading fire. I just looked it up. Also the protection or concealment afforded by defilading."

"A real corker, ain't it?" I said lapsing as usual into the argot of the street whenever I talked to those whose employ-ments were what you might call extra-legal. "So what's the scam?"

"It's big," he said. I am protecting his identity for obvious reasons. "Bigger than the Superbowl."

"Gawanne," I said. "Nothing's bigger than the Superbowl."

"Well, locally, you're wrong, boy. Odds are being given, bets made. There's money to be won...or lost."

"So wha's the scam?"

"Zukovsky's derriere."

"What about it?"

"Well is it gonna, ya know, collide wid da foist fiddler'r not?"

"What're da odds?" I inquired.

"Seven to four against she hits the foist fiddle wid da butt…ah, derriere."

"Well thanks, but no thanks. I got nothing but sympathy for musicians. I've been to performances where soloists have been writhing in dangerous proximity to their fellows, and it gives you the giggles. But face it, Manny," (not, of course, his *real* name) "they gotta stand somewhere. And when one is standing with his or her back to one who is sitting—and you got a large orchestra and a small stage…"

"Three to two against the derriere is the best I can do…"

I didn't bet. There was no collision. But it wasn't the end of it. He called again.

"You see all da fuss in da paper over da review?"

"Yeah."

"We got a little thing goin' 'bout who wrote da review. Wan in?"

"Whaddya tink?" Practice makes perfect.

"We got alla kinda odds for alla kinda Joes. Martin Bernheimer, L.A. *Times,* ten to one against. Might a wrote it for a lark, but probably too big a shot wid dat Poolitzer Prize he got."

"I'll agree to that." I agreed to that.

"Den deres youse. Five to four for. Dem's tight odds."

"Thanks for the flattery, Manny, but I wasn't even there."

"Didn't haf to be. I tolt youse da important stuff on da phone 'bout da fanny an' all. You coulda' made up da rest."

"Well, I didn't. I'm a musician, Manny. We don't savage fellow musicians."

"So there ain't two stiffs in PV knows da woid defilading."

"And I'm not one of them," I admitted.

"How 'bout jealousy? Someone from da Symphony?"

"Odds?"

"Three to two against. Could backfire," he said. "You read da editorial reaction—and da letter from da Chamber Orchestra board member?"

"Yeah."

"Dey kept saying 'He' alla time. Notice dat? He dis, he dat. Coulda been a broad. Most of da music reviewers is broads."

"But none of them write like that."

"True, true. But, *T.* Hyperbole coulda been Talulah, Tanya, Tracy—or maybe somebody called Jane or Diane."

"Could."

"Natch, I'm amused on da editorial ya know, sayin' da bad guy outta unmask hisself. As if da paper don't know who wrote da review. I gotta halfer mind dey done it theirseles. I got two to one for it's a inside job. Look at dat editorial. Ya know da Bard of Stratford on Avon said, 'Thou protesteth too much.' Such a goin' on. Called the writer 'Stone' once, den 'Smith.' Guy who wrote da letter said T. Hyperbole *Jones*," he said. "So youse don't want in on da action?"

"Nah."

"If I find out youse wrote it, what shall I tell da paper?"

"Send me da check."

Cough Medicine Works Like This

TAOS, NM: "You know how it works, Dad?" It is my daughter Esmeralda (not her real name) going on about cough syrup.

The scene is a rented van in Taos, New Mexico, which we are told was the only Third World country you could visit without a visa.

We are visiting *en famille* to observe the winter solstice, with the express purpose of cutting down on the quasi-obscene volume of gift-giving the family had observed, heretofore.

Well, my wife, Ginny (that's her real name), is not to be reasoned with. She has so many gifts packed, I have to break my vow of cold turkeying the holiday gift orgy to buy her two suitcases to transport the additional stash.

We have so many bags when we pull up to Delta Airlines that I suggest to the porter it might be easier if they just taxi the plane up to the curb. I don't know if they took my advice or not because we went in before we saw what happened to our bags.

(Note to Editor: You might want the boys and girls in Advertising to make a pitch to Delta for an ad to accompany this free pitch.)

Each of our daughters is enamored of presentable young swains, and of course my wife, who has absolutely no sense of privacy, invited them to share the blessings of the winter solstice with us. Under some apparent sense of misguided graciousness, each one accepts.

No one has the brains to calculate in advance this doubles the personnel and, ergo, doubles the amount of gifts. And with so many gifts, there is nothing for it but to get a tree to shelter them from the elements.

The *jeunesse* set out to buy a tree, but none are available so late in the Third World, so they buy a saw instead. They reputedly prune a tall tree half-way to the ground and cover it with flat ornaments transported for the occasion. A string of lights, the greatest scientific advancement since heavier-than-air flight, is purchased. It is electronically programed to flash on and off in alternating sequences, at three alternating speeds: buggy, buggier and instant insanity.

Now you may wonder where the paterfamilias is for all this fun. The answer is, he is nursing a cold which soon blossoms into an explosive cough. After two days of merciless hacking, my daughter asks the question that appears at the head of this communiqué from darkest New Mexico.

Let it be understood, I do not cough *all* the time. No—only when I change the position of my body from standing to sitting or lying, or vice versa. And talking does it too. And coughing. And maybe it does seem endless, but there are gaps, I know there are.

"It's probably an allergy," I tell my daughter, between coughs.

"Yeah," she says, "to bacteria. Take some cough medicine."

"I don't take medicine. It's a sign of weakness, and that goes especially for some mysterious formula they hawk on television." So what if they are getting a little weary of my bloodcurdling coughs that sound like the rapid explosion of antiaircraft shells. I am the host.

When we get to the restaurant that evening my Esmeralda diplomatically asks me, "Will you stay outside until we get a table?"

"Why?"

"We might not get one when they hear you coughing."

Driving us home after dinner, Esmeralda continues her lecture. "Cough medicine works like this: (I am coughing through this whole recital) When you cough, you aggravate the throat so you can't cure it. The medicine stops the coughing so the throat can heal."

"And it makes you sleepy," says Jambalaya, from behind me in the van. "You always say sleep is the best thing when you are sick."

"Okay, I'm sold," I say. "It's liable to turn me into a sniveling, drug-dependent weakling or a boozer, but I'll do it."

The stuff is predictably wretched, with a sickly-sweet pseudo-cherry flavor. The dose recommended was two teaspoons. I have difficulty taking one, it is so awful. Instant cure! On half a dose!

Twenty minutes later I start hacking again. What do you expect from half a dose? I take the other half. No help. Still the antiaircraft explosions pierce the night like forgotten bombs. And two teaspoons do not make me sleepy. I never had any trouble sleeping before I took the medicine. Next time, I'm taking the full dose if it kills me.

There is a gentle, fine snowfall. The first of our trip. Somehow, I fall asleep. I awake to new pristine snowfall covering this high ground like the dandruff of an omnipotent snow god. My cough is gone.

Esmeralda and Jambalaya are coughing.

"Why do you do that?" I ask. "It's very annoying."

(Note to Editor: Could we sell some ads to the cough medicine industry to run as a companion to this piece? I'd be willing to split the revenues.)

Editor's note: That's the funniest line in the entire piece.

Forbidden Fruit

I'm glad to see the porn pickets at the Holiday Inn. It was getting so tough to find a good porno in the area, especially since the L.A. *Times* stopped running their ads. Now local citizens are carrying placards so no one will miss the show.

It reminds me of when the P.V. Library was showing a bunch of drawings and a couple of them were, er, well, adult entertainment. That is, if you find drawings that smack of the gynecological aspect of the species entertaining.

At any rate, the display was tucked off in the meeting room, not a place too many patrons frequent. There are, after all, no books in there; it is reserved for piano recitals, community meetings and art shows for tough-minded adults.

I got to see it courtesy of a righteous woman who was standing in the entrance telling everyone to be sure and catch the exhibit, it was simply scandalous.

To get a handle on the latest scandal, I zoomed down to the Holiday Inn on Hawthorne Boulevard to get the real story from the pickets.

The troops were slugging up and down the sidewalk carrying their homemade placards. They were, for the most part, demurely dressed and as proud as any auto worker or airline pilot.

Their cardboard signs tacked to thin lumber sticks contained various persuasive messages, most written in uneven block letters with black marking pens.

<table>
<tr><td>PORNO
MUST
GO</td><td>PORN
IS
CORN</td></tr>
</table>

And the most creative:

MR. CORN ONCE CORNERED PORN
AND NOW HE IS RICH AND MISERABLE

The group seemed loosely organized. When I asked to be taken to their leader, there was some confusion.

Finally, a middle-aged woman with an aged middle stepped into the breach.

"I'm Annie Smutz," she announced proudly. "I hear you are from one of the big papers and you are here for the big story."

"Yes," I said. "What is your goal in picketing this hotel?"

"We want people to become more aware of the sinister forces afoot right here in our very own community. It is absolutely scandalous the filth and degradation these people are showing on TV in these hotel rooms. Have you ever seen anything more shocking?"

"Well, I haven't seen them, have you?"

"Well certainly I have."

"You watched a whole movie?"

"Six of them."

"But if they are so smutty, why do you keep watching them?"

"Civic duty." She fixed me with a flaming righteous gaze. "Someone has to sacrifice themselves for the public good."

"Tell me something," I said, surveying the shock troops, "I don't see any men in your ranks."

"Oh, we had men, but they've gone into the hotel to hassle the management."

"Is your crusade with these pickets having the desired

effect?"

"Oh, yes it is," she said, justly proud of her accomplishment. "You can't imagine the number of converts we got to the paths of righteousness with our little picket line. Why, hundreds of people have gone inside while we've been here!"

"To register their protest with the management?"

She tightened her pink-glowing lips and nodded the nod of the pure.

"Hundreds, you say?" I looked toward the front door of the hotel. "Funny, I don't see any coming out," I said.

"Well," she said with a twitch of her cheek, "they are probably backed up at the manager's desk, giving him a piece of their minds."

At that moment, two waiters and a bellman came toward the picketers. They were each pushing a cart laden with delicacies of every stripe: luscious fruit, sumptuous cheeses, cakes and pastries.

Annie Smutz was confused. "What's this?" she asked the bellman.

"Compliments of the management," he said.

The pickets were baffled. Their placards were beginning to droop.

"But why?" Annie Smutz inquired.

"Sheer gratitude, me girl," he said smiling. "We're sold out. Business is so fantastic the customers are doubling up—six in a room sometimes."

"Six people in one bed?" Annie Smutz was clearly scandalized.

"No, six watching one TV set."

Teddy Kennedy On Mars

—Almost Mt. Rushmore: Jon Eric Beckjord, the director of the Crypto-Phenomena Museum in Malibu, California, recently announced that a volcanic formation was discovered on Mars that looked remarkably like Senator Ted Kennedy. Beckjord, whose "specialty" is Big Foot and Loch Ness Monster photos, which he shows in his museum (situated in a Malibu restaurant), said of the 3.6-mile-wide formation, "This is serious. This is not a joke." The crater of the volcano "gives the impression of a square face, with jowls, fat jowls, a chin protruding out of the jowls," he remarked. "This is a characteristic look of Kennedy." Citing the chances of such a formation happening by chance as "one in a trillion trillion," Beckjord stated, "It is very likely that a creative force in the past caused this formation of rock, lava and sand to form in that manner, possibly knowing that the Senator would be famous around this time in his life."

—The New Republic

I was unable to entice Jon Eric to the phone. He was busy with the lunch crowd at his Malibu restaurant slash museum. I was fobbed off instead on one Eldon Halflife, Jr. who is the curator of the Crypto-Phenomena collection, and, I am happy to report, he was every bit as knowledgeable as his boss.

"Mr. Halflife, is that really your name?"

"Yes it is."

"There's no need to get edgy about it, I have nothing against it. I was just wondering, since you are Eldon Halflife, Junior, if that didn't make you quarterlife?"

"Cracks about my name are not appreciated, buster. I'm doing a serious job here—this is no joke, and I'd appreciate it if you want to talk to me you take it seriously."

"Yes, sorry," I said. "I have looked at the evidence you say proves that the volcanic visage on Mars is Senator Kennedy, and I must say it is unmistakable. And I'll buy that the Mars creator took Teddy out of four billion plus mortals and smacked his kisser there. What I'm not sure is why. Can you shed any light on that?"

"Yes, well, I can try," Eldon Halflife, Jr. said. "We have speculated that we are being warned about the dangers of obesity and the pitfalls of profligacy."

"Could there be some message there about the obdurate obstinacy of the Massachusetts electorate?"

"Yes indeed," he said, "and the far-reaching effect of that obstinacy on the universe."

"Tell me, Mr. Halflife," I said, "I can see that anyone with half a brain would have to acknowledge your theory about the Senator's mug on Mars…"

"Sure, it's a trillion trillion to one shot that it could be anything else."

"What is not as clear to my Palos Verdes constituency is the true identity of Big Foot and the Loch Ness Monster. There is speculation down here that one or both of them might also be the Senator."

"Yes, we are working on that," Halflife said. "The Lord knows he's big enough. Now it is a matter of tracking their movements to see if they coincide at all."

"I guess neither the monster nor Big Foot have ever been sighted in Palm Beach or Washington?"

"Nor Hyannis Port or Chappaquiddick for that matter. But there isn't any reason to suspect that when things get too hot in Florida, Senator Teddy couldn't hightail it to the Northwest or the Loch Ness area. All I can say at this point is we are working on it. It's still something less than a trillion trillion to one sure thing, but we're closing in on it."

To wrap up my story, I called Senator Kennedy's office in Washington. The nice young woman who answered the phone did not seem to have heard of the Crypto-Phenomena Museum. The Senator himself was in, she said, but he was so terribly busy, he couldn't talk to me. "He has his hands full," was the way she put it.

I begged her to relay one question to the Senator so I might have his firsthand response for my readers. She said she would try, but couldn't promise anything.

"Does the Senator think there is any chance that the three-point-six-mile rock, lava and sand formation on Mars that looks like him could actually have been put there by a creative force knowing that the Senator would be famous around this time in his life?"

"…mouthful," was all I heard her say.

"The Senator has a mouthful, did you say?" I asked.

"No, I said, 'That's a mouthful.' I don't know if he'll have time to digest that, but hold on, will you?"

In a few minutes she was back on the line. "He wants to know if there are any barrooms on Mars."

Justice
Or Mercy

A professional organization I belong to has asked me for a photograph.

This group recognizes my outstanding competence by allowing me the privilege of paying them $250 a year. In exchange, I get four letters to put behind my name.

I have never used the letters, but it wasn't because of any innate modesty. I just can't remember which letters they are. I'm better with numbers.

For this stipend they put my name in a directory and send it to those similarly endowed, so they may see who else is paying $250 a year to have their credentials recognized by others with the same credentials.

This year they have asked for a picture.

I looked for a suitable likeness to send them. I had an adorable one taken when I was 5 years old, and since then they've gone steadily downhill.

I had another cute one kneeling in a flight jacket before a T-34 airplane, a flight helmet on my knee. But, it wasn't the right size and I didn't want to trim it because I'd have lost half the plane, half the flight jacket, or the whole helmet.

Our Choral Society program had one where I look like I am being shot out of a cannon.

Once my mind was set, I practiced my smile in every mirror I passed.

Painstaking care was taken with my wardrobe. When I modeled it for my wife, Ginny, she said:

"I guess if it's a black-and-white picture they won't see your red face." She considered a moment and added, "Maybe you should buy a larger shirt, or don't you care about breathing?"

A pretty young woman was at her desk in the photographer's studio. When I walked in she looked up at me and giggled.

On the wall was a giant picture of a woman. I didn't realize a photograph could be blown up so large.

"How much for that?" I asked.

"They're regularly $800 each, but they're on special today."

"Oh? What kind of special?"

"You buy ten, you get one free."

No matter how hard you try, you can't get away from these comedians.

A nice-looking young man came from the bowels of the studio, looked me up and down and pronounced judgment. "You don't look so bad," he said, glancing at his receptionist as if to correct her.

"Compared to what?" I was beginning to wonder. The studio was in fearsome proximity to the Peninsula *News*, my newspaper, and who knows what they might have told him.

"Some guys come in here without shaving," he said. So much for the compliments.

He sat me on a stool amidst a bunch of inverted white umbrellas, and I wondered if the roof leaked.

It was an exciting day when my proof sheet arrived. Ten little pictures of little me. And not too bad, I thought.

I decided I preferred the one where I looked deep and thoughtful—you might even say intellectual.

The smiles I so studiously rehearsed had, for the most part, failed me. There was one with sort of a grin that made me look like the victim of a sudden gastritis attack, but not a real toothy smile in the carload.

I took them home to my loved ones.

My wife, Ginny, and daughter Jambalaya (not her real name) took a look at them.

"Well," Ginny said at last with a pained expression on her face, "he didn't take your personality."

"Count your blessings," Jambalaya said.

"You look a little like Attila the Hun," Ginny said.

"I think he looks like he lost a prizefight," from Jambalaya. "Have you ever considered a face-lift?"

"I had one," I said.

"Shame it didn't take," Jambalaya said—"you look like the meltdown of a nuclear reactor."

"Why didn't you wear your glasses?" Ginny asked.

"Because they turn dark when the flashbulbs go off, and I look like a Mafia don."

"Mafia would be an improvement," Jambalaya said.

A week after I sent my picture to the exclusive directory I got the following note:

"Dear CCIM—we are in receipt of your photograph. We are experiencing some difficulty knowing which end is up. We are extending our deadline two weeks in order for you to submit a reasonable, usable picture."

Self-doubt was creeping in. I decided I *was* much

better looking after all.

I went back to the photographer with the letter.

I handed it to him and he read it without comment.

Then I handed him the proof sheet and said, "These pictures don't do me justice."

He looked at the pictures and frowned, then looked at me and said, "What you need isn't justice."

"What *do* I need?" I asked, falling into his trap.

"Mercy."

If He's Ticking He's Still Kicking

Under the most wonderful headline "Pooch Takes a Licking, Keeps on Ticking," the Peninsula *News* has run a delightful article about a Rolling Hills dog getting a pacemaker (Saturday, March 22).

I was somewhat surprised to find my name omitted from the article and no mention of the credit I am due for the vanguard research I did in pacemakering.

During my years in medical school, before I qualified for my plumber's license, I was among the *avant-garde* in the original research team investigating the installation of pacemakers in animals and fish.

I was, in fact, well-known in my specialty for the creative paper I delivered to PUSS, the Peninsula University Science Society. My work was entitled "The Necessity For Ground Wires in the Installation of Pacemakers in Aquatic Creatures." It was greeted by the society with a modicum of caution.

It was a direct result of that paper that I came to the attention of Marineland of the Pacific, here in Rancho Palos Verdes.

After verifying my credentials, they gave me a large grant to research and experiment with adapting pacemakers to killer whales. Whales are expensive, and prolonging their lives would be worth big bucks. My background has been in experimental animal surgery—I was the first unlicensed surgeon to do a triple bypass operation on a duck.

Duck soup.

I then experimented with dogs, cats and gerbils, and my first foray into aquatic creatures was with a turtle. Real, not the mock.

So, I am quite surprised, and more than a little offended that my name did not even warrant a footnote in the Licking Pooch Ticking article. Especially since one line was lifted practically verbatim from my original research: "...he refuses to down the special dog food prescribed for him...he's back on hot dogs, salami and cheese—the sharper the better."

One of the difficulties in the application of pacemakers to fish is you are never quite sure when the fish needs one. A dog may stagger, but a fish floats. I had experimented with a gray-cheeked parakeet, but I waited until the little fella was on his back in the cage, with his feet in the air. The vet who did that operation warned me there might be brain damage, but it turned out the bird's brain was so small we never could tell if it was damaged or not.

That was a bird of a different stripe (orange) and this is a different kettle of fish.

My preeminence in the field is due to my experiments on goldfish. (I refuse to flaunt my erudition by parading a list of Latin names.)

The big hurdle here was the time required for implanting the pacemaker in the fish, which was longer than the fish could live out of water. So, the procedure had to be performed underwater.

The operation went smoothly until it came time for the final hookup of the pacemaker to the heart. There was a sudden blue flash that electrocuted all the fish in the pond.

I got some nasty burns.

It was that incident that led to my study on ground wires.

Once conquered, in subsequent successes with goldfish, I was ready for the big one: the killer whale.

In retrospect I know what went wrong. But, hindsight is always 20-20.

I knew from the literature that the heart rate of a hare was faster than that of a tortoise. But in those days, research into the heart rate of a killer whale was poorly documented.

Quite simply, I miscalculated the size of the pacemaker required. A whale so big, and his heart so small. After the surgical team got the pacemaker planted and hooked up in the Marineland tank, the whale got to shaking so violently there was this tremendous tidal wave that almost washed away the Wayfarer's Chapel.

The implant team didn't know if the whale was dead or alive. But I stepped in with my unchallenged theorem for determining if the recipient of a pacemaker was still alive: *If he's still ticking, he's still kicking.*

Many of my fellow scientists ask me what my next project will be. I have a guppy that is showing signs of slowing down.

It should be a real challenge.

Jimmy Carter Is A Busser

Just today I received yet another letter from Jimmy Carter. I must have gotten six or eight of them since he left the White House involuntarily. They all start out the same way:

"Dear Friend,

As a former U.S. President..."

I always feel rather sad that he has to remind his friends who he is. I, for one, have not forgotten him. And now, he and his helpmate, Rosalynn, are schlepping all over the world with hammer and nails, building houses for the poor, without regard to race, color, creed or political alignment.

Some say he is putting his time to better use than any other ex-president in recent memory, and I am hard-pressed to argue with that.

But today, in the same mail, came an *HG* magazine, that used to be called *House and Garden* before abbreviation fever swept the country.

It revealed something so scandalous to me about Jimmy Carter that I can't help passing it on to you.

Jimmy Carter was apparently (still is, for all I know) an inveterate kisser.

The *HG* article is about greetings. How some of us old-timers were taught to give a firm handshake—look 'em in the eye, and all that. Then the writer (Martin Filler) goes on to say that nowadays there is a big kissing game going on. When people greet now, instead of shaking hands they have begun kissing. It is one of the reasons I never leave the house anymore.

Of course the kissing is supposed to be sort of air-kissing; no real physical contact outside of perhaps a glance on the cheek with the kisser's cheek. You don't want all that lipstick smudging, and cast-iron hairdos are off-limits.

Jimmy Carter apparently (according to *HG*) has his own style—he goes right for the lips. Apparently he planted a championship smacker on the Queen Mother in London and the grande dame was shocked out of her crown. Said she had only been kissed like that by her dear departed husband before he was so dearly departed, some twenty-five years before. There is apparently a photograph of Jimmy pulling the same trick with Jackie Onassis at some Kennedy memorial ceremony, and Ms. Onassis is seen to back away and grimace at the mere thought.

This is a shame. Perhaps she didn't know who he was. Maybe she didn't get one of the letters identifying him as a former U.S. President. It's understandable. Celebrities like Jackie O. can't go kissing every Tom, Dick and Harry, or Jimmy, for that matter, who come along. Aside from the threat of germs, there is the assault on one's dignity to be considered.

A Plains, Georgia, contact of mine slipped me the phone number of Jimmy Carter's social secretary, Ester "Willy" Forbusser, so that I might inquire into the nature of the aggressive kissing practices of this former U.S. President.

She answered the phone, "Former U.S. President Jimmy Carter's Social Secretary Ester 'Willy' Forbusser, how may I help you?"

"Thanks for asking Ms. ForBUSSer."

"The accent's on FOR. FORbusser," she corrected me.

"I was wondering if you could give me any background on former U.S. President Jimmy Carter's kissing practices?"

"Well, I never…" She was a little put out.

"*HG* magazine has a piece about him planting a whopper on the Queen Mother. Can you tell me, do you think he found her attractive?"

"I couldn't tell you."

"Or did you, as his social secretary, advise him that was the proper protocol with the British Royal Family?"

"No, I did not." She was being emphatic.

"I understand Jackie O. reacted rather negatively to one of Jimmy's proffered smooches."

"Agh, she doesn't know what she's missing."

"Why, is he a good kisser?"

"How would I know?" she answered with a flash of anger.

"This was the president, I believe, who said something in a *Playboy* interview about lusting in his heart for a bunch of women…"

"He said that about others, not himself."

"So you don't think that has anything at all to do with this kissing blitz?"

"Not at all."

"Ever consider advising him of alternate forms of greeting?"

"Oh, we've been all through that…"

"Like hand-kissing…"

"Agh," she pooh-poohed that, "that went out in the thirties with Ernst Lubitsch Paramount comedies."

"How about just shaking hands?"

"We talked about it. He even tried it for a while."

"What happened?"

"Jimmy's got a real weak handshake because he's been pounding nails so long for his pet project, Habitat for Humanity, the muscles just went sort of slack."

"So, Ms. Forbusser," I asked carefully, "can you tell me, ah, not from personal experience, of course, but from say, ah, reputation—what kind of kisser is the former U.S. President, Jimmy Carter?"

"Superb!" she didn't hesitate. "His lips are extremely strong from holding all those nails in his mouth."

"How about you, Ms. Forbusser?"

"What about me?"

"Do you kiss at all?"

"Kiss off, buster," she said.

My Wonder Woman

It was the headline that caught my eye:

"Wife Scares Attackers By Leap From Balcony."

The story was of a woman who saved her husband from three attackers by jumping off the balcony and frightening them away.

Wouldn't any reasonable man wonder if his wife would do the same for him?

"Ginny!" I called, across several crowded rooms.

There was no answer. So I picked up my clippings from the Santa Barbara *News-Press* and headed for the kitchen, homing on the sound of some English novel being read aloud to our resident dishwasher.

I am especially proud that Ginny still does her own dishes. So many of her friends are sending theirs out.

In the kitchen some British chap was reading Thomas

Hardy's *The Mayor of Casterbridge* to Ginny. She thinks her listening to all these British novelists and British narrators will make me think she's British.

When Ginny saw me coming she switched off the tape. It was a diversionary action she usually took in deference to the prospect of live discourse.

"Ginny," I said, taking the bull by the horns, "would you jump off the balcony if I was under attack below?"

She gave me one of those sanity-questioning looks where the eyes sort of slide off your face to prevent further embarrassment.

"We don't have a second story." She had a maddeningly realistic streak.

"All right, would you jump off the roof? Now don't tell me we don't have a roof."

"What would I be doing on the roof?"

"Will you stop nit-picking?" I asked suavely. I don't care what she said later—I *was* suave.

"Just imagine you were on the roof and two, maybe three, people started attacking me."

"Because of those silly articles you write?"

"Okay"—I conceded, just to get my answer. "For any reason."

"No," she rejected the idea. "There's not a word of truth in them anyway."

I was on the verge of giving up. But I think every once in a while a marriage should be put to a test.

"Look, Ginny," I pleaded. "Is there any circumstance that would cause you to jump off the roof?"

She rolled her eyes while rinsing pots and pans, the splash of the water denigrating my life-or-death queries.

"I suppose if the house were on fire," she conceded.

"To save your life?" I pressed her.

"Sure."

"Aha!" I seized my advantage. "But not to save mine?"

"You're over-dramatizing again," she said.

"Am I?" I insisted. "I suppose you don't think it could happen?"

"Right."

"Well, it happened in Franklin, New Jersey, all right," I said, flourishing the clipping.

"It's right here in the paper—see what she says." I consulted the Santa Barbara *News-Press*, not to misquote.

"'No other woman wouldn't do the same thing to save her husband,' said the 33-year-old mother whose husband now calls her 'Wonder Woman.'"

Ginny turned up her nose—"That's a double negative—too hard to follow."

"Don't you want to be called 'Wonder Woman'?" I asked her.

"No."

"I'm going to call Mrs. Grbac in Franklin, New Jersey, and tell her I found a woman who wouldn't jump to save her husband."

"Don't be silly."

"Listen to this," I read from the article again. "'There was nothing else to do, I had to help.' Now there's a real woman," I said.

"I wonder," Ginny said.

"Make light of it if you will," I smarted. Then I compromised. Sometimes that is necessary to save a marriage.

"Would you step out of the first-floor window to help me?"

She turned off the water, dried her hands and sighed, a long-suffering British sigh.

"Sure," she said and patted me on the top of my head.

Something seemed to soften her. I deny, as she later accused, that I had tears in my eyes. I suspect she wanted to go back to *The Mayor of Casterbridge*.

I pressed my marriage test.

"Would you or wouldn't you jump on my assailants from the roof and scare them off as Mrs. Grbac did?"

"Sure," she said, "I'd do anything to save you." In her voice was a certain lack of conviction.

"Jump out of a second-story window?"

"Yes." Her surrender was total.

"Off a mountaintop?"

"Absolutely." She gave in graciously, if without any real enthusiasm.

"Into a pool of sharks?" I pulled all the stops.

"Well," she hesitated. "That's a little different."

"Aha," I caught her temporizing. "You don't love me enough to jump into a pool of sharks to save my life."

"Oh, it's not you," she said.

"What then?"

"I'm just not that crazy about swimming with all your relatives."

You Have To Be Dead To Collect

"Hello—I'd like to talk to someone about this notice I got in the mail today—"

"Yes?"

"This special offer to seniors. Ten thousand dollars for burial expenses."

"Yes?"

"Do I have to look at condos in the desert or something?"

"No."

"Nothing to buy?"

"Just the policy."

"So let me get this straight—to get this $10,000 from burial insurance, what do I have to do?"

"Die," she said.

"Do I need any proof?"

"No, we'll take your word for it."

"Is it possible to get an advance on that ten grand?"

"Before you are dead? I don't think so."

"I guess it wouldn't do me a lot of good after I'm dead."

"I guess not."

"Well, suppose you want to economize on the funeral—say you go only eight, nine hundred—can you get the rest in cash?"

"I'm sure we could work something out."

"Your mailer says, 'Ages forty to eighty-five.' What does that mean?"

"The ages we cover."

"So if you are over eighty-five, you can't die?"

"Sure you can—we can't stop you—we just won't pay anything."

"It says no physical exam needed."

"That's right."

"Well, I guess I have to somehow prove I'm still alive."

"That would be preferable."

"Like I have an uncle who's been dead for three years but he doesn't know it yet."

"But you have to answer three questions."

"Yeah, the flyer says three simple questions—how simple are they?"

"Very—would you like me to give them to you now?"

"Ah, well, maybe—could I kinda peek at the anwers first? I mean, I don't want to mess up."

"Oh, don't you worry about that. You can take the test as often as you want."

"Oh well, in that case, go ahead."

"Question One: Are you still alive?"

"Well, as far as I know. I feel like it anyway."

"Very good. Question Two: Have you ever been dead before?"

"Not to my knowledge."

"Hey, just a minute. It sounds like you might be waffling a bit there, fella. It's a yes or no question."

"Oh, ho, ho, is that the forty years of courteous service I hear in your voice?"

"Certainly, sir—would you like to answer the question yes or no? It's *entirely* up to you, sir."

"No."

"You wouldn't?"

"No, no is my answer. I've never been dead before."

"Very good, sir. Are you calling from an intensive care unit, psycho ward or any mental institution?"

"No, I'm at home. Just give me the last question."

"That *was* the question."

"Oh. Let's suppose now, just for the sake of argument, I send you the money, then I change my mind about dying. Can I get it back?"

"What do you mean, change your mind about dying?"

"Well, you say you don't cover anyone after eighty-five—just suppose I hang on that long, what do you do for me?"

"Count your blessings."

"That's it? You count my blessings? No money?"

"Look at it this way, pal. If someone told you for a lousy ten thousand dollars they would guarantee you'd live to be more than eighty-five, would you give them the money?"

"Well, I suppose I might."

"Good, send it to this address…"

"Suppose I send you the money—when I die, how will I know you pay off?"

"Well, we could give you the names of other stiffs we've paid off."

"And their phone numbers?"

"Some things you have to take on faith."

"I don't know her."

"She's dead."

Prizewinning Messages

My wife, who is known in the horticultural and botanical book trade as VLT Gardner, has asked me to stop making recorded messages on her answer machine.

This is a great pity, for I had not only done some dazzling work in that field for her, heretofore, but I had some prizewinning ideas for the future.

I am willing to share some of them with you here, on the condition you do not tell Virginia Louise Twining

Gardner about them. Her loss is your gain, and you may feel free to adopt these messages for your own enterprise.

(Read with lazy Southern accent)

VLT Gardner Books here. All our operators are busy right now, but if you'll stay on the line, your call will be answered in the order it was received, but just between us, your call was received after about a dozen others, so it's going to be one long wait, honey chile.

*   *   *

(Read rapidly, a breathless pitchman)

Hello, VLT Gardner Books here—Announcing our twoferone special. Buy two copies of *Stubble Mulching in the Great Plains* for only $34.95 each, and get a third copy absolutely free, while the supply lasts. Slightly higher in the Great Plains. In order to treat all our valued customers fairly, we ask that you make this a one book to a customer offer— So to take full advantage of the special will require the participation of three people, so hurry, call your friends. Sorry, due to the tremendous volume of orders we anticipate during this very special sale, we will regretfully be unable to accept checks, money orders, certified checks, cashier's checks, credit cards, barter or cash.

*   *   *

(Slowly—deliberately)

Hello. This is Agent Foster Cartwright of the Federal Bureau of Investigation. We have found it necessary to tap the phone of VLT Gardner Books. In order to assist us with our investigation, please leave your name, address, phone number, age, sex and the date of your last fingerprinting.

*   *   *

(Folksy, friendly)

Hi. VLT Gardner Horty and Botany Books on the line. If you are looking for Ginny, the chief executive officer of this enterprise, you aren't the only one. Last Tuesday she went into the stacks to find a book to fill an order she received in March, 1976, and hasn't been heard from since. If you should happen to see her, tell her to call home please, we're out of spaghetti.

If you are calling about an order you placed anytime after April, 1976, we remind you patience is a virtue, and virtue these days, as you well know, is in short supply.

*   *   *

(Reverently)

Good day. This is VLT Gardner Horticultural and Botanical Books, reminding you that you can lead a whore to culture, but you can't make her think.

*   *   *

(Laconically)

VLT Gardner Horticultural and Botanical Books here. We can't come to the phone right now because Ginny is in the stacks taking a long overdue inventory. Please leave your name and…(sounds of crashing books)

*   *   *

(With a kiss of the bureaucracy)

Greetings. This is Special Agent Phoenix Snethkamp of the Internal Revenue Service. We're here to investigate VLT Gardner Books in an effort to determine how it could be humanly possible to sell so damn many books and make so little profit. If you have any information that will help us in this investigation, please leave your name and phone number, your tax I.D. number, and a brief explanation on how you chiseled us on your last three tax returns.

*   *   *

When she goes to the market, I like to use this one. It keeps the phone from ringing so bloody often:

(Like a voice over a travel film)

VLT Gardner Books here. With thousands of titles the proprietor, VLT herself, is off scouring the continent of Australia to bring you the finest books money can buy. She'll be back in a month or so.

(Shift voice to the friendly cop)

But in the meantime, don't get any ideas about ripping

the place off. In the first place, you can't move in here there are so blasted many books; so even if you were able to put your hands on a couple volumes, you'd never get back out.

We are also surrounded by attack dogs and guards with automatic weapons purchased just before they blew the whistle on those little toys.

Leave a message, and if one of our unfriendly attack dogs doesn't chew this tape, she'll call you back.

Ginny, that is, not the dog.

Not Exactly A Doctor

"Jambalaya got a job for the summer," the distaff exclaimed with undisguised pride.

Jambalaya (not her real name) is going into her senior year at the University of the Pacific. To keep the same distance between her and her parents, she has opted to work in Northern California.

"Great," I said. "What's the job?"

"On a magazine."

"Wow, a writer like her dad."

"Not exactly."

"What then?"

"She's going to work in the advertising department."

"Ah well, just as well—that's where the money is."

"Not exactly."

"Sure it is. Ads grease the skids for editorial—newspapers as well as magazines. Everyone knows that."

"Not exactly."

"What do you mean 'not exactly'? You are talking to a newspaperman who knows. She'll be rich before you know it."

"Not exactly."

"She on commission?"

"Not exactly."

"Salary then. That's okay to start, but take my word for it, the big money is made on commission. But it's reassuring to have a little salary—I don't expect they'd offer too much to start."

"No."

"Four, five hundred a week is all?"

"Not exactly."

"More? Well, that's more like it. No reason they shouldn't pay her a decent wage. Getting her dirt cheap I'll bet—cost them an arm and a leg to pay *her* on commission. So what's the scoop? Sort of a salary and commission arrangement?"

"Not exactly."

"Not exactly? Not exactly? Can't you say anything else? Can't you just tell me straight out how much they are paying her?"

"Oh, don't be so crass. She's young. She doesn't have to make a million dollars on a summer job, does she?"

"Of course not. So what's she making?"

"Oh, why don't you call her if it's so important to you."

"You bet I will."

"Only do me a favor. Don't deflate her. She got the first job she interviewed for. You know she went to a lot of work to send those résumés all over the country, and you know how competitive it is to land a job in the media. So do us both a favor and soft-pedal the money thing. Money isn't so important when you are young and working for a summer."

"I guess you're right. Maybe she could get by on a couple hundred a week. But you gotta be careful too they don't take advantage of you. It's a proven fact if you sell too cheap they don't respect you."

"She's always worked at jobs just to make money. Now she found one that will help with her career."

"Yessir. I'm proud of all the girls. All workers. And every year they make more. She *is* making more with the new job?"

"Not exactly."

*　　　*　　　*

"Jambalaya—congratulations on landing a job with your first interview. Your mom and I are proud of you."

"Thanks."

"Quite a feat for a 20-year-old going into her senior year of college—getting on a big magazine for the summer."

"Thanks."

"I don't want to be crass, but you know how I've always had a thing about statistics—"

"Yeah."

"Minimum?"

"Not exactly."

"Well, a girl with 3 years of college *ought* to be worth more than minimum."

"It's an internship."

"An internship? Like a medical doctor or something?"

"Not exactly."

"So, what's it pay?"

"Oh, Dad, don't be so mercenary."

"*Mercenary*? You mean you are working for nothing?"

"Exactly."

Hometown Drunks

I was so disappointed to read an article in the Saturday, May 3 edition of the Peninsula *News* (and, of course, the highly-touted Rolling Hills *Herald*) headlined:

"PVE Police Show No Favoritism to Hometown Drunks, Chief Says."

Since I have always personally favored hometown drunks, I thought I'd better speak to the chief and get to the bottom of this.

"Is the chief in?" I asked at the desk of the PVE Police Department.

"No," the nice young man in uniform said. "He saw you coming and ducked out the back door." The man at the desk certainly didn't look old enough to be a policeman, but they seldom do, nowadays.

He was one of the few cops under 50 I've seen who didn't have a moustache.

"What has the department got against hometown drunks?" I asked.

"Hey, if you are referring to that article in the Peninsula *News*," he said, backing away from me as though he suspected leprosy, "you better talk to the chief."

"I *want* to talk to the chief," I said.

"He's not here."

I won't say I can never be fooled, but I could smell cover-up here a mile away. And, I said so.

The young officer blushed. "Look," he whispered, as though his hushed tones could intimidate a reporter as intrepid as I, "we don't have *anything* against hometown drunks."

"Then why won't you show them a little favoritism?" I asked at the top of my lungs, startling everyone in the room, including a minor boy who was being fined for drinking beer on the cliffs.

"Look," he was whispering again, "that headline might have been a little misleading. Did you read the whole story?"

"Darn right I did," I said. "Every word."

"Then you know the city manager said, 'I think we have an outstanding police department and I want to see that it continues.'"

"Yes."

"And you read the memo that said law enforcement must be impartial, decisive and firm, no matter who the violator—to do less would demoralize the police department?"

"Yes, and I read Councilman Culver's declaration that preferential treatment had never been discussed in her six years on the council." I looked our young policeman square in the eye. "But nobody said *anything* about hometown drunks and why you can't show them any favoritism."

"Are you trying to stir up trouble, buddy?" the desk man asked me through a dubious, cocked eye.

"I don't think all drunks are created equal," I confessed.

"I mean, on the one hand you have a drunk drive up here from Pedro or Hermosa, maybe. He bought his booze off the Hill—he is wearing out our streets and doesn't pay a cent of taxes to keep our police department well-oiled."

"'The law is the law,' Councilman Florance says," the young officer sputtered, blushing with guilt.

"Yes, but on the other hand you have the hometown drunk. He probably bought his hooch right here on the Hill, putting all the sales taxes into local coffers. He is, in effect, paying the salary of the police officer who stopped him."

"Listen, buddy, I don't have all day."

"What have you got against hometown drunks?" I asked.

"Nothing," he said. "Some of my best friends are drunks."

"Well then," I sighed in vast relief, "surely you give your friends a little preferential treatment if you stop them driving under the influence of strong spirits."

"What if I do?" The officer's face flushed again.

"Then you *are* giving preferential treatment to home-town drunks!" I have to admit I was more than a little proud of the way I had, with consummate skill, trapped him into admitting the favoritism so vehemently denied by all the politicians and policemen.

"Naw," he said. "All my drunken friends are from Pedro. I throw the book at these locals."

I couldn't hide my disappointment. I may even have said something intemperate.

"Say, fella," the young police officer said, "your breath smells a little funny—would you mind stepping in the back room for a little breath analyzer?"

"Hey, wait a minute. I'm a local boy."

"Hometown?"

"You bet."

"Where do you live?"

"RPV."

He slapped the cuffs on me, and said, "This is PVE."

Clint Eastwood Owes His Fame To Me

Carmel Mayor Clint Eastwood and I were once very close. I'd estimate closer than two feet or so.

I got one Christmas card from him. It was the only sign that he ever understood the enormous debt he owed me for making him famous.

In my golden youth, and his, we both worked on a CBS television show called *Rawhide*. He played a subsidiary character named Rowdy Yates, and I was a big gun in the film production cost control department.

Rawhide was the cultural highlight of Friday night television. Naturally they sought the top writers in town. It is unimportant that I was one of them. What is important is that I made this minor television performer into a star.

In one of my scripts, I wrote a particularly engaging lip curl for Mr. Eastwood's Rowdy Yates. It was a snarl that catapulted him to stardom.

Clint has never actually acknowledged the large part I played in the promotion of his career, but I have been very big about it—until he was elected mayor of Carmel.

I once gave him an opportunity to repay his debt to me. Some years ago, I sent Clint one of my better novels with a personal note about how he would be just right for the lead in a movie based on my book. I tastefully reminded him of our past close association.

As I recall, I also generously offered to make myself available to write the screenplay.

Inexplicably, Clint never responded to my letter. Sometimes an unacknowledged debt weighs so heavily on a man, it tongue-ties him. I suspect some misguided underling thought he was protecting Clint from a crackpot.

I did get a note from some stranger saying Mr. Eastwood was not interested in doing any more cop movies.

When I asked to have the book returned, someone said they couldn't find it.

Since then, my book has been mercilessly plagiarized by some of Clint's writers. The biggest ripoff being the smile he was sporting in Carmel during his campaign for mayor.

Whenever anyone asked him for an autograph he would say, "I'm sorry, I don't give autographs." Then he would break into the most engaging smile—the smile *I* wrote for him—the smile he has *never* thanked me for, and he would say, "But thanks for asking."

When I read that account, I decided the time had come to collect on my markers from my old friend Clint.

I put in a call to Carmel City Hall. I asked for my old friend Clint by name.

For some reason he didn't come to the phone. Shyness, I suppose. Instead, a sissified apologist came on the line and said, "The mayor is in conference with the city council."

"What is on the agenda?" I asked.

"A Frisbee festival in the park. As you know, one of the antiquated laws they had up here was the prohibition of Frisbee tossing in the park."

"Is Clint a big Frisbee tosser?"

"Not really, but he's a champion of the little guy. Got a chunk of the hippie vote with that one."

"Let's analyze his stunning victory. How did a man who is for business progress win so big in a small residential community?" I asked.

"Frisbee in the park for the hippies and fast-food outlets for the business community were big issues in the campaign," he said. "But there was a lot of voting on the silent issue."

"What was that?"

"The autographs," he whispered. "During the campaign Clint was besieged for autographs. Whenever anyone asked him for one, he'd smile that big-as-all-outdoors smile and say, "I don't give autographs *during the campaign*." Then he'd smile so broadly again and say, "But thanks for asking."

"So what?"

"Then an aide who followed him around would pass

out a card that said, 'Clint does not want to influence his election with his stardom. If he is elected mayor, he will be glad to sign his autograph for any constituent. This card entitles you to one free autograph from Mayor Eastwood.'"

"It worked?"

"Like a charm."

A good reporter always verifies a story—so I put in another call to my old friend Clint. He was in conference with the amazing blue ribbon Frisbee-in-the-park committee, but a minor functionary at City Hall fielded the call.

I told him I'd like to congratulate my old friend Clint on his stunning victory, and added, "I was the man responsible for the small snarl that made him so famous."

"I'm sorry, Clint doesn't give autographs," the voice said, "but thanks for asking."

I think I reached a recording.

To Spread Manure Or A Gift Of God?

Dear Ted:

I was browsing in the *Oxford English Dictionary* the other day, looking up the various meanings of the word "Teeming," when, en route, I came upon a strange definition of "Ted."

"To spread manure."

Seth, your publisher, and I have been kicking around the appropriateness of this appellation for our family newspaper. On the one hand it seems a terribly accurate portrayal of what you do; and on the other it seems, well, rather coarse. Do you have any other names we might use?

Fairly sincerely,

Reid Bundy,
Executive Editor
Peninsula *News*

Dear Reid:

Theodore means "gift of God."

Dear Theodore:

The name we are looking for should be believable.

Dear Reid:

Let's not get too frisky here. I have just looked up both "Reid" and "Bundy" in my *Name Your Baby* book. "Reid" says, "See: Read—red-complexioned." It's a good thing Joe McCarthy is dead and gone. A red-complexioned newspaper editor has got to be suspect in this conservative community.

"Bundy—the Old English 'Bondig,' free man—a man who earned his freedom from his overlord."

So that makes you sort of a left-wing slave, as I see it.

How about something more appropriate and descriptive: Ted Reid—left-wing manure spreader?

Dear Gardner:

Your letter has me in stitches. Seth thinks I should read (Reid—get it?) it first before I fall down laughing—but I don't have to, your handwriting just does that to me.

It occurs to both of us that Ted Gardner is simply a manure spreader in the garden and so very appropriate in every way.

At any rate, we are looking for a new name for you, not me. My name isn't plastered all over the page in 20-point type. And underscored. I don't get any by-lines or sign my editorials.

Dear Slave:

Oh, it's jealousy, is it? And just whose name is on the masthead with "Executive Editor" tagged behind it? I don't notice "Executive Writer" behind my name anywhere. And who gets his picture in the paper with burning pencils, with Santa hats, and laughing so ingratiatingly beside comely wenches?

Dear Manure Spreader:

Seth is considering an agricultural section so we might run your picture between the sows and the cows. The company should flatter you.

Dear Mr. B: (B-movie, get it?)

Are you talking about Seth Baker?

I won't even get into the obvious meaning of "Baker"—a guy who bakes bread—and just between us, I wouldn't squawk if he sent a little bread my way, if you take my meaning.

Dear Mr. T:

I showed your darling note to Seth Baker. He agrees that bread would go well with a guy as cheesy as you. Enclosed find a gift certificate for day-old Wonder bread at your local outlet.

Okay Farm Boy:

I was perusing <u>my</u> *Oxford*, looking up the many meanings of "Reactionary," when I stumbled on the first definition of "Read," to wit: "The stomach of an animal."

Maybe you want to join me in my picture of the sow and cow *if* we can find an animal big enough to swallow you. Or one that can stomach you. Yuk, yuk.

Fortunately, I've run out of space and am unable to print Reid Bundy's last reply. But since my name is up there in 20-point type, and you need a Seeing Eye dog to find his name anywhere, it is only fitting I should have the last word.

Editor's note: Ted Gardner is on vacation, probably spreading manure in his hometown. (Busman's holiday.) The word processing for his column is being done by a meat grinder.

Social Phobias On New Year's Eve

"Ginny!" (She's the distaff.) "Why did you leave this article on social phobias from the *New York Times Magazine* open on my desk?"

"I was just starting to read it," she said.

"Oh, ho, ho," I snickered, "you weren't trying to needle me into going to the neighbor's New Year's Eve party?"

"No."

"Believe that and you have a nice New York river bridge on sale."

"Take my word for it—nobody cares that you don't go to parties."

"And you don't mind going alone?"

"No, I rather like it."

"Oh you do, do you?" I expressed some doubt. "Then why did you leave this article on my desk—giving people tranquilizers to get them over their social phobias? I'm not afraid of people, I just don't want them to be afraid of me. Just because I don't go to parties doesn't mean I'm afraid of people."

"Oh, what does it mean then?"

"Well, it doesn't mean what this article says."

"What does it say?" she asked. "I haven't read it."

"Umhumm. 'The true social phobic is disabled by fears of being rejected,'" I quoted liberally the article by Dava Sobel in the "Body and Mind" section; the page Ginny left open so innocently on my desk. "You certainly don't think *I* have disabling fears do you? Social phobias?"

"Of course not."

"Ho, ho, look at this—one of the social phobias is signing checks. Now that's something I could relate to."

"Amen," she said with a certain lack of human warmth.

"But you don't seriously think that the reason I don't go to parties is because I suffer from intense, unreasonable fear of social situations as your article says?"

"No, dear." She was assuming that acutely patronizing tone again. "And it's not *my* article. I didn't write it. I didn't even *read* it."

"It says here only two to three percent of Americans are thought to have social phobia—that is, to be, in effect, paralyzed by their fears of what others will think of them. And I'm not..."

"I know, I know," she cut me off. "You're not afraid of what people will think of you, only of what you will think of them."

"Well..."

"I suspect most people can bear up to your opinions— so why don't you come with me to the New Year's Eve party this year? I've gone to the last six alone."

"I don't know. What do you think of this?" I asked her, reading from the article she claimed not to have read. "'Experts then tend to think of it in two extremes: either as anxiety anyone might experience at some point—walking into a party, say—or as part of the constellation of features of "avoidant personality disorder." Some investigators lumped it with agoraphobia—the more generalized panic of being out alone.' You have to admit, that certainly is not me."

"I never said it was."

"No, you just left this article open on my desk accidentally."

"That's right."

"So how many people actually enjoy parties? All you have to do is take your own informal survey, as I did before I stopped going altogether."

"What survey?"

"I asked people—the people at the parties—if they enjoyed parties."

"What did they say?"

"The responses range from, 'Not really,' to '*Some* parties.' No one ever said unreservedly, 'I *love* parties.'"

"So what?"

"So I'm not so far out of the mainstream, I'm just

more honest about it. You might say I have the courage of my convictions, as do precious few of my peers."

"You used to say you were without peer."

"Never."

"Yes you did." She frowned in reconsideration. "Maybe that was before you knew what it meant."

I ignored her. I had discovered some years ago it was the only solution to her solecisms.

"Hey, get this," I said, reading aloud to her the last paragraph of the "Body and Mind" piece:

"'For me, social phobics are the most rewarding people to work with,' Dr. Heimberg says. 'Their oversensitivity to other human beings makes them almost pathologically nice. As the therapy helps the pathological part go away, their basic niceness emerges and they do very well.'

"Well, what do you think of that, Ginny?" I asked. "Do you think I could be called pathologically nice?"

She pondered for a moment, her features slinking deep into ersatz concentration.

"I suppose..." she said at last, "that's half true."

Jackie Robinson Made It, Why Not She?

The World Series used to be a big deal.

That was before the women took over the sport.

Years ago, I was a first baseman because I am left-handed. Being left-handed is a sign of genius, as any left-hander will tell you.

A lot of lefties like me were first basemen: Einstein, Leonardo da Vinci, and Michelangelo, to name just a few.

I had a first baseman's mitt that had a signature burned in the cowhide:

Phil R. "Lefty" Cavaretta, Jr.

That mitt marked the beginning of my signing my name:

Teddy R. "Lefty" Gardner, Jr.

So much for my credentials.

Now, as I say, the women have horned in. A seemingly harmless statistical item buried at the bottom of a new feature in *Harper's* magazine claims:

"Percentage of men who say the biggest sports thrill would be to get the winning hit in the World Series: 31.

"Percentage of women who say this: 37."

The implications are staggering. We should have realized this would happen when we gave women the franchise.

Equality has become inequality. Or, as a friend of mine said, "I'm all for equality of the sexes. My wife has been treating me as an inferior for years."

More women than men want to make the winning hit in the World Series. And what I didn't find out until today was that there was a training camp right here in Palos Verdes Estates whose secret goal is to do just that—prepare a woman to make the winning hit in the World Series.

On the Lunada Bay Little League field was gathered a group of women of assorted shapes, sizes and ages. Some were hitting baseballs from tees. Some were being thrown slow underhanded pitches. Some, more advanced, were hitting at overhand throws.

Surveying all this with balled fists on her waist was a well-set-up female of uncertain years with a sun-kissed leathery face like a Sunkist orange.

I introduced myself; she squinted at me.

"Yolanda Berry's my name," she said extending her dusty hand and almost ripping my arm out of the socket with her rocket-launching shake. "They call me Yogi," she grinned.

"I'll bet," I said. "Yogi, what's this all about?" I waved at the women at batting practice.

She spit a chew of tobacco at my feet.

"Women tired of taking a back seat in sports. Menfolk sittin' front o' the teevee tube and pay no attention to 'em—

decide they play ball, men'll sit up and take notice."

"Gosh, Yogi," I asked. "There aren't any women playing major league ball. How do you propose to crack the big leagues?"

She spit another wad of tobacco.

"Jackie Robinson did it 30 years ago," she said, referring to the first black to make the big leagues. "Now it's our turn. You heard of Civil Rights; now you hear of Equal Rights."

I looked over the women batting. "Say, you've got a tiny kid over there at the tee. That bat's bigger than she is."

"That's Baby Ruth," Yogi said. "Shows a lot of promise."

"What *do* you promise these women?"

"Don't promise them nothing. They only paying me $200 a day."

"What do they expect?"

She looked at me as though I hadn't understood anything she was saying.

"The girls practicin' to hit the winning run in the Series, I told you."

"How you going to get them in the game?"

"Disguise them as men at first—you never seen *National Velvet*?"

"You have a husband, Yogi?"

She nodded with a frown. "I don't have anymore time for you. I gotta work with Marilyn DiMaggio over there. It gets late out here early."

"Will you have any ready by the final game?"

She winked at me. "Remember, the game ain't over till it's over."

"What does your husband think of all this?" I asked.

"He's down by the high school kicking field goals."

She had to run, and I watched them only a few minutes more—but I must tell you, some of those ladies could hit.

So when, in the final game, a pinch hitter steps up to home plate, take a real close look.

You might be surprised.

Answer Machines Could Have The Answer

HIS MACHINE: Alan! Are you there? Pick up the phone, Alan, I've got to talk to you. Geez, Alan, this is important, give me a call.

HER MACHINE: Sharon, did you call? I'm having trouble with my machine. Sorry I missed you, I'll try again.

HERS: Sharon, Alan again.

HIS: Alan, this is getting ridiculous. I've got to see you. Lunch tomorrow? Noonish at the Biltmore. Regrets only.

HERS: Geez, Sharon, I just got your message, and since it's half past twelve already, I guess you're at the Biltmore.

HIS: Thanks for the message, Alan, and for standing me up. I was going to ask if you made up your mind about the photographer and the caterer. We've got to reserve them. There are a lot of weddings around ours, so we've got to start thinking...Do you think we can keep our appointment with the jeweler? If you don't show, don't worry, I'll just take that thirty thousand dollar ring I'm so crazy about. We can get a fifteen-year loan to pay it off.

HERS: Sharon! Don't be ridiculous. I'll be there. Don't do anything rash if I'm a little late.

HERS: Sharon! Where the H were you? I waited at the jewelers for an hour.

HIS: Sorry I missed you, Alan. I guess I was a little early. Frankly, I didn't expect you. It's been so long since I've seen you, I don't know if I'd recognize you. You'll just love the ring I picked out—it's a real beauty. I just had them mail the loan paperwork directly to you. Miss ya. When can we get together?—we've got a lot of plans to make.

HERS: Sharon, what *is* this? A *forty thousand* dollar ring—are you outta your mind? You have any idea how long it takes me to make forty thousand dollars? Say, where are you all the time anyway? All I ever get is your machine.

HIS: Where am I? I can't remember the last time *you* picked up the phone. While I'm at it, Phyllis my girlfriend—you remember Phyllis, she's going to be my maid of honor—she's the one you think is so cute. She says she saw you last night out late with a 'pretty hot-looking number,' was what she said. *And*, Phyllis also said the hot number came up to your eyeballs when you kissed her. No wonder you never answer your phone!

HERS: I think there's something wrong with my machine again. I've never gone out with Phyllis. I told you, I'm up to my eyeballs at work and I've got to keep the old nose to the grindstone if you want me to ask for time off for the honeymoon.

HIS: Alan, are you avoiding me? Phyllis says it was definitely you, and you certainly weren't working.

HERS: Hi, Sharon, it's Alan—just a quick message. My sister is in town and I'm going to be spending every free moment I have with her for the next week or so. Oh, by the way, why is the jeweler bugging me? *I* never agreed to a forty thousand dollar ring in the first place.

HIS: Alan. Do you still love me? I already have the ring and it was custom-made, so it's not returnable. I was so looking forward to showing it to you, but I know you're up to your eyeballs at work. So I hope you aren't going to be a poor sport about the ring. They put it on your credit card and will take some modest payments for ten years—it's only seven, eight hundred a month, you know I'm nothing with math. Hey—it just occurred to me you don't have a sister.

HERS: Cousin. I said cousin. Better check your machine. I think it's hearing things.

HERS: Hey, it's me again. What's this about eight hundred a month on my credit card? You gotta be out of your mind. My sis—cousin doesn't spend money like it was water, I don't know why you have to.

HIS: Hey listen, buster, what do you think I'm going to do when you are up to your eyeballs with 'relatives'? Sit home and mope? It was your idea to give me the credit card, remember? That was when you called me 'Honey Cakes,' and said I had the cutest big toe in the world. You remember that, Alan? The photographer, the caterer, the florist, the hall, they all wanted deposits, but I put it all on the card, up front. 'What the heck, no problem,' I said, 'no way will we cancel *this* wedding.'

HERS: You are out to lunch, Sharon. I've just reported the credit card stolen, and I gave them your description as a suspect, so I wouldn't try to use it again. And, look, Sharon, I still feel kindly toward you and all, but I'm afraid I'm not going to have time to get married real soon. It's nothing personal, but I am up to my eyeballs at work and I have this cousin who is taking up a surprising amount of my time. But hey, we can still be friends, go for a drink sometime? Anytime I have a minute, really. Just call me up.

___ Gardner

"Hey, Ginny," I yelled at my wife of several winters, masking my excitement as best I could. "Look at this. There's a crossword puzzle in the Peninsula *News*, and it's got my name in it."

"Wow," she said, apparently not sharing my excitement.

"I appear to be the only local reference," I said. "I'm in here with Verdi and an Old Testament book—pretty big company."

"Wow," she repeated.

"Gardner. No 'e.' At first I thought it might be a misprint and they meant gardener. But it is capitalized, and there it is, by golly—77-across, and it's 3 letters for Ted. I've read it twice, and I am the *only* local person mentioned."

"Are you sure?"

"Of course I'm sure. Look here, it says the answers are on page 22." I turned to page 22 and found a page full of ads, but no crossword solution. So I tore through the rest of the *News*, but I couldn't find the answers anywhere.

"Let's just work it out," I said.

"I'm gonna write Ted in here and see how the rest of

it comes out. Let's see, 66-down will have a 't' as its third let-ter. Sixty-six-down is Japanese port. I didn't know they made wine."

"Not wine, silly," my wife corrected, "a seaport."

"Oh—do you know any?"

"Well, there's Hiroshima and Nagasaki."

"It's only 5 letters."

"Tokyo?"

"Naw, the third letter in Tokyo is a 'k.' Let's try 67-down—Ben blank, Scottish peak, 5 letters again."

"No."

"Me neither."

"All right, we'll get one of these. Sixty-eight-down—5 letters, the third letter will be a 'd.' Let's see—outburst."

"Madder?" she said.

"That's 6 letters."

"Sorry, I was trying to get your 'd.'"

"Angry, but it's a 'g' instead of a 'd.'"

"Shout."

"An 'o.' We need a 'd,'" I puzzled. "Hey wait a minute."

"What?"

"Teo is a nickname for Theodore. Maybe they used Teo—that would fit with shout."

"Hm. Reaching a little, I suppose. No one knows you as Teo."

"No, but these things are tricky sometimes. They put stuff like that in just to throw you off."

"Hm," she pored over the paper. "Let's try the one underneath Ted. It might give us a clue to the other words. Here it is, 81-across—demon, in Arabic myth. Know it?"

"No."

Glum. We were both glum. I don't mean to suggest I was being carried away with something as unimportant as seeing my name in the paper, but let me just ask you how many of you ever got your name in a crossword puzzle? I think it's a neat idea to keep readers interested—I mean, every week they could use another local name along with—

Guinness and Verdi. "Oh ho, here's actress Meryl, you know who that is—?"

"Hm—Streep—not a very common name," Ginny said, as though a light went on in her dark brain—"Gardner is, well maybe more common—"

"Well," I protested. I thought of other Gardners—there are the writers, John and Hy—4 letters and 2—this is 3; Ted is 3. There was that government servant—John—also 4 letters.

"Was there a Joe or a Jim?"

"Well, my brother is Jim, but who knows him in Palos Verdes?"

"Sid, Wil, Don, Ben..."

"You see, there aren't any 3-letter names. All that's left is Ted."

"Wait a minute. Why couldn't it be a woman?" she said.

I smiled, the smile of indulgence. "Ginny has 5 letters," I point out, "and Virginia has 8."

"But maybe it's someone else. Someone not local."

"Oh, Ginny, don't talk so dumb. This is a local paper. Why would they put in a local man's name and then put some out-of-town woman for the answer?"

"Well, you said yourself, sometimes they get tricky." Ginny picked up the paper and leafed through it as though she weren't looking for anything special. "Hey, look, here are the answers on the next page—let me see, 77-across..." She dropped the paper and started giggling. Then burst out laughing.

"What's so funny?" I said, picking up the paper. Seventy-seven-across had the wrong answer. It would follow, if it was on the wrong page, the answers could be wrong too. I suspected it was another of Reid Bundy's devious games.

Seventy-seven-across, three letters before Gardner, said, "Ava."

Does Fail Fail When Banks Fail?

...James M. Fail of Phoenix, is under investigation by a Senate subcommittee that is studying how he acquired 15 insolvent Savings and Loans, using $70 million in borrowed money and a personal investment of $1,000.

—Jeff Gerth
New York Times

I'm sure it's no news to you, T. R. Gardner, that your present financial status places you far above the average in terms of means, influence, and credit resources.
...The greater your success today, the more likely you are to rely on credit to achieve your personal and financial goals.

—Letter from
TRW Credentials Service

"Hi—you don't know me, but I'm a guy with a spare grand lying around, and I just wondered if you could tell me how I can get in on a little savings and loan action."

"Action?"

"Yeah, you know, some of that 1.86 billion action for the, like, you know, thousand dollars down."

"Dreamer."

"No, no there's this guy who did it. His name's Fail—Fail, the way I see it, can't fail. I just want to know how a guy like me can duplicate that coup."

"Well, who *are* you?"

"I thought that might come up. Well, I have plenty experience borrowing from savings and loans, so I thought it might be fun to own a couple—like Mr. Fail. Oh, I understand there are risks and I'm willing to take the risk. I thought about it for some time and I decided, what the heck, a thou against one-point-eight-six-billion is not too shabby, so I'm willing to stand the risk."

"We get a lot of crackpots since the Fail failure."

"Well, just hold your horses. I'm no failure. Let me quote you from a letter I just received: 'Dear T. R. Gardner: I'm sure it's no news to you, T. R. Gardner, that your present financial status places you far above the average in terms of means, influence, and credit resources. Precisely because you've already achieved such an impressive measure of success, you stand to reap important benefits from charter membership in a new kind of service.'"

"So they send out millions of those. What's the big deal?"

"Wait a minute. I'm not relying solely on my impressive measure of success. I told you, I also can put my hands on a thousand bucks. So I want to know how to qualify for a couple of those savings and loans."

"Listen, what you read in the papers is often misleading. We can't sell a savings and loan to any Tom, Dick or Harry with a lousy thousand bucks in his pocket."

"You need connections?"

"Well, it's certainly a start."

"To President Bush, would that help?"

"You'd have to ask him."

"Well, I just want you to know I received an autographed picture from him and Barbara. I don't mean to name-drop or flaunt my connections or anything, but I figure with my credentials I should be a natural for one of the savings and loan deals. No less an institution than TRW Credentials Service said in black and white I was far above average."

"Yeah, when you factor in the street people."

"Listen—do you realize I could get a copy of my personal credit report just for the asking?"

"Wow."

"Not that a guy of my influence would ever need one, but it sure doesn't hurt to be well-thought-of. So how do I go about getting a couple of these banks?"

"You submit an application to the FDIC."

"Mr. Fail had been indicted when he got his 1.86 billion worth of banks for one thousand bucks. I've never been indicted, you know."

"That could help you."

"Say. You sound quite knowledgeable. Who am I talking to, anyway?"

"I'm Neil Bush..."

Linda Evans On A Clearer Channel

Hot Property

Actress Linda Evans has moved to a house she bought a couple years ago in Washington State and is looking for a tenant for her Beverly Hills-area home.

"Our give-away price is $12,500 (a month)," said Stephen Shapiro...who is handling the monthly lease.

"Linda's is cheap because she just wants a reasonable rent and a person as a tenant that she feels comfortable with. She doesn't like to play the real estate business." Homes in nearby neighborhoods have rented for as much as $100,000 a month...

Evans, a follower of the metaphysical fad of channeling, bought her home near the Yelm, Wash., ranch of J.Z. Knight, who claims to be a channel for a 35,000-year-old named Ramtha...

—From the Los Angeles Times

Through the auspices of a small-time aspiring guru, I spoke to the Legend direct.

"Can you hear me, Ramtha?"

"I hear you loud and clear," the eerie, distant voice responded, faintly.

"I notice you talk a little funny, Ramtha, but I'm delighted we speak the same language. I had no idea English was in currency 35,000 years ago—in fact, I was a little surprised folks were talking at all in those days."

"Yes. My native tongue was pretty much grunts and groans, but I figured there was more demand for my unique brand of communication in the English-speaking world."

"How did you learn?"

"Berlitz."

"I didn't realize that Berlitz language school had a branch in your neck of the woods."

"Mail order," he said, his voice fading.

"You'll have to speak up, old guru, there's quite a distance between us, apparently, and it's kinda hard to hear you."

"THAT BETTER?!" he shouted.

"Much," I said. "What I wanted to ask you about, old guru, was Linda Evan's house. You are acquainted with Linda, aren't you?"

"Of *Dynasty*—you bet! Never miss it."

"What I'd like to know is did you have anything to do with setting this ridiculously low rent for her house? Apparently she's motivated to *give* her house away. Other houses in those star-studded neighborhoods are going right up to $100,000 a month. Why should she rent hers for $12,500?"

"Simple—you get a better class of tenant that way."

"Oh?"

"Yeah—at a hundred grand a month, face it, you're probably looking at a coke dealer, whereas for a paltry twelve-five you could get a nice respectable working couple—both employed, say, in accident-injury law or some kind of healing racket. Maybe even a TV evangelist."

"But your real big movie people could pay a hundred thou a month, couldn't they?"

"We don't rent to movie people."

"You any idea what sort of person Linda is comfortable with?"

"Someone who can pay twelve-five a month, I expect."

"Yes, but I wonder if there were some who could pay, say, twenty, twenty-five grand a month, why wouldn't she be just as comfy with them?"

"Well, you figure to pay twelve-five you only need an income of five, six hundred thou a year. And that's husband and wife, where applicable. So technically each spouse could be earning as little as a quarter of a million a year—and that's from all sources, whether it be income, trust fund, lottery ticket, whatever. Now there are some real nice people in that bracket, and Linda would be real comfy with them."

"That would exclude the President of the United States—that's more than twice what he makes," I said.

"Linda's not into politics," he said. "But back to your question—to pay just twenty gees a month you are talking more like a million a year, gross. Now when we get in that bracket Linda gets a little edgy, you know—"

"*Un*comfy?"

"Exactly!" he said. "And Linda doesn't like to play the real estate business."

"A million a year gross is too..."

"Gross," he said.

"Do you figure Linda Evans moved to Yelm, Washington, to be close to J.Z. Knight, your channel, so she could be closer to you?"

"What channel's she on?"

"J.Z. Knight?" I said, surprised. "I thought you knew."

"No Linda—I used to get her on Channel 7, but they must have changed networks or something, I can't find her anywhere."

"According to the article in the *Times*, she's off the air."

"Oh man, what am I going to do with my Friday

nights?"

I used to be skeptical about this channeling stuff, but talking direct to Ramtha sure made a believer out of me.

Dear Santa: Is There Really A Virginia?

Dear Abby:

I am a man who does seasonal work in this singular occupation. I've gained a certain amount of notoriety. I try to be gracious when kids take a poke at me or squirm on my lap. "Ho, ho, ho," I say, trying to maintain this jolly reputation.

Some years ago a letter was published in a newspaper, raising a question about my existence. It was 1897 in the New York *Sun* that the letter appeared.

Dear Editor:

I am eight years old.

Some of my little friends say there is no Santa Claus. Papa says "If you see it in the Sun *it's so."*

Please tell me the truth; is there a Santa Claus?

It is signed by Virginia O'Hanlon.

Now, the answer to this letter, Abby, is famous enough: "Yes, Virginia, there is a Santa Claus. He exists as certainly as love and generosity and devotion exist, and you know that they abound and give to your life its highest beauty and joy." And he blathers on about faith, poetry and romance.

So anyway, Abby, my question is not whether or not there is a Santa Claus, I oughta know all right, and in case I might forget, every Christmas I get the stuffing knocked out of me by wiry kids as a reminder.

No, my question is, was there really a Virginia?

I don't know if anyone's ever asked that before, but I got to thinking, maybe the whole thing is just a little too pat.

I mean, it may have resulted in the most famous newspaper editorial of all time, but think about it—analyze the alleged letter.

First, she starts out with "I am eight years old." If she were truly eight years old, would she lay that out up front? Kids who are eight have long tried to pass for twelve or more. Kids that age don't brag about their age. And let me tell you, I don't get too many eight-year-olds on my lap. In my experience, the skepticism begins on the first day of the first school grade. The teacher seats the kids, calls the roll, and someone leans across the aisle and says, "Pst, there's no Santa Claus."

Now, her second sentence: "Some of my little friends say there is no Santa Claus."

Look at that sentence closely, please. It is the tip-off. Have you ever heard an eight-year-old refer to her friends as "little"? First of all, they probably aren't "little" to her but just about her size, and she, as mentioned above, aspires to be twelve, if not old enough to drive a car.

So even if her friends were "little" to a grown-up, they were big to her. But a grown-up writing that letter wouldn't think of that. Eight-year-olds would be little to grown-ups.

Now if that isn't enough evidence to convince you that the editorial writer for the New York *Sun* or one of his cronies wrote that letter, consider the next sentence:

"Papa says 'If you see it in the *Sun* it's so.'"

You think there were guys kicking around in those days who believed everything they read in the papers? The *New York* papers?

And why didn't Papa just tell Virginia there was a Santa Claus? Did he have some doubt?

No, it is so obvious with that self-promoting plug "If you see it in the *Sun* it's so" that the letter was not written by an eight-year-old but by some hard-bitten newspaper reporter bent on making a name for himself.

Instead he seems to have made a name for Virginia.

"In this great universe of ours man is a mere insect, an ant, in his intellect, as compared with the boundless world about him, as measured by the intelligence capable of grasping the whole truth and knowledge."

Now that could have been written by an eight-year-old. What do you think, Abby, was there a Virginia?

Expectantly,
Santa Claus

Dear Dad,

Thanks for your letter. I'm really busy at school—four finals and two papers this week—so I don't have a lot of time to write. It sounds a little like you popped your cork. Of course there's a Virginia. You're married to her, and she's my mom.

Hope this finds you in better spirits, and Merry Christmas.

Love,
Abby

Father Gardner's Secret Candy Recipe

So many of my friends who have experienced my culinary magic have asked me why I wasn't represented in the special "Taste of Summer" recipe supplement to the Peninsula *News*.

The answer is, of course, I wasn't asked.

It should be obvious by now there is a concerted effort at this paper to keep me in my place. And though certain editors have no objection to wolfing down the products of my fabulous recipes, they seem peculiarly guarded about sharing my talents with others less fortunate than they.

My culinary career is a long and honored one.

I was one of the first to discover the underrated health-giving properties of fat, which I wrote about in my quasi-bestseller, *Thin is In, But Fat is Where it's At*.

Since its publication I have been admiringly called

"California Fats."

I sent Executive Editor Reid Bundy an autographed copy of the book, but it was not reviewed in this paper though I sent a favorable review right along with the book.

Sugar is also an underrated foodstuff, and I rectify years of its neglect in many of my famous recipes.

Rest assured my forthcoming book on the subject, *Sugar is Sweet, But You Ain't Seen Nut Thin Yet*, will be sent to Mr. Bundy, autographed, along with a glowing review. And you can almost positively rest assured he will ignore it.

And so I am taking just a tad of this space to share with you the recipe for my most popular candy, which I market under my own label:

FATHER GARDNER'S
CANDIES
No preservatives have
been added
except to Father
Gardner who was
pickled anyway.

Each box comes packed with an inspirational message, as well as the following money-back guarantee:

"This product is manufactured to the highest quality standards. In the unlikely event that this product is not fresh or in good condition, return entire package top for replacement. Print your name and address and tell us why you returned it, you cheap chiseler."

Father Gardner's Caramels

1 lb. sugar cane

1 lb. sugar, powdered

1 lb. sugar, beet

16 oz. corn syrup

16 oz. honey

1 lb. brown sugar

1 lb. tan sugar

1 lb. yellow-D sugar

1 teaspoon cream

INSTRUCTIONS: Cream the sugar. If you don't have the cream handy, you may substitute half-and-half (low-fat milk will bollix the texture). If you have no dairy products available to cream the sugar, you may cream it with a wooden baseball bat (plastic will compromise the integrity of the candy).

Simply pile the sugar in a convenient place. Remember, if you use a garbage pail for this step, it should be clean. The candy will taste much better if it is.

After the sugar is piled, carefully pour the corn syrup and honey on the pile. You should note here that faulty or careless technique in this step will cause some of the honey to drip onto the floor and make a sticky mess. You can guard against this by using older honey that has already solidified.

The corn syrup presents another sticky problem. Some cooks avoid this pitfall by eliminating the corn syrup and doubling the sugar. I would caution against that. Twelve pounds seems just a smidgeon too much sugar.

Once you have successfully piled the sugar on a table or in a *clean* garbage pail, you cream it with the baseball bat until it is smooth.

Then pour it into a copper kettle and light the fire.

Cook on low heat or until the cook turns a pale shade of blue. The hue is vital. If you cook to the royal blue stage, you can be sure the candy will be too hard to chew. If you are lighter than baby blue, you will be eating soup.

Cooks with yellow jaundice should compensate by cooking the mixture until they turn a pale shade of mint green. Not forest green, mind you.

If the mixture burns—you've cooked it too long. It would behoove you to start afresh.

When you have completed the process and both the candy and you have a shiny finish, salt and pepper to taste.

Serves one.

Enjoy.

One final word. If you suffer from, or have a tendency to, diabetes, this recipe might not be for you.

Bach In Muzak
Attack On Slurper

> *They tried police patrols, curfews on arcade games and bright lights.*
> *Now officials at South-land Corp. are hoping that ...youths who hear the violin strains of a Brandenburg concerto at their local 7-Eleven store will take their Slurpees and run.*
>
> —"Muzak Attack"
> by Psyche Pascual
> Los Angeles *Times*

I park the big wheel in two spaces. So some friggin' broad in a friggin' Mercedes don't nick the friggin' daylights outta my vehicle.

I am comin' to check the chick action down by the 18 store. There's this one bimbo I been eyin' a couple nights now—

The action's cool at the 18. Plenty asphalt. Good sounds eminatin' the shopkeeper's stereo, plenty a slick broads poured into them flesh-huggers, an' it's altogether a cool ambiance, if you dig.

I alight my vehicle and, what's this? My eardrums is assaulted with these friggin' sounds YOU WOULD NOT BELIEVE! I mean, it's like you wanna puke.

I am so positively ticked off I make a header straight for the shopkeeper. "Man," I say, "what *is* this noise you got comin' outta here in substitution for the *gen-U-eyene* article?"

"Bach," he says, and he's wearin' one of them pukey self-satisfied grins on his kisser. I mean, you just wouldn't believe it.

"Bach?" I says. "What's Bach?"

"Oh, probably the greatest composer who ever lived," he says, and he is still grinnin' like a nerd.

"But what's that thing that sounds like a dying calf?"

"Violins."

When he tells me what a violins is I am put straight off my feed. It's like a electric guitar without electricity, an' 'stead of grabbin' the strings like a man an' makin' some *real* sound, they pull somethin' made of HORSE HAIR!! over it. It's just about the most awful sound you ever heard. It was so unhip I almost neglected to patronize the establishment with my regular purchase of a Slurpee.

Slurpin' my Slurpee out on the asphalt, I get cognizant of my surroundings, most especially one cool chick by the name of Psyche. I mean, that's what she says her name is, but I can't hardly believe it because who would moniker a kid Psyche unless it's some kind of a headcase? I saunter, supercool, over to make a converse with her an' my heart is kicking into high gear.

"Welcome to the Eighteen," I says, an' she look at me peculiar with them hazel green marbles beaming right in on me through them flaxen tresses that is her hair.

She is reacting by turning up that excruciatingly adorable buttonish nose. "What's 18?" she asks with that honey-coated gurgle that bespeaks volumes of erudition—

"Shortcut," I shrug my scapular. "Seven an' eleven is eighteen. Saves three syllables." I pronounce it sil *ah* bells, just to be engaging to the chick.

"Your math is admirable," she says. "But if you *subtracted* the seven from the eleven, you would get four. Four is a word of one syllable. Eighteen is two syllables. If you really want to save syllables, why don't you call it Four?"

I am admitting on the spot her brilliance dumbfounds me. I am also ruminating that in them old-fashioned days, when this bozo Bach is writing them awful sounds for the electric-less guitars with horsehair gizmos, the chicks is not so erudite. Not so uppity as they is these days. I'll just betcha no chick of this old Bach would tell you to subtract after you've done a pretty cool addition of a seven and a eleven.

"Where you gonna be tomorra?" I venture.

Psyche looks at me kinda weird.

"I mean, if the shopkeeper here at the Eightee…ah, *Four* keeps pumping this bilge out onta the asphalt, it ain't a gonna be fit for man or beast to abide on these premises, dig? I mean, it's like they spraying customer repellent around the place."

"Hey," she says, "I kinda like it. I mean, it's very soothing. You know, you don't get all jangled up inside when it plays."

"Oh man," I says, "you're weird."

And that's the trouble with a lot of them chicks today. They's so weird you can't even talk to them—Psyche? I should have known—I'm gonna hunt me up a chick named Eliza or something. Dig?

More Stress In Women

"Hey, Ginny," I called to my wife of many winters, "look here in the Peninsula *News*. It's what I've been saying for years."

"Hm?"

"It's a scientific study that proves women feel more stress than men."

"Oh—"

"I mean, do you realize this is vindication of all my opinions? Wow—I'm going to write a column on it. I've got to do it right now—how about a quote—or your reaction?"

She was reading a book—the only one that wasn't on the floor or strewn across tables and chairs.

"Our trip is coming up and I've got to get another one to the *News* because we won't be here. So what do you think? I mean you as a woman. Do you feel more stress than a man?"

She looked up with those squinty eyes that let you know what she thought of your question. "How would I know how much stress a man feels?"

"Well, take us, for example. I'm a man and you're a

woman—"

"I swear, you get more insight every day."

"I'll ignore that, but just because I'm a man and I hardly ever feel any stress at all. None to speak of. But you have some idea just from observing me. I mean, it should be obvious that you as a woman experience more than I do."

"You're the man in this riddle?"

"Heh, heh, that's real funny," I said, calmly. "I mean, look here in this paper," I waved the Peninsula *News* at her, not angrily as she later said, but merely to get her attention.

"It's under the heading 'Health Watch' and the sub-head says: 'Women feel more stress than men.' Stress on their time, for example—63 percent of the women feel it—only 51 percent of the men. Now tell the truth. Don't you feel the pressure of time from time to time?"

She didn't look up from her book, but she couldn't fool me playing blasé.

"Good gracious," I said, looking at my watch, "I've only got ten minutes to knock this thing out or I'll never make our trip. I haven't even started packing yet."

"I'm finished packing," she said, cool as a frozen cucumber, and turned a page without wetting her thumb.

"You know, I really would appreciate a little attention from you on this stress thing," I said. "I've got no time left and I've got to get something to the paper. Can't you at least give me some reaction?"

She looked up. "You don't have to shout."

"I'm not shouting," I shouted. "I'm just trying to get your attention."

"What for?"

"Stress," I stressed. "I need the woman's view if I'm going to finish this article before our trip."

"Oh," she waved her hand at me, the ultimate insouciant dismissal.

"Make it up—you always do."

"Now wait just a minute," I put my foot down. For it was one thing to keep the peace at home, and quite another to let your spouse walk all over you.

"Can't you be rational about this for a minute?" I asked her. She had gone back to her book. It was her way of overcoming the tremendous stress women feel. "Finances. According to Mass. Mutual, the women have the men out-stressed 62 to 52 percent."

"Oh well," she said in that subtle smarty-pants voice, "I don't know about that."

"Oh?" It was my turn to turn cryptic.

"This might be a good time to show you the Visa bill for the month." She was using it for a bookmark and, well, what if I did get a little angry—the charges were astronomical.

"Family problems, women stress out 7 percent more than men."

Ginny wasn't looking up from her book anymore. Not until I grabbed it out of her hand. Then she looked. She was doing a great job of hiding the horrible stress she was feeling. Of course, I felt nothing. Zero stress.

"What about family problems?" I pressed. "Surely you will admit women are more stressed out over family problems than men."

She just looked at me with those steady, stress-filled eyes.

"Go on—deny it then."

"The only family problem we ever had," she announced with a super cool delivery as though her vocal cords were mink and her breath was crème fraîche, "is you."

"Oh yeah," I riposted. I was, after all, the man of the house.

"You understand," I announced, standing over where she understood, "that women are more stressful in every category, bar none. Retirement preparation, women 9 percent more stress. Health, women 5 percent. Speaking of health, what in the world did you give me for dinner?"

"Why?"

"I have this most excruciating heartburn."

Odds And Ends

Under the headline "Combine and Conquer," the *Los Angeles Times Magazine* ran an article by Julie Logan about multifaceted enterprises she calls "binary businesses."

There is a picture of a pet and bike shop. The caption reads, "Fish Gotta Schwinn." A religious objects store is joined with a live birds and fowl shop. That picture is titled "Saints Necessarily Grow."

The most intriguing of the lot, I think, is the evening-dress store that combines with a pizza parlor. There is a picture of a young woman dressed to the teeth in a silky blue number, scalloping down the front and off the shoulders, and the same teeth are munching on a pepperoni pizza.

Behind them is a sign with a quaint spelling:

EVENING-DRESESS

The mutations are endless. I used to work in a place out in Venice where we sold evening dresses and pizza. While the women waited for their pizzas to be ready, they tried on the dresses.

Then when their pizza number was called they got so excited, often as not they forgot to change clothes, and many of our evening dresses had tomato sauce down the fronts and all the clothes began to smell like mozzarella cheese.

So many dresses had to be sent to the cleaners, we decided to open a cleaners with the pizza parlor and evening-dress salon. There was enough steam from the busy pressing iron to run the pizza ovens.

Then someone had the bright idea to take on some fish to eat the scraps of pizza crust that were piling up all over the changing rooms—then we stocked some cats to take care of the overfed fish. The thing just grew like Topsy. We went right through the chain down to rattlesnakes and mongooses, but nothing we did ever got the smell of mozzarella cheese out of those evening gowns.

Strangely enough, the women didn't seem to mind the smell. In a kooky way they seemed to like it. That's when we decided to experiment with other smells.

We put the smell of hamburgers on a plunging purple jersey with a diamanté kick pleat, and fish and chips on a single-shoulder sequined job, and buttered popcorn on a cute chiffon. One of our biggest sellers was a strapless fried chicken.

A lot of clothiers have begged us for the recipe on that one, but I'm sorry, it must remain a trade secret.

The intriguing names given these commercial combos remind me of two friends of mine who combined their offices to save on the rent.

One was a psychiatrist, the other a plastic surgeon who made a specialty of the reconstruction of gluteus muscles.

Their biggest argument came over what to call the enterprise.

The psychiatrist opted for "Nuts and Butts." The plastic surgeon wanted "Queers and Rears."

They compromised, after many recriminations, on "Odds and Ends."

The psychiatrist, always a squeamish person at best, felt he got the short end of the arrangement and decided to break away from the gorgeous-gluteus guru.

On a temporary basis, the beleaguered plastic surgeon moved into the back room of a branch library where he hung the sign "Shush and Tush."

His next office was a liquor store where the sign was "Rum and Bum."

But he was a restless man who found it cheaper to move than pay the rent.

He was offered space in a gas station. Although the rent was the most reasonable so far, he finally had to reject it because he couldn't think of a descriptive rhyme for gasoline.

Nothing seemed to satisfy the surgeon until he found an open space in a bakery. It was the sign he dreamed of from the beginning of his career.

It read simply:

"Buns and Buns."

Meanwhile, the deserting psychiatrist opened up shop with a female psychiatrist on Silver Spur underneath the Peninsula *News* before it was repainted.

On entering their office through the door marked "Entrance," you came upon a small waiting room with no receptionist. There were just two doors.

One said, "Men"—the other, "Women."

I went through the men's door and was in another room with two doors. One said, "Psychoanalysis," the other, "Psychotherapy."

I chose the first, and, on going through it, was confronted with two other doors. One said, "Male doctor," the other, "Female doctor."

I chose the female, and when I went through that door, two more appeared. One said, "Your income over $25,000"—the other said, "Your income under $25,000."

I went though the under $25,000 door and found myself back on the street.

Batman In Stockton

You might consider Stockton, California, a long shot for taking a flyer celebrity hunting, perhaps not worth the trip, but then you aren't a world-class celebrity spotter like I am. Coupled with my sixth sense about the thing, I had the excuse of attending my final daughter's graduation from the University of the Pacific. It was the culmination of my contributions to the cause of higher education.

At the graduation exercises there were no celebrities on the roster. The first honorary doctorate went to a 91-year-old drama professor emeritus. The second two to fellas who had forked over a million plus. But no politicians, no movie stars. It was refreshing.

That evening, we opted to imbibe some ice cream. There were two options: Baskin-Robbins and Häagen-Dazs. I was driving. This is where the incomparable sixth sense comes in. I drove to Häagen-Dazs.

There are five of us and we are the only patrons in the joint. Until in walks this dude in a straw cowboy hat and cowboy boots, sunglasses (it is dark) and the standard faded blue jeans and red jacket.

He clumps up to the counter and orders while we are slurping our goodies. Ginny, which is the name of my current wife, is watching the dude primp in the mirror. She claims, for a minimum of thirty seconds. When, lo and behold, he turns around and my daughter Esmeralda (not really, you know, her name) says, "That's Michael Keaton."

Now this is why I say it isn't important that the celebrity spotter knows who he is spotting, as long as *someone* does. I am afraid I had never heard of him. I was educated in short order that he was Batman in the film of the same name. I didn't see *Batman* because David Knoles, former managing editor of this journal, had bought all the tickets.

My other daughter in attendance, the graduate in this scenario, Jambalaya (which name is also, natch, fictitious), and her gentleman caller say, "No way," because said celebrity has turned his back once again. But shazam! He gives us the full face again and they say in unison, "You are absolutely right."

What does Batman look like in real life? Well actually, he looks something like a bat. Only smaller. It is not unusual for performers to take on the characteristics of roles they play.

We speculate on what Batman is doing in Stockton, alone, inconclusively. But that's not important. What *is* important is I have just bagged another movie star.

The next day we fly out of there, and who do you suppose is on our plane? And the same who-do-you-suppose checked in his rental car right after me. And who do you suppose neglected to record his mileage for the boys at the desk and had to hightail it back to the lot? Not I. When the instructions say, "Record your mileage," I record my mileage.

The waiting room at the Stockton airport is in two sections. We all sat on the right, facing the other section, when Batman comes slogging in and sits in profile in the empty section, like he is on stage and we are the audience.

He takes off his cowboy hat and fiddles with the brim, checking it for just the proper rakish dip in the front.

It is a plane configured like a Greyhound bus, and Batman sashays to the back of the bus, where he spreads out across the rear seat. We are just in front of him.

I read in the airline magazine an article about stars who changed their names. Michael Keaton's real name, it seems, is Michael Douglas.

Then, in the *New Yorker* I see a short movie review of Mr. Keaton née Douglas' last film, *One Good Cop*. The review begins, "One big flop." No matter. They can't dampen our enthusiasm that easily.

My daughter Esmeralda and I exit the plane together, right after Batman. She thinks it is really something, but is acting blasé.

When we reach the terminal building, we notice again one side is full of people, the other side empty. Batman has slithered over to the empty side and has turned to face us as we march down the aisle. Why he hasn't left the terminal we don't know.

Then as we approach, Batman starts toward us and cuts in front of our path, close enough to touch him (the acid test for being in the presence of a celeb).

Then I go to the phone, Esmeralda departs and Batman goes back, retracing his steps to another phone.

How do you explain it? He must have heard that I was a celebrity in my own right, having authored *The Paper Dynasty*.

Those who suggest he might have been trying to get a closer look at my daughter Esmeralda are quite simply mistaken.

Mugs Meaning...

"Hey, Ginny," I call out as I so often do to my co-conspirator in hearth and home.

"What!?" she yells out as she so often does when she is across the house and plugged into a cassette player funneling into her sensory acceptors some fruitcake reading a novel of questionable intellectual achievement.

"Could you come here a minute?" I ask with my customary consummate consideration.

I can hear the machine click off and the audible sigh that so often accompanies that procedure when she is called upon to fraternize with the ranks of ordinary mortals who opt to grapple with the weighty issues of life and who accordingly shun escapist entertainment.

As I hear the reluctant footsteps approaching, I am quick to cover two objects on my desk. If she saw them, the game would be up and she would return to her stage personality lisping the woman's parts alternatively with the strained bass of the ingenue's lover. The setting is some exotic location and the woman's dress is falling off, the man is shirtless and one of them is on horseback. Somewhere there is a cactus.

"Ginny," I must grab her attention and hold it. "If you had to pick a couple adjectives to describe me, what would they be?" Her face is as blank as a freshly-painted barn door. It is as if she is pondering the answer most calculated to please, the most honest, perhaps. She is coping with the many flattering descriptive adjectives that crowd into her head.

"Are you serious?" she asks at last.

"Nevermore," I respond with a catchy phrase.

"For this you called me from the kitchen?"

"Just a couple adjectives—what springs to mind?"

"Oh, I don't know. Weird, maybe. Goofy. Bizarre. How many do you want?"

"That's very funny, but I was thinking along more serious lines."

"Serious," she says. "That is definitely not a word we could use to describe you. Silly, maybe. I wouldn't say stupid—off the wall, perhaps…"

"Okay, okay," I hasten to interject because she is, as you can see, way off base. "Let me throw out a few myself and see what you think applies. Gifted…"

She snorts, an unbecoming sound in a distaff.

I continue, "Talented, especially gifted, a flair for art and crafts, perfection, mastery—any of those connect with you?"

"Me," she says. "Sure, a flair for art and crafts—what were the others?—but I thought we were talking about you."

"We were," I say wearily. I am beginning to wish I hadn't detached her from her lisping thespian.

Without further ado (she would never get the drift, I am convinced), I throw off the cover to produce a mug which I couldn't resist purchasing. Inscribed on the side was the following:

TED
MEANING: GIFTED

It must give you a mental lift to be so talented.
With such special gifts.
When it comes to craft or art, you have a flair;
In everything you do you take pride and care.
Whatever your interests or talents may be,
You shall reach both perfection and mastery.

I hand her the mug and she reads it, frowning skeptically at first, then laughing out loud as she comes toward the end. When she is finished, she runs her fingers across the letters as if to see if the paint is still wet.

"Surely you don't take this seriously?" she inquires.

I have met and conquered skepticism before. "I just thought it fit pretty well, that's all."

"Fit what? You?" She has a healthy release of laughter. "Why not start reading horoscopes? They deal in pleasing hyperbole. This is as accurate as a Chinese fortune cookie."

"Oh, I don't know about that," I say, and I hand her,

without any flourish to speak of, another mug. I bought this at the same time. They were side by side on the shelf. Such touching serendipity I couldn't resist.

She reads:

VIRGINIA
MEANING: GENUINE

You never hold back, but express what you feel.
You are always yourself, someone truthful and real.
Instead of playing games and acting out parts,
You share the true feelings that come from your
heart.
Because you're so genuine, thoughtful and true,
Others are happy to know the real you.

There is not a laugh, not a snicker, nary a snort.
"Well?" I ask. "Horoscope? Fortune cookie?"
"Funny," she says.
"What's funny?"
"How they could get me so right, and you so wrong."

Perfect For Supreme Court

While it was nip and tuck for a certain Supreme Court nominee, I got a phone call. It was from Eldon Sassoon (rhymes with bassoon) Frasconi, my old fraternity buddy who had wormed his way though the councils of government until he found himself talent scouting for President Bush.

We called him Sassy Frass, which he didn't care for, but tolerated because he called us much worse.

"I'm in a bind," he said.

"How's that, Sassy?" I asked.

"Supreme Court. We may need a new candidate and I've canvassed every possibility. No one wants it."

"Oh?"

"Lot of guys figure with the confirmation hearings getting longer and longer they wouldn't live to take their seats on the court."

"Get someone younger."

"We tried that. They accused him of talking smutty to a fem. So we were looking for somebody the fires of youth had banked a little, you know what I mean?"

"Uh huh."

"That's where we ran into trouble. What with all these ax grinders who threatened to 'Bork' Thomas, our judges are getting gun-shy. President says, 'Okay, if no one wants it, we'll go with eight judges. Save some bucks.' Me, I don't want to give up so easily. I said, 'George, let me call my pal Ted out on the Coast. He comes from a family of lawyers and judges, he may be the key to this thing.' 'Key?' George asks kind of puzzled. 'Trust me,' I say. And hey, I wouldn't be where I am today if I didn't have some well-placed trust, you know what I mean?"

"Uh huh," I said. "But how do you figure I'm the key?"

"Key," he said, "you're *perfect* for the Supreme Court."

"Ho, ho, a good one, Sassy. Still hitting the sauce, I see."

"I'm sober, and I'm serious."

"Come off it, I'm not even a lawyer."

"Perfect!" he cried. "There's too damn many lawyers on the Supreme Court now. If I'm not mistaken, they're *all* lawyers. That's a large part of the problem right there."

"Oh, Sassy, you'll never change."

"So I gotta screen you a little, you know. Get the FBI in on it—nothing to be afraid of, but I got to ask you one thing—ever talk kind of, you know, 'suggestive' to any women?"

"Sass, I'm not a lawyer—"

"So? That's minor. These are the important things, like talking sexy. I told George you worked with a lot of women in your time and you were too wimpy for any overtly aggressive behavior."

"Now just a minute, Sass."

"Well, am I wrong?"

"Wimp isn't a very nice word."

"Don't sweat it. It didn't hurt George. I told him if there was any sexy talk, it probably came from the women—and you wouldn't know what the words meant."

"What's this got to do with the Supreme Court?"

"Everything! We're looking for a nonentity. A guy on whom, when they go through his garage, they won't find anything. You know they dug through the video store records on Bork—found he only took out G & PG movies. Held it against him. How could a narrow guy like that sit on the Supreme Court? He wouldn't know pornography if he fell on it."

"Didn't he rent those videos for his kids?"

"Neither here nor there. His kids wouldn't know pornography if they fell on it. Clarence Thomas, who knows, maybe watched a couple pornos. So they couldn't use the same ploy. Bork wasn't sexy enough; maybe Thomas was *too* sexy."

"So how did they Bork him?"

"They didn't. They Pee-wee Hermaned him. In this world, you're either too sexy or not sexy enough for the Supreme Court. But listen, pal, we figure your confirmation will be a breeze."

"How's that?"

"You don't know anything. If they throw you *Roe v. Wade,* you can let your jaw drop—and let them try to prove you know anything about it. Besides, these things go in patterns, you know what I mean?"

"No."

"The Prez throws them a controversial, high-profile candidate. One they can sink their teeth into. Bork was such a man. Thomas is such a man. The hearings drag on and on. There is a plenitude of passion on both sides of the aisle."

"Plenitude of passion? Sassy Frass, come on."

"Hear me out. The Senators make fools of themselves. They see the tapes and are embarrassed. The Prez throws them a low profiler—Anthony Kennedy was such a man. Ted Gardner is such a man. Presto! Chango! Romance in the hearing room. The guy answers no questions. The Senators are wrung out—and still embarrassed about the last snafu, and they vote him in unanimously. Ted, my boy, you can't lose. You see what I mean?"

"I see what you mean."

Patsy Claus Tells All On Santa

The regular guy who fills this space is celebrating the holidays in such a fashion that makes it next to impossible for him to compose intelligible prose, let alone compose himself.

We are fortunate in having a guest columnist who is usually in the background and has heretofore had very little opportunity to tell her side of the story.

The Famous Fabulous Fatso Fable

How would you like to be married to a man who lies around the house all year, then, in one burst of hyperkinetic activity, goes tearing around the world in one night, in and out of chimneys stuffing optimistic-sized socks?

I don't want to seem like a whiner or a complainer or anything, but if you think it's easy, I'd like to see you try it. Try running a household with an ageless adolescent man underfoot 364 days a year—frozen in time—and not frozen in the *best* time, I can tell you. And sometimes I fear, in spite of all hype to the contrary, that he isn't as agile as he once was, and negotiating all those chimneys gives him a real pain in the sacroiliac, as well as in other anatomical locales. And who gets the complaints, I ask you? You-know-who gets the complaints.

And now with this *glasnost* business, I am worrying that *more* countries will be pipe-dreaming my man down *their* chimneys, and even though the long night so close to the winter solstice gives Tubby more working hours, adding

Russia and Eastern Europe could cause big problems. Sometimes it's easier having the world at loggerheads.

And that brings up another problem. In eleven years we are adding a billion people to our world roster. Now all those billion are newborns, not to mention the other newborns that replace those who keel over. That's a lot of customers for Fatty. A lot of believers. Sure, they're not all believers, but you factor that into *your* business and see what comes out.

And don't forget we run a *charity* operation here. Santy works gratis. I mean, how long can you live on Christmas Eve junk food? Think of it. Toys underfoot constantly. The endless hammering and sawing all year long. I don't have a moment's peace.

And can you imagine my prima donna in the once-a-year command performance? Everyone fawning all over him, saying what a great guy he is and all. *You* try to put up with that for the rest of the year. I mean, it's about six months afterglow—and trying to diet off those superfluous calories—and six months anticipation to the big show. I might as well be married to a doctor.

I don't want you to think I'm one of those cranky libbers or anything, but put yourself in my position. He's underfoot all year long. You know what the Duchess of Windsor said when she dethroned her king? She married him for better or for worse, but not for lunch.

Lunch? I got him breakfast, lunch, dinner and all the hours in-between. And he's got this weight problem and I can't do a thing about it. Lord knows I tried.

And did you ever try to wash the soot of a million-odd chimneys out of your man's clothes? Fun! Not to mention the half million pieces of mail—gimme this, gimme that—all in one month!

And I'll bet you think he's just a barrel of fun with that ho-ho stuff all the time. Ha! That's his public face. After all that ho-hoing, he's a real downer at home—hoed out, to the max, you might say.

And if there is anything in this everloving world that

has been romanticized more than Santa Claus, it's reindeer.

I'll admit they look like ideal animals, sleek, shining, steadfast studs on those watercolors that illustrate that "'Twas the Night Before Christmas" sentimental rhyme. But let me tell you the truth about reindeer. They stink! There just is no prettier way to put it. And guess who is assigned the joy of cleaning their stalls?

You guessed it. You'd think Fatso would lend a helping hand once in a while, but he only lies in his favorite chair and says riding behind them once a year is more than should be expected of any man.

He is, as you may have gathered by this time, something of a sexist pig. I suppose if I were in his position, I'd be a sexist pig too where reindeer are concerned.

And I guess if you want to be charitable about it, it's no bed of roses for the reindeer either, pulling that tub of lard around the world at that breakneck pace, then lying around the rest of the year with nothing to do but munch grass and get as fat as he is.

Well I've finally had my say. Thanks for listening. So if your husband isn't always what you think he should be, just think of *my* situation. Maybe it will make you feel better.

Patsy Claus
(The *real* patsy)

Foolproof College Essay

College application deadlines are upon us. My daughter Jambalaya (not her real name) is hard at it, filling in the blanks and striving for a scintillating slant for her essays.

The colleges are getting so tricky, it is almost impossible to adapt the essay for one school to another.

Jambalaya and I fall into a discussion about the possibility of an essay being read, or, more germanely, the possibility that it would have any effect on the decision to accept or reject an applicant.

I say she ought to try writing something zany—off the wall. Get them to fall on the floor laughing. They might, as a result, sit up and take notice.

Jambalaya suggests that I am messing with her future in an inappropriate, not to say dangerous, way.

"It's *my* future," she insists, rejecting my idea.

I drop the subject. It is her future.

Then I get an Education Supplement with the Sunday New York *Times*.

The front page flags the article "The Hardest Thing You'll Ever Have To Write."

"Oh God, the essay," the article begins. There follows the lament of Peter Muth, Dean of Admissions, University of Virginia, who says that he can recite the essays in his sleep, so similar are they.

"First Paragraph: The band taught me leadership. Second paragraph: The band helped me organize my time. Then two more paragraphs, then the last paragraph: To summarize, the band…"

I call for Jambalaya. "Look at this," I say—"they are urging applicants to take chances."

She reads the article and drops it with an exaggerated air of insouciance.

"It's *my* future," she emphasizes.

I am about to give up, when an attractive packet of admission forms arrives from a school of more than passing interest to Jambalaya. In it is a form for a parent to complete.

I see my opportunity. I will get the admissions office to sit up and take notice. I sit down and fill out the form in my flourishing psychotic handwriting, using different colored ink for each question.

1. *What is your attitude toward the applicant's desire to attend college?*

Lukewarm—we would save an awful lot of money if she just took a job as a waitress.

2. *Has the applicant chosen a career objective? What is it and what is your attitude toward this choice?*

(a) Yes.

(b) See answer to #1 above.

3. *What are the applicant's special aptitudes or talents?*
I wish I knew. Perhaps her dramatic talent should be noted here. She was cast in numerous important dramatic roles in her high school drama class, culminating in her triumph as the offstage chicken in *Tender is the Thigh—and Second Joint*. Her mother and I were terribly proud.

4. *What are the applicant's special interests? How is his/her leisure time spent?*
(a) Your guess is as good as mine. If I had to guess, I would say her special interests are: (1) young men (2) boys (3) not-as-young men; in no particular order.
(b) Squandered on society. She has never even tried to write a symphony.

5. *Has the applicant changed schools for reasons other than change of residence? If so, give reasons.*
None, other than the unfair suspension for drug abuse. (She was framed. She is too fond of drugs to abuse them. She even works in a drugstore.) And the picky Principal who threw her out for excessive truancy. Oh, there was the time she flunked all her courses, but I am explaining that in a separate letter.

6. *Is there any information which you wish to share which would assist the residence hall staff or faculty advisor?*
No. It is definitely to her advantage if we say as little as possible.

Cleverly I offer to mail Jambalaya's completed application, surreptitiously slipping in the Parent Assessment Form.

A week later, Jambalaya receives in the mail a postcard with check marks beside the forms they received. The Parent Assessment Form is not checked.

They can't ignore my work like that and get away with it.

I send them a copy of the original, registered mail, return receipt requested. *I will* make my point to Jambalaya.

A few days later I get a postcard from the dean vindicating my position.

It says simply:

"Can you pay?"

Making An Impression

My father doesn't remember me. I still remember him, but his memory has slipped a rung or two more than mine.

While I was driving him to the Emmaus, Pennsylvania, Rotary Club, to which he has belonged for fifty-seven years (thirty-five or so with perfect attendance), he asked me my name.

It was done with charm and grace. He was always a gracious host. "This is an embarrassing question," he said, "but what's your name?" I was neither surprised nor offended.

"My name is the same as yours," I said.

"Is that right?" he seemed pleasantly surprised. "You mean like a junior?"

"Exactly like that," I said.

He let that sink in for a moment. "I just wanted to know," he said, "in case I have to introduce you."

"Sure, you can just tell them my name is the same as yours."

"How about that?" he said smiling. "Theodore Gardner."

"Theodore Roosevelt Gardner."

"I'll be darn."

We walked through a dark barroom to get to the stairs that lead to the Rotary meeting room. There we met the president of the club—to whom I introduced myself.

I verified with the prez that I could hawk my book *The Paper Dynasty* to the assembled membership for a few minutes. He said indeed I could.

It was the purpose of my trip to the Rotary Club, this crassly commercial grasp for book sales. Though as a corollary benefit I could spend this time alone with my father who used to recognize me.

There were perhaps five or six tables of men (with one woman) and the president sat at our table. My father introduced me. "He has the same name as mine," he said several times. He did not provide the names of any of the people I met, but when you are the dean of the club, they should remember *your* name, not necessarily vice versa.

The president graciously called me to the rostrum to give my pitch.

I opened with a few remarks about how my grandfather (my mother's father) founded the club and how my father joined the year I was born, I suppose to get out of the house. I told them I was a Rotary Club Boy of the Month in high school, but that was not that special because in those days there were more months than there were boys.

I asked them how many read. Two hands went up. I asked how many knew *how* to read. Two different hands went up. I have discovered this is par for the course at Rotary Clubs. There are usually two guys who are willing to admit they read.

I told them what Mark Twain said: "The man who can read and doesn't, is no better off than one who can't read."

And Groucho Marx, an inveterate reader, said: "Outside of a dog, a book is a man's best friend. Inside of a dog it's too dark to read."

I told them Barbara Bush was barnstorming the country to promote literacy and I was barnstorming the country to promote reading—especially of my book *The Paper Dynasty*. I told them where they could buy it, where I was having book signings, and how it made a fantastic Christmas gift.

I said it was fitting for Mrs. Bush and me to have the same cause since I had so much in common with her husband.

He is President of the United States, I was president of my Emmaus High School class.

He and I belonged to the same club in college: The

Book-of-the-Month Club.

He went to Yale, and I applied to Yale. Three times.

The president was standing over me. My time was up. I finished by saying that the most intelligent people read books, so they should all go out and buy copies of *The Paper Dynasty* for their wives.

The president said I was too modest and gave *The Paper Dynasty* another rousing plug.

After the meeting, the two Theodores retraced our drive the four blocks to the house where my father and mother have lived for fifty-four years. A week later, my mother called to read from the Rotary Bulletin which chronicled my appearance thusly:

"Jack Gardner was here from California to tell us about the origins of our club."

How Big Is Your Hotel?

Is Something Brewing Between Hon, Monaghan?
By Anne La Jeunesse

There have been conversations between the parties about possible arrangements between the two parties, but there are no deals and no arrangements with the parties…

Representatives of both developers refuse to reveal what conversations between Hon and Monaghan have been about.

—Peninsula *News*

JM. Hon baby, how's it going?

BH. Not bad, Jimmy, how about yourself?

JM. Can't complain, comin' down the homestretch on the luxury hotel. You?

BH. Homestretch, yeah. The Ritz, Jimmy, *real* luxury.

JM. I was just wondering if you'd done any studies on your thing?

BH. Studies? You mean feasibility and junk like that?

JM. Well, yeah—I mean, it just occurred to some of my staff that we may be sticking up a real potload of hotel rooms here and, well, to put it bluntly, the City is looking for a nice piece of change from us, bed tax-wise. And not to put too fine an edge on it or anything, you know, you do gotta have someone in the beds to spawn any bed tax.

BH. Yeah, I hear you talkin'. But you know other than our parcels, there is zilch oceanfront hotel land left in California.

JM. Think there's a reason for that, Hon? I mean, we got a coastline of what, seven, eight hundred miles? And we two lucky guys get hotel sites within a mile of each other. I mean, that's almost back to back.

BH. Yeah, I hear ya talkin'. It's almost too good to be true.

JM. You really are an amenable guy, Hon. You know that picture of you and your family you sent around the Hill, that was real nice, Hon. You must be one swell family man.

BH. I do my best, Jimmy.

JM. Atta boy, what else can we do, eh, Hon? My mother used to say, 'Do your best, your very best, and do it every day.'

BH. How can you argue with that?

JM. Can't.

BH. So what's this call all about, Jimmy?

JM. Well, yeah—you remember Marineland?

BH. Sounds familiar.

JM. It was an aquatic park of national repute. People came from all over the world to spend the day there to watch the fishies.

BH. Wow, that would have been the time to have a hotel.

JM. They *did* have. They had a little ten, twelve unit motel.

BH. Ten, twelve units. That's all?

JM. Yeah, and guess what?

BH. What?

JM. They closed it.

BH. Why on earth…?

JM. Not enough business.

BH. You're not serious.

JM. Yeah, and they had a fancy restaurant.

BH. Don't tell me…

JM. Yeah—same result. Kaput. So now I'm starting to wonder about my thousand rooms.

BH. And my five hundred…

JM. Yeah, and like so what's gonna be the attraction, the magnet to pull people in—the nude beach at Abalone Cove?

BH. Well, we're building golf courses.

JM. Golf courses? There's one on every corner now, haven't you noticed? They're taking the place of the gas stations.

BH. Hm—there must be something…We're going to have tennis courts—horseback riding—hiking trails—real luxury stuff.

JM. Sure, and I'm putting in a fish tank, but if Marineland in its heyday couldn't fill ten rooms, it gives you pause, Hon.

BH. Yeah. So what's your slant on the thing?

JM. The City has gotten so worked up about the thing, they are scheduling extra meetings to bicker about it. Every other week from December to May.

BH. It's a long, long time from May to December.

JM. And vice versa. They're kicking the South Coast Choral Society out of Hesse Park after seven years so they can yak more about hotels.

BH. Don't you get tired of music anyway?

JM. Yeah, you're telling me. Up to here with Mozart. They got it out of the schools, this was the next logical step.

BH. That's a point.

JM. And while the City is bickering about can we have a thousand beds or five hundred, maybe we'll have time to do a feasibility study on whether or not the site will really support a ten-room motel.

BH. Luxury, Jimmy. *Luxury* motel.

It's Not Worth The Money

My mother called me.

Prime time in the middle of the week from Pennsylvania. That is an occurrence reserved for catastrophe. My mother, you may remember, was the one who told a date of mine, seven years my senior, that I wasn't twenty-one. She is also the mother who sent me a subscription to *Modern Maturity* years before my time.

"Your newspaper sent me a bill."

"What for?"

"Twenty-one dollars."

"What was the twenty-one dollars for?"

"A six-month's subscription." I could tell by her voice this event had not made her happy.

"Don't pay it."

"I won't, don't worry."

"I'm giving you the Peninsula *News*. They can just deduct it from my pay. Of course they may not want to wait that long for payment."

"I mean," she went on as though the connection was inadequate, "it isn't worth it to me."

"I'm paying it."

"I don't find it that interesting."

"You don't like my articles?"

"Oh, I love your articles. I liked the last one especially."

"Which one was that?"

"Oh, I can't remember now. What were some of the most recent ones?" I mentioned a few, but none seemed to touch a nerve.

"The one about the dungarees," she said at last.

"Denim," I corrected, "blue denim."

"That's it. That was a real good one."

There was a silence, which over the long-distance wire is always painful.

"I suppose I could pay it," she said grudgingly.

"I told you I'd pay it. They shouldn't have sent the bill to you. I paid it before. There is a large body of opinion on the newspaper staff that holds I should be grateful to be paid in copies."

"Yes, but twenty-one dollars for six months is almost a dollar a week."

"I know."

"Will they pay that much?"

"I'll let you know. I also sent it to my mother-in-law and a daughter."

"Oh dear."

There was another painful silence. My father would be in the background asking if my mother was intending to underwrite the phone company single-handedly.

"You know, I do enjoy some of the things in the paper."

"Oh?" My curiosity was piqued.

"That Homeline column. I always read that. There are a lot of good tips in that."

"Yes." That was okay, I thought. She had spent many years as a domestic scientist and Homeline would be near and dear to her. I didn't mind at all that she didn't mention my little column first. She would mention it second.

"And I like the editorials. They're well-written."

"Um hum."

"And the letters to the editor. There is some lively stuff in that."

"You think so?"

"Oh yes," she said. "There really is a lot of good stuff. I don't know what all. There's the entertainment pages, they're good, and that writer who talks about the Polish King—Ann Somebody, and that dentist."

She was warming up so much, I knew any minute she would mention her own son.

"Now that I think about it, I'll send the twenty-one dollars. That's not a bad price for all that."

"Aren't you forgetting something?"

"Nooo…What am I forgetting?"

"My column—"

"Your what?"

"You didn't mention *my column*. For six months I send you the paper and all you talk about is Homeline and the editorials. *What about my column?!*"

"Oh?" I could tell I had come down too hard on her and remorse was setting in. I was, after all, flesh of her flesh, bone of her bone.

After another painful pause, she said:

"What was it about?"

She Didn't Look Hungry

"Hey, you!" a woman yelled across the main street of a posh California resort town. She was so loud I looked in her direction to see at whom she was yelling.

"You!" she insisted, and as I looked around, I discovered I was quite alone, thank you, and she must have been yelling at *moi*.

When I looked back at her, she was pointing at me and yelling, "You, come over here!" I saw she was a smallish woman who had managed to infuse a large command into her voice.

"Me?" I spoke across the traffic, medium light that evening. "Are you talking to me?"

"Yes you. Come over here."

I looked at her again, wondering if I knew her. I am frankly not accustomed to being yelled at, except by very close relatives, but she didn't look particularly like a relative. Or even a friend, for that matter.

"What do you want?" I insisted. I have my pride. Let it not be said I am a pushover for strangers. I don't just go running across the street because some assertiveness-trained female commands me.

I think she got the message, because she changed her tune in a hurry. "Wait there," she said, "I'm coming over."

And coming closer I got a closer look. (One of the

fringe benefits of being closer.) She was in her middle years and the best was not yet to come, it was long gone, if it indeed ever transpired at all. But she was neat and clean enough, with a pair of reasonably-fitting aquamarine polyester pants and a white rayon blouse, open at the neck.

"What do you want?" I asked bluntly when she faced me as though in challenge.

"Give me a quarter for a cup of coffee."

I gave her the once-over. She didn't look like a street person—too well dressed and groomed. She wasn't emaciated. She looked happily fed.

"You yelled at me to cross the street so I could give you a quarter?" I injected a dose of incredulity into my voice.

"Well," she said, not to be put down, "I came over here instead."

She had an air of engaging belligerence about her.

"You don't look hungry," I announced, lest she get the idea she could have the upper hand.

"I'm not hungry," she affirmed, "I want coffee."

*　　　*　　　*

Now, the purpose of this exercise is to test your perception. The story has many possible endings, but I will list only a fraction of them for you to guess what the actual upshot was.

The correct answer can be found at the bottom of this column (no peeking). Many tests of this sort put the answers upside down so they won't be so easy to see if you peek.

My executive editor rejected this suggestion. He said the cost of running the page through the presses a second time, upside down, would be prohibitive.

Remember to select the ending you think actually happened, not the one you prefer.

1. On closer questioning she spilled her story. She just walked out on a drunken, abusive husband, and though she had been battered, abused and abandoned, she didn't want sympathy, only a quarter for a cup of coffee—so I gave

it to her.

2. Feeling philanthropic, I took her to an automatic teller, withdrew my life's savings and gave it to her with my blessing. She gave me effusive thanks, opened a dress shop and lost her shirt (rayon).

8. I didn't give her a bloody farthing as it is unpatriotic to encourage begging. Let them find honest work. Not everybody should own a dress shop.

5. Flabbergasted at her chutzpa, I reach into my pocket for a quarter and she pulls a knife, starts slashing it back and forth under my nose and persuades me to give her my wallet, which I do without further ado. The wallet is full and she opens a first-class dress shop. She loses her shirt, but this time it is silk.

3. The wallet is empty. She sells it at a swap meet and with the proceeds she opens a dress shop and makes a fortune. When she makes her first million (after taxes), she gives me my twenty-five cents back, but not the wallet (which is long gone via swap meet). Her parting words are—"Here you are, you cheapskate."

I buy a postage stamp with the quarter, send a pyramid letter, and get back $7,051,097 in the first year.

I open a dress shop and put her out of business.

Answer: Editor's note: Try as we did, we simply couldn't read Gardner's handwriting. It could be a two, it could be a three, a five, even an eight. When we called for clarification, the phone at Teddi's dress shop had been disconnected.

The Truth About Michael Keaton

Dear Editor:

This letter is being written in the hope of clearing up some mistaken "facts" printed in Ted Gardner's column.

First, my name is not Esmeralda and he isn't using that and the other phony names for my sisters because he is trying to protect us from the glare of publicity, but simply because he has so much trouble remembering our names.

The idea that he is a world-class celebrity spotter is ludicrous. He wouldn't know a celebrity if he fell on one. It was *I* who spotted Michael Keaton first. Old Dad didn't even know *who* he was. Had never even *seen* him in a movie. And the line in his column that says: "…this is why I say it isn't important that the celebrity spotter knows who he is spotting, as long as *some*one does," is ridiculous. How can you spot a celebrity if you don't know he or she *is* a celebrity?

And, hey, I knew that was Michael Keaton the minute he walked in the door. I waited until his back was turned to tell the others. They all said, "Nah," except you-know-who said, "Who's Michael Keaton?" World-class celebrity spotter? Hah!

As for saying Michael looked like a bat, only smaller— he obviously never saw him in the black Batman suit. Maybe everybody looks like a bat to a guy who is built like an elephant.

When we got off the plane, Mr. Keaton stopped to let me go first. I said, "No thanks, I have to get my stuff." He didn't wait for any "author" at that point.

But the final blow was when this so-called columnist says at the end of the column that Michael Keaton walked in front of us so he could get a better look at him because he was the author of *The Paper Dynasty*. Can you imagine Michael Keaton looking at a guy who could be his father rather than at his twenty-five-year-old daughter?

Julia Gardner (née Esmeralda)
Redondo Beach

Ted Gardner replies:

Okay, I don't mind taking half my column for letters from crackpots, but throwing the space to my daughter, who is obviously laboring under some serious delusions, is a very questionable practice. And, believe me, I understand you don't have to *pay* those people who write letters, and I just love to get bumped by scabs, but this is really too much. I can just see my check for what is left of this column today. About six dollars and change.

I mean, to try and take the credit from her father for celebrity spotting defies reason. I was a celebrity spotter before she was born.

Who is more attractive to a movie star—a young woman who has lived a mere 25 years, or a seasoned, erudite author of a novel?

Pretty girls are a dime a dozen to Hollywood stars. What is more important to a star than a pretty girl? I'll tell you what—a good story. Writers are tough to come by. A good script can *make* a star.

Ridiculing my celebrity spotting talents springs from the depths of ignorance. I have probably spotted more celebrities with one eye tied behind my back in the time what's-her-name was gestating than what's-her-name has in her whole life. And there are lots of celebrities I know that *she* wouldn't know if she fell on them. Would she know Barry Goldwater, Goodie Knight, Emmitt Schlegel? How about Eric Fleming and Fats Wannemaker?

And where is her gratitude? For the nurturing, the sacrifice, the clothes, the shelter, the food. It goes without saying that a grateful daughter of a first-class celebrity spotter would not cast aspersions on his abilities.

So Keaton waited for her to get off the plane, but not for me. So what? That's plain chivalry. But it wasn't chivalry that made him wait for me in the airport, then cross in front of me with that awe-struck look, praying in his star's heart for a part—*any* part—in the movie of *The Paper Dynasty*.

You can't fool me, Esmeralda. And what if I did get your names a little mixed up? There were *three* of you, for heaven's sakes. It is for *your* benefit that I not overshadow you with my celebrity. One doesn't get by in this world on one's looks. He does it with *TALENT!* Michael Keaton recognizes that; that is precisely why he was trying to get my attention.

So, if you want to blab your real name on these pages, it isn't going to change my mind. I'm just now wondering if Julia is really Esmeralda. Or is she Jambalaya or Hortense? It does get a little confusing.

But don't think blabbing your name is going to get Michael Keaton's attention. He seldom reads The Rolling Hills *Herald*.

What he reads these days is *The Paper Dynasty*. I just sent him a copy with a note about how our paths crossed in the airport.

P.S. I threw in a picture of Esmeralda on the off-chance Michael could use it to help jog his memory.

Is The Bird Fresh Or Frozen?

Weatherwise, Ginny is under it. Ginny is the name of my real wife. With the distaff under the weather, the guy who heretofore wore the pants in the family is conscripted to bring home the turkey.

Now heretofore I had brought home the bacon on a fairly regular basis, and I have been known to *talk* turkey, but my services have never been impressed to actually purchase a bird. My forte was Christmas trees. December 24th. There is nothing like waiting until the last minute to get the ultimate flavor of the season.

My trepidation is understandable. So much of the holiday fare rides on the quality of the dead bird. The difference between happy holidays and the blahs is the difference between top turkey and a tough old bird.

A novice has every justification for a little nervousness.

Especially since it is the afternoon before Thanksgiving.

Frozen birds, I imagine, are a dime a dozen. Fresh, on the other hand, could be scarce. We have, at our house, a fetish for fresh. No frozen meat knowingly passes our lips. So my mission is especially crucial.

Luckily I arrive just as the turkeys are being unloaded. I mingle with the old-time holiday throng and put my mitts on a plastic package. The label says, "FRESH," but the package is cold and hard. I fish around in the bin and find some plumper birds that are soft and squishy to the touch, a test I imagine the seasoned shoppers use in judging the relative merits of turkeys and toilet tissue.

My suspicion is fueled when a woman in our gaggle comments, "They must be frozen." I sink into mild panic. I thought this was going to be easy. Would a supermarket lie to you? Banks used to be the last bastion of integrity in the marketplace, and look what happened to them. If supermarkets started flim-flamming, could the end of civilization be far behind?

One of the women who obviously has shopped for turkey before and is therefore conversant with the intricacies of the game game or fowl game, as the case may be, confronts the meat manager.

"These birds frozen?"

"No, ma'am, they're fresh."

"They feel so hard."

"We keep them at thirty-five degrees," she says. "They get a little cold."

If you have never shopped for a bird, you can appreciate my precarious position. Thirty-five degrees is three lousy degrees over freezing—maybe the thermometer was off.

Darkness is encroaching in more ways than one. Do I buy a turkey that says, "FRESH," but feels frozen, or a turkey that is *not* marked "FRESH" that feels fresh? Maybe the soft one was frozen and defrosted and that Jell-O-like consistency is melted ice.

So I opt for the bird marked "FRESH." If the turkey is frozen, how can I be at fault? It is clearly labeled "FRESH."

But what if the turkey, the centerpiece of our Thanksgiving festivities, is dried out as frozen stuff is wont to be? Who can I blame? Not Ginny. She is out of the loop on this one.

She seems suspiciously nonchalant when I tell her the story. She keeps halfheartedly reassuring me that everything is going to be all right. But we both know "all right" won't cut the mustard with our finicky standards.

I call my sister, across the continent. I tell her the story.

"What do you want with a fresh turkey?" she asks.

I am dumbfounded. My sister comes from the same long line of gourmets. How can she promulgate this heresy?

"You don't buy fresh turkey?"

"Nah—frozen," is the response. "It's safer," she says.

"Safer? A frozen turkey is safer?"

"Yeah—you don't get salmonella."

"I thought that was from chickens."

"Maybe you got a chicken," she says. "You know the story about the guy who ordered the turkey sandwich in a restaurant? The waiter returned from the kitchen and said, 'I'm sorry, we're out of turkey.' 'Okay, I'll have the chicken then,' the customer said. 'Lady,' he said, 'if we had chicken, you'd have had your turkey.'"

"But frozen meat is so dry."

"Nah," she says, "you can't tell the difference."

Heresy.

Our FRESH turkey is fantastic. Do I get smothered in praise for picking such a stellar bird?

You know I don't. I am just another of the many unsung holiday heroes. "It's fine," is as good as it got. Fine? I think she has the blahs. It is the best turkey we ever had, bar none.

From now on, I'm shopping for the turkeys.

A Ghost Story

Dear Mr. Bundy:

There has been so much talk lately about ghostwriters, plagiarism and just downright friendly borrowing of words, phrases, ideas, paragraphs and, heck, the whole *oeuvre*, that it set me to thinking.

And I don't agree with you that any time I start thinking, it hurts the newspaper. Not necessarily.

This time it could help us all.

An article entitled "The Culture of Plagiarism" in some magazine, by a guy I don't want to give undue credit to, points out that nobody writes or speaks their own lines anymore.

He mentions that when Senator Joe Biden borrowed from Robert Kennedy, he was actually borrowing from a guy named Adam Walinsky, who wrote the lines (without attribution) for Kennedy in the first place.

No president or even presidential candidate in our memory wrote his own speeches. Even though we were led to believe Adlai Stevenson wrote his, they were apparently the work of a man named Sidney Hyman.

Does any of this give you any food for thought?

Dear Ted:

No.

Dear Mr. Bundy:

That's okay. I just thought you might be quick on the uptake for a change and spare me belaboring a point.

Anyway, you know that curious Washington novel we all thought was written by Maureen Dean, John Dean's wife? Get this. *Washington Wives*, which starts with a sensational sex scene and slides south from there, started out as a movie treatment by a Hollywood producer. They knocked the plot out with a committee in true-blue Hollywood fashion, then found a publisher. *Then* they signed up Mrs. Dean as the "name author."

Then, and only then, did they bother to look around

for someone to actually write the book.

Take, for instance, that industrial god Lido Iacocca, whose uncle sells the best hot dogs in my hometown (under the name Yacco's, because that's the way the Pennsylvania Dutch pronounced Iacocca). He made 10 to 15 million badly-needed dollars on a book written by William Novak. Novak, with all his perks and bonuses, reportedly got around $30 thousand.

After Iacocca passed 10 million, Novak (if the folklore is to be credited) wrote to the Industrial Baron asking for another crumb from the pie, and the letter went unanswered.

I can see Iacocca somewhere behind a desk in his navy blue pinstripe suit saying, "Hell, it's my story they bought. Anybody could have put it on paper."

Including you, Lido?

Dan Rather isn't speaking his own words. Jack Anderson's column is written by someone else. Many court opinions that may change the course of history are written by 24-year-olds fresh out of law school and still wet behind the years.

The better judges, I hear, do read the opinions before they are published.

Most of the newspaper columns written by celebrity non-writers are written by someone else. Ghosted. Now do you get my drift, Mr. B?

Dear Ted:
     NO.

Dear Mr. Bundy:
     I don't mean to exaggerate my stature or anything, but I was just wondering if you could find anything in the Peninsula *News'* budget to help support a ghostwriter for yours truly?

Think of the status the Peninsula *News* would gain as soon as word got out it had a ghostwritten column on its pages.

If you are suffering from your usual short-sighted-ness, you might check with Seth Baker to save me the proto-col *faux pas* of going over your head.

I realize I may not be quite up there with a Senator or presidential candidate, but a case could be made that my luminosity was on wattage par with the wife of John Dean, *n'est-ce pas*?

Dear Ted:

You know Seth and I are just nuts about your letters. We realize they aren't ghostwritten or anything because there isn't anyone else that nuts.

My instinct is to say nuts to you, but Seth says not to be hasty. It is something we might look into. He says that maybe even a raise would be warranted if we could get some-one to write your piece in intelligible English.

Reid

And P.S. If we can take your name off the thing, there might be a little more in it for you.

R

Reducing The Debt

To: Nicholas Brady, Secretary of the Treasury

Dear Secretary Brady:

I'm a guy who has done some serious borrowing in my time. Maybe not Latin-America serious, but serious enough for a bloke in my straits.

Now let's face it, the most unpleasant thing about borrowing is paying it back. And I've been doing my bit in that regard—you might say every month like clockwork.

Now I hear a couple of your world-class borrowers have been kinda slow pays, as they say in the banking game. And I don't begrudge 'em anything you want to do for them in that regard. And the highfalutin language you are using boils down to sorta forgiving the debt.

Now I got to thinking how we were talking big-time bucks with these Latin loans and how that could set the old bankers back a week or two, when I come up with a solution I think you'll like.

I do want it understood right up front that I don't require any kind of thanks or personal publicity about my scheme, it can be just between you, your treasury department and me, as far as I am concerned.

Simply stated, my proposal is this:

When you first announced your idea that the banks ought to forgive those giant loans, a large groan went up all over the country—like everyone discovered their pocketbook had been pinched at the same time. Like they realized the little guy would be paying for the big guys' folly.

Now I don't mean to suggest your idea is a bad one—quite to the contrary. I think it is a stroke of genius because, as that famous Marx brother Hart Schafter N. Marx once said, you can't get honey from lemons (or was it blood from a turnip?)

Of course, the real challenge of those big shot giveaways is making it palatable to the public. And therein, if I may modestly say so, lies the innate beauty of my plan.

While the banks are shutting their eyes to hundreds of billions of Yanqui dollars in loans to those banana split and fruitcake republics, there has got to be a bit of sugar for the little guy, to—as the immortal sage Mary Poppins once said—make the medicine go down.

I am selflessly offering myself as that very sugar. Oh, I'm sure there are many worthy subjects out there in this great land of ours, maybe even personally acquainted with you, Secretary Brady, but they would not all be able to take the intense glare of the public spotlight.

So instead of opening with your big guns in the hundred billion buck range, I am suggesting you start more modestly—

With me.

Just get these pompous bankers to go easy on me—forgive my puny loans—you know, tell me, "Ted, it's okay, you've been paying us for decades. And to make an example of those little bitty guys who send it in month after month, year after year, why, you don't have to pay us another nickel. We forgive YOUR ENTIRE DEBT. We hope, incidentally, that you will reciprocate and forgive your debtors, but that is entirely up to you, and ours is a no-strings-attached deal."

I'm sure you see the beauty of this idea, Secretary Brady. Especially at tax time when you have a lot of soreheads complaining about forking over your pound of flesh (I am not one of those soreheads, but I guess you can tell that from my writing style).

The beauty is—a regular guy, just like the chump next door, is rewarded for paying. Not for *not* paying his loans. People will rise up and cheer you. I wouldn't be surprised if you were drafted and elected President by acclamation, next time around. But without my plan, I wouldn't want to run for dogcatcher if I were you.

Then, you know on the Latin thing, if you have to do it, you have to do it. But forgiving my loans first (symbolic of so many chumps who have paid like lambs) will take the sting out of all the flak that you would otherwise be a sitting duck to catch.

Feel free to use my name if you have to. I don't seek any personal publicity, but I realize it would be tough to forgive my loans anonymously. No one would believe you.

> God Bless America (including, but not limited to, Latin America)
>
> Ted Gardner,
> Your faithful servant

It is a tribute to my persuasiveness that I got a prompt response from the Treasury Department. It wasn't from Secretary Brady himself exactly, but it was from one of the Treasury Department's more prominent divisions.

Dear Mr. Gardner:

Your Income Tax Return has been selected at random for audit. Please contact this office to arrange an appointment…

Gaffing The Decorums

Dear M:

Thanks for the kind invitation to your daughter's *vinculum matrimonii*. Since you just came to our nuptials, I don't see we have a lot of options. I mean, it's not like a funeral where if you go to his, he isn't coming to yours. So we accept your kind invitation, conditionally.

Oh, we don't have any qualms about the wedding part of it. But the insert of cautionary restrictions for trespassing the portals of L.A.'s California Club has given me pause:

> **The California Club, House Rules**
> *Members and Guests must conduct themselves with decorum at all times. Gentlemen are required to wear jackets and ties at all times. Acceptable attire for ladies includes only skirts or dresses; pants outfits are not acceptable.*

Now you know, M, I have no trouble with this decorum business, it's my wife, Ginny, that concerns me. You will remember Ginny as the nonconforming Girl Scout leader to the bride-to-be; the intellectual whose housekeeping rivals your own. The Ginny whose favorite outfit is the white tie and tails she sports at the least opportunity. And that spells P-A-N-T-S.

We had a guy at our daughter's wedding who wore a tux jacket and shirt, cummerbund, string tie and jeans. How does the California Club stand on that? I was toying with the idea of borrowing it, it was so smashing. But how will they cope with Ginny?

It doesn't mention how they stand on jewelry. I take it Ginny may wear her Santo Domingo Indian squash blossom? May I wear earrings?

May we bring the Indian? She never wears pants, though her skirts are made by Oram the tentmaker. They are a little coarse, but so is she. And they *are* skirts.

The little card doesn't say anything about polyester

blouses. Is that jake with the Club? You know you don't have to iron them, and these days with so much time being taken up with decorum, time is of the essence.

Now when they say, "Only skirts," are they talking topless? I mean, I am not trying to be risqué or anything, I'm just checking, you know, decorum-wise. How about just a halter top for modesty's sake? Would it be permitted? Should we get it in writing that you don't have to wear *only* a skirt?

Oh, I know rules are rules, but it could be cold in late December, and, for instance, shoes and socks might be welcome.

And hey, when it says, "Gentlemen are required to wear jackets and ties at all times," does that necessarily include me? Ginny says we could make a strong case that I wasn't a gentleman.

When you say, "Jackets and ties at all times," you don't say anything about pants. I am hoping I am not out of line in assuming that pants are optional. Would shorts be OK? Only if it is an especially hot day. Kilts? Could Ginny make believe she was a man and wear the tails? If I wore the skirt only?

But I don't mind putting on a tie now and again. The only problem is the muscles in my neck have built up with the necking exercises I have been doing, so the collars on my shirts are a tad tight. When I wear the shirts my complexion takes on a rather rich blue hue and I am prone to shortness of breath.

So I am especially relieved there is no mention of the Club requiring *shirts*, only jackets and ties. If I read that correctly, I'll have no trouble with conforming to the California Club constrictions.

Oh, and just one more thing. Technically I was hoping I would be *your* guest and not the California Club's. That would make things a lot simpler. I can see the Club making their own members wear "jackets and ties at all times," but for guests it could become a little bothersome at bedtime.

Well, I just wanted to be sure up front (before we buy

a gift and all) that we wouldn't be gaffing the decorums.

Best to bride,
Ted

By return telegram:

Dear Ted:

Please disregard wedding invitation. Stop. It was sent in error. Stop.

Please.

M—

Man's Best Friend

The following slice of everyday life is pure unadulterated fiction.

Once upon a time there lived in a far-off land two neighbors; one with a barking dog, one without.

The neighbors with the barker, Mr. & Mrs. Ob Livious, went off to the city to earn their daily bread, leaving their dog behind to bark for his.

The dogless pair, Mr. & Mrs. Agri Vated, were not so fortunate in their employments and spent most of their workdays at home, listening to the barking of the neighbors' dog.

Tolerance for barking dogs was not counted as one of this suffering couple's strengths.

There are as many remedies for barking dogs as there are hiccup cures, and they are just as effective.

Mr. & Mrs. Agri Vated tried them all:

1. **Friendly communication.** Mr. & Mrs. Ob Livious, with the barker, were nice folks. They promised accommodation. And they kept many of their promises. It was just such a pain to put the little barker inside every time they left home. Besides, it wouldn't be fair to the dog. He was, after all, an outside dog.

"Call us anytime he barks."

Agri Vated called once too often. The lady of the

house hung up while he was still talking.

Mr. Agri Vated felt poorly that he had upset Mrs. Ob Livious. He decided to endure. For after all, it was one thing to be upset by an uncomplicated animal, and quite another to upset a real person.

But, predictably, in time his patience wore thin. When he stopped calling, the dog was left alone outside more often. The barking increased mid-day.

Other remedies were sought.

2. **Sue.** He called an attorney. Why not bring suit for mental distress, harassment, pain and suffering in ability to think and do productive work?

Attorney's advice (free) was "Shoot the dog."

3. **Buy a dog whistle that has a frequency so high it annoys the dog.**

It was the premiere item on Agri Vated's Christmas list.

It was 100% effective. When the dog barked, he just took his whistle out back and blew it. The dog stopped barking immediately (for 10 seconds).

So all Agri had to do was stay out back with his whistle for an hour or so and he soon found the disease almost more acceptable than the cure.

More than once Agri Vated tore his house apart trying to locate that blessed whistle while the dog barked more and more. He just couldn't ever seem to remember where he put it.

4. **Petition the neighbors and send it to a sympathetic agency.** Agri thought it a little tacky to pit neighbor against neighbor. One neighbor said—"I can see why it drives you nuts, but we had dogs for 48 years and I'm too sentimental about them to complain."

5. **Record the dog and play it back in stereo outside their bedroom window.**

Agri made definitive recordings of continual barking, which may be listened to every time he gets lonely for the sounds of barking dogs. That eventuality has not yet arrived.

6. **Train the dog.** The dog owners agreed to take their dog to have it trained at their expense. The training

consisted of surprising the little darling by dropping a tin can behind him every time he barked.

But the dog's pen faced the house and they couldn't sneak up behind him when they were home. When he barked most of the time, they weren't home to drop the tin can anyway.

7. **Throw poisoned hamburger over the fence.** But what if he is a vegetarian?

8. **Play music to soothe him.** Agri Vated tried all the composers on the hope of hitting one the dog found favorable. The Romantics were out, Bach was too brittle, Beethoven stirred him up. It wasn't until Agri played Prokofiev's "Seventh Piano Sonata" that some peace was attained. It wasn't that the dog liked the music and stopped barking, but rather that the music was so loud the Agri Vateds couldn't hear the dog barking.

Of course Mrs. Vated couldn't remain in the house when Agri played the Prokofiev, so the Agri Vateds were back where they started.

Since all these suggested remedies failed, one day the lady of the beleaguered household, being ever so much more brave than the man, climbed a fence and a dog pen, stick in hand. The barking beauty cowered in a corner. With heroic gestures, Mrs. Agri Vated opened the unlocked door and signaled with her stick for the doggie to go inside.

The dog seemed tickled to death after gaining entrance to his home.

Now, as soon as the dog owners' car door slams as they flee once again from man's best barking friend, he starts barking for that nice, if somewhat intimidating, neighbor to put him inside.

Sometimes it's a dog's life.

A Sense Of Direction

Dear Prez:

It was nice of your club to sport me to lunch, to comp me three free raffle tickets (even though they didn't have numbers on them, it was a lovely gesture) and to give me all those wonderful gifts. Really, it wasn't necessary to give presents on top of letting me blab about my book *The Paper Dynasty*.

And incidentally, you have a very literate group there, relatively speaking. Most clubs like yours have two, maybe three, people who fess up to reading books. You had *three times that!* Why, that's almost ten percent of your attendance! You can be very proud.

I had been promised there would be no heckling, and yet as soon as I stood up, a guy up front who looked suspiciously like Ken McNeil starts in on me. Well, naturally, my composure went to pieces and I barely got through the talk, so it was especially reassuring of you to give me four (4) gifts at the end.

And by the way, I had no idea just how swanky your club was until I saw my famous and esteemed publisher, Michael DeF. Griffin, sitting at the same table as the aforementioned heckler.

"The check's in the mail!" my publisher shouted. (The PV *News* uses a private mail service that takes two months to deliver.) Michael DeF. Griffin was very gracious to me afterwards and did volunteer he would go to bat to get me a salary increase in the neighborhood of $1.50 a week. I thought something like $2.50 would have been more sporting after seven (7) years, but I held my tongue.

You can imagine my surprise to see him sitting there as a member of this highfalutin group. I hope you can also appreciate the last-minute alterations I was forced to make in my talk.

I had never met Mr. Griffin before. Way back, it was decided by the *News* management that for the benefit of all concerned, it would be best if I stayed away from the *News* office.

The gifts were really something and I am especially grateful for the last one you gave me. Oh, the pen stamped with the name of your club was great, though it isn't my first pen. And the cap, stamped with the name of your club, is champion. And the low-flow shower heads and toilet dams hit the spot. But the thing I am most crazy about is the car compass. My sense of direction is on the nil side and I find it so helpful to have a compass to set me more or less straight.

I have had two or three car compasses heretofore, but I couldn't get any of them to work. When you are driving into the sunset at five in the afternoon, even I know the little gizmo telling you you are going north is on the fritz. I wasn't too bothered because I had paid less than $4 for them, and anyone will tell you what a bargain that is.

So you can imagine my excitement when you hand me a real upscale-looking car compass. I couldn't wait to get home to tear into it.

There I notice the plastic cover on the cardboard has been removed and taped back on with Scotch tape. Jake with me. I am not a guy who thinks he is too good for hand-me-downs. Thoughtfully, the directions are intact. (I have already looked at the handsome instrument and ascertained that something is catawampous.) I have a fair idea of where south is, and my new gift gadget says east.

When all else fails…I turn to the directions. There, in no uncertain terms, I am told to take my new compass out where there is nothing—at least twenty feet from automobiles, corrugated steel structures, houses—out in a field. After I do that, I am to point it north.

North? I was sort of hoping the compass would help me with that. Just exactly where north was, you know. Now I am to take a screwdriver to a couple plastic screws and adjust the thing to point north. Then I am to repeat this with the other cardinal points and "correct for one-half the error," whatever that means.

Now, my question is, even if I had a PhD in astrophysics and *was* able to make these sophisticated adjustments (not to mention having an uncanny knack for spotting the North Pole in this vacant field), what happens when I get the thing back in the car? I mean, if I have to set it twenty feet from the car so it won't get screwed up, won't it get screwed up in the car? (I have an older car made when they were still making engines of metal.)

So, all in all, Prez, I was wondering if I could bundle it back up, good as when I got it (I will put on brand-new Scotch tape and turn it back to you), and maybe—subject to your approval, of course—you would give me the cash instead?

Nothing But A Dumb Old Man

I start the New Year with my customary panache.

One thing must be admitted up front, as they say: I am not the world's best driver. I concede the sanity of mankind might be better served if I never sat behind the wheel of a car.

But on New Year's Day I am driving to a movie with my wife, daughter and friend. I am a little late. The parking lot is full. Cars are everywhere. I am going the wrong direction and seek (naturally) to remedy it.

In the course of straightening out my car to go down the right aisle, I back up a few times. In the process, I come close to nicking a family—mother, father, child and mother-in-law. Just how close I come to drawing blood, I cannot say, but Ginny (wife) buries her head in her lap and groans. The family gets into their car and pulls out. I am luckily situated so I could take his space. There is a jamb-up to exit, so he is still there as we leave the car.

He rolls down his window. "You better learn to drive, you F'ing idiot, you almost hit me twice."

I must be looking at him with provocative astonishment, because he jumps out of his car and comes within ten inches of my nose. "You F'ing jerk, you almost hit me twice." Here he holds up two fingers in a victory sign. "Twice," he repeats, "you dumb F."

"F" is not exactly what he says, though I don't see any evidence he has not memorized the alphabet—but his actual language leans more toward the colorful side. Sort of bluish.

"You're nothing but a dumb old person," he says—stating with slight exaggeration the truth of the matter, though I think it best not to call him on it at this particular time.

You can tell that "old person" is his favorite insult. There is the stream of profanity climaxed with a profanity-free phrase—"You're nothing but a dumb old person." It is as though the word "old" is profane unto itself.

I take a step back, and maneuver a parked motorcycle between us. Not in fear, you understand, more in terror.

"You better learn to drive, you dumb F." He has an ostinato style and keeps pounding away at the same measly notes.

I have several options. I can say, "Look, you loud-mouthed bozo, I can take you with one arm tied behind my back." While perhaps not strictly true, I think I can hold my own with one arm tied behind my back, as long as he has both his arms tied behind his.

He is a squarish, squat, muscular fellow, and as he previously pointed out, from his perspective I am an "old person." This, of course, makes him a "young person" by comparison.

I have with me my daughter Jambalaya (not her real name—we don't want any repercussions) and her boy friend Lochinvar (ditto). Lochinvar has a couple inches on six feet, and even Jambalaya is taller than the villain. So I figure Lochinvar can bust the heavy in the mouth after I faint. Of course the heavy's eyes look like his bravado might be the result of some controlled substance, and he keeps feinting like a boxer ready to throw a Sunday punch—and it was only Tuesday.

My second option is to agree with him. I can't really say he was that inaccurate. Yes, I am a lousy driver—yes, I better learn to drive—easy enough. I can even agree to the stupidity epithet. I can tell him only a stupid person could think they are intelligent.

But when he calls me old, with such smug satisfaction that he doesn't need the crutch of his profanity, something inside of me snaps and I (choose one): 1. Haul off and poke him in the nose, breaking it. 2. Poke him in the nose and break my hand. 3. Push the motorcycle over on him. 4. Say, "Your father's moustache." 5. Cower, cowardly, and say nothing.

At the peak of my bravery, when he says the third time, "You almost hit me twice, you stupid F," I mutter, "I didn't hit you, did I?" I know I have him there, because if I had hit him, he would not be saying "*almost* hit me twice" all the time.

So what is the big deal? I am trying to say *almost* doesn't count in cars anymore than in pregnancy.

His response: "This is your lucky day," I take to mean he is sparing me the indignity of using me for a punching bag in public.

Perhaps he means I was lucky I didn't hit him with the car, because then he would have killed me.

For my part, I would feel a lot luckier if I hadn't met him.

I am, however, considering a New Year's resolution to improve my driving.

King For Poland

In order to stay on top in these fast-moving times, one has to have a timely gimmick.

Eastern Europe! Everything is Eastern Europe. They are throwing the rascals out. Rolling back the clock, and that is just where I come in.

I have reasoned that, as Jimmy Bakker, the incarcerated evangelist, says, "The way to be successful is to find a need and fill it."

Eastern Europe needs leadership. I am a little rusty with their languages, so instead of being a leader I have decided to become a middleman. A broker. A headhunter for heads of state!

Making a deal requires two consenting parties. In my case, I need a country, and I need a leader.

So naturally, I thought of Ann Rutkosky, who gallantly commands this space on Thursdays.

Poland, I reasoned again, might do very nicely with a king. Ann has been living with a Polish king for years. It was my ticket to riches.

I called Ann.

"What with Communism disintegrating before our very eyes, what with the tough economic straits the Poles are experiencing, a monarchy might be just the ticket to see them through the thicket. How do you and your king feel about that kind of thing?"

"Sure, and butterflies give milk, Ken," she said.

I said, "I'm Ted."

"Right," she said.

"No, really—let's just suppose the Poles thought the way out of their mess was a royal family. Would you be available as a Polish queen?"

"I'm Italian."

"Send the spaghetti recipe."

"Bring the water to a boil and cook about seven, eight minutes. A little bite and it should have some snap to it. *Al dente*—don't overcook."

"No, Ann—the *sauce*."

"I don't make sauce."

"Okay, so as far as I'm concerned, you could be Polish. Gosh sakes, it wouldn't hurt you to make believe you were Polish if it got you crowned Queen of Poland. Look at it this way, you would be performing a service to mankind—helping the Poles out of the doldrums."

"From the doldrums I don't know, Ken, but I can tell you this: At our house there is a Polish king. There is no Polish queen. Period. End of report."

"I am, between us, something of a power broker force on the international scene. Sort of a quintessential head-headhunter."

"Like Kissinger."

"Henry?"

"No, Sam Kissinger. But he's changed his name so often, people are starting to ask—I wonder who's Kissinger now?"

"Is that so? I didn't know...oh, Ann, wow, 'who's Kissinger now?' So anyway, let's get back on the track. I'm a power broker. I match heads of state with states."

"And Poland is one of your clients?" Ann asked.

"Will be, soon as I find 'em a king."

"Oh, my..."

"Well then, would you make the trip with him—if the Poles offered him a crown?"

"What's this crown you're talking? He's got a mouth full of them already."

"Ann, Ann, can we stay on the track? I'm talking about your husband really being crowned King of Poland. Shore an begoorie, you take my meaning."

"Wrong accent for Poles, Ken. And Italians."

"Okay, forget the accent. Would you move to Poland with your husband if he really were the King of Poland?"

"What would we get, a castle in Warsaw, I suppose?" she asked.

"Perhaps a remodel in Gdansk."

"Silliest thing I ever heard. Where did you even get

the idea he would be a Polish king?"

"From you."

"From me?"

"In the papers."

"You know you can't believe what you read in the papers."

"Okay, Ann—but would you consider it? I mean, it would give my career a real boost to match a Polish king with Poland. At least let me make the overtures. You can put off your final decision until I get a firm commitment from the Poles."

"Okay," she said. "I've gotta run give the grandkids a bath."

"Hot dog," I said to myself after I hung up the phone. "I just made half a deal."

They're Singing My Song

To Andrew Lloyd Webber:

You may not know me personally, but it is obvious you know my music. I speak, of course, of your plagiarism of a tune I wrote for my wedding, when you were an up-and-coming nobody and I was just a nobody.

The sad news is, Andrew, you have ripped off the melody of my wedding song for your ever-popular "Memories," from *Cats*.

Oh, it's no coincidence, I'm sure, that "Memories" is the only ballad in *Cats*, and the only song which does not use the words of the T.S. Eliot "Cats" poems.

There are no words to my music, so you are home free on that score as far as I am concerned.

Now, Andrew, we both being musicians as well as businessmen, are well aware we live in a litigious age. Deep pockets (like yours must be, eh?) are the targets of constant assaults from the poorer classes, whether justified or not.

And this leads to a lot of unwarranted settlements by insurance companies and their lawyers who rightly think it is better to settle the thing than hassle with the time and expense of court.

I should state, right up front here, that this is in no way a threat. Nothing could be further from my mind at this juncture.

So you are probably wondering what I have in mind—"Get to the point!" I can just hear you say.

Well, frankly, Andrew old boy, I was reading how with your big Broadway hits and all—heck, what am I saying, Broadway, that's peanuts for a guy who is all over the world—but anyway, I am reading you are hauling in the shekels to the tune of two, three million a week just in royalties alone, and I expect you got a coupla sweet investments to boot which probably kicks it above that, hey? *Well* above, I'd venture to say.

So if I wanted to be crass and grasping—which I certainly do not (get that straight right now)—I would ask you what you thought my "Memories" was worth to you, royaltywise. Everybody who has seen the show *Cats* knows it is the hit song—and heck, I don't begrudge you using my tune at all. (Everybody at my wedding liked it too. It is so popular, we played it at my daughter's wedding.)

I am just thinking that a guy as well-off as you are probably has a lot more money than he can spend and would probably welcome the opportunity to share it with a guy who has contributed so materially to your success.

Of course, you know as well as I that it is no easy matter putting a precise dollar amount on my contribution. A lot of people tell me I should hold out for a piece of the action—you know, be paid everytime someone sings "Memories"—like you are paid everytime someone sings it. A funny thing just occurred to me, and that is how funny it must feel to you to be getting paid everytime someone sings *my* song. I realize royalties might be the way to go, because I see by your ads for *Cats* that you say, "Now and forever," and that forever could be a very long time.

But I am nothing if not reasonable. I am not a gouger or a skinflint. A lot of people consider me very openhanded, so I don't at all mind a lump sum settlement. You know, a buy out kind of thing where you would write me a reasonable check (I believe you Brits spell it "cheque," and I just want to clarify that so there won't be any sort of misunderstanding), and I would be willing to put my John Hancock on the dotted line that it was in full satisfaction, or whatever fancy language your barristers could come up with.

I don't know but that five or ten million might be a good starting point ("Now and forever," and it's that "forever" part we ought to keep uppermost in our minds) for our negotiations. I am considered a fair negotiator—"Tough but fair," a lot of people say, so you don't have anything to fear on that score.

And I hope you won't think, Andrew old chum, that my willingness to sell out so cheap in the scheme of things—maybe your greatest hit for a paltry five million (whoops!—there, I've shown my hand already)—in any way denigrates my "Memories" tune (or your "Memories" tune if we make this deal). Please just consider me a marshmallow.

*　　*　　*

Dear Marshmallow:

When you are as successful as Andrew Lloyd Webber, you are plagued with a lot of paranoids. Let me assure you, Mr. Webber was not at your wedding, and from the look of your handwriting he wasn't even born then.

S. Hy Eister
Attorney at large

Our $3,000,000 Chair

"Hey, Ginny—"

"Hm?"

"How old is that chair in the living room?—The one your grandmother gave us."

"I don't know how old it is—we've had it re-covered and it looks all right to me. Since when have you taken an interest in furniture?" she asks.

"Since this," I say, showing her the current issue of *Connoisseur* magazine (one of those glossy coffee-table magazines for the nouveau pretentious) wherein is trumpeted the most recent idiocy, art-salewise; viz., an old chair that went for $2,750,000.00 (two million seven hundred and fifty thousand dollars and 00/100 cents).

Ginny, between us, often belittles my loftier ambitions, and this is no exception.

"Oh, yeah, but that's a priceless antique. Our old stuff is just old."

"Wait a minute, who says so?"

"Well anybody who knows anything about furniture."

"I am overlooking any condescension implied in that statement," I say. "I just want to put you on notice that at two-point-seven-five mil a pop, I am going to know something about furniture."

"Puh," she chortles.

"Look at this picture—what do you see?"

"A chair," she says.

"You see, that's the prosaic mind," I enlighten her.

"And what's the word from the poet? What does he see there?"

"Close to three million smackers," I say.

"But it's an antique."

"Sophistry," I say. "You know it's in the eye of the beholder."

"But no eye is going to behold our old chair as art, antique, beautiful or valuable," spoke she of the limited vision. "You need provenance, rarity, history, quality, condition."

"And the rest is hype."

"Hype?"

"Certainly." My superior knowledge of these matters does not prevent me from speaking modestly. "That's what these high-priced auctions are, hype. Paintings for fifty million, chairs for two-point-seven-five. They get the bidders all psyched up with hype—I read that it cost that Japanese company about one hundred and twenty-five thousand dollars every day, weekends and holidays included, to look at that Van Gogh picture."

"Well, hype or no hype," she says, calling up her long-suffering tone now, "you aren't going to get three million for that piece of junk."

I go to sit in it. "You know," I say, "it's pretty comfortable."

"Nobody's going to sit in a three million dollar chair," she says.

"Well, look, I'm not going to be greedy. We'll just take it to Christie's or Sotheby's and see what the market will bear. I might even let it go for a million and a half. Practically wholesale, when you think about it."

"A real sacrifice," she says.

Ginny has many good qualities. But she is not a visionary.

"It is not for nothing I have been called a man of vision. And it is the men of vision who find and sell these rare old chairs and things."

"Who calls you a man of vision?" she asks. "Your ophthalmologist?"

"That's very funny," I say, "I'll be sure and pass that on to the auctioneer. I'm sure he'll be amused. He will doubtless have a smile on his face ruminating on your witticism while he gavels my chair down around the two or three million mark."

"*Your* chair," she says with a sudden burst of passion. "The chair is *my* chair."

"Well," I mollify my thrust, "community property," I say in a decidedly non-threatening tone.

"No, private and personal property. The chair was a gift to me—and me alone."

"But I'm sure you'd want your cut if I sold that card table my aunt gave me."

I don't wait for her answer. I am on the phone to my mother to ask her the pedigree of that old chaise of hers.

I figure since it is twice the size of the 2.75 mil chair, it should knock down at around 5 mil—and I thought it best to deal direct with the owner to save any surreptitious circumvention of the community property laws.

And as I tell Ginny, when my ship comes in, I won't be stingy with the cargo.

"Where are you going?" she asks as she sees me head for the front door.

"The guy that paid two-point-seven-five mil for the chair in New York was a Philadelphia neighbor of the guy who sold it. If he had been as astute as I, he could have saved the quarter-million commission."

"How?"

"I'm going to case the neighborhood. There ought to be someone right on this block with an eye for a bargain."

A Bentley For The Diffident

Dear Reid:

I'm in a bit of a bind. My car just celebrated its 11th birthday, so I started kicking around for a new one.

First I stopped at the bank. Money is easier now, and I just thought I'd see what they could do for me. Well, first thing they wanted to know was what you paid me. I thought that a little cheeky myself. What have you got to do with it? I want the car. You, I understand, travel only by limo.

When I told them what you paid me, I thought

they'd die laughing. They were still laughing when I stormed out, telling them in no uncertain terms I would take my business elsewhere, thank you very much.

But I got to thinking; before I did anymore shopping, I ought to have a chat with my old friend Reid. Not old in any chronological sense that you are old in years, Reid old buddy, just that the warm and deep friendship, based on mutual admiration and respect, goes back a long time. Which brings me to my point: do you think you could see your way clear to a little increase in the stipend so they won't laugh me out of the bank?

Now I realize you might have a tough time in the present circumstances getting me enough to cut any ice with bankers. But I notice on the *News* masthead the position of executive editor seems to be vacant. Of course it is perfectly understandable that the boss doesn't want any ex-retirees in that position, but, Reid old buddy, I haven't retired yet. And no cheap shots, please, about seeing if you could rectify that. You do know I was managing editor of my high school newspaper—the "Hi Jeff" (Jefferson High School, isn't that cute?) and isn't this the next logical step? It would only have to be temporary—just until I qualify for the loan.

Do you know anything about cars, Reid? I was thinking along the lines of a Bentley. I understand it's a pretty good car and, since the Revolution, the British always seemed to be there when we needed them. I was considering buying one of their cars as a gesture of good will.

I am very international in my tastes, having in my time purchased cars made in America (Studebaker—remember those, Reid? They ran on steam), and made by the losers of World War II: Italy (Fiat), Germany (Volkswagen, Audi, Daimler-Benz), Japan (Honda).

So I am thinking it is England's turn. What first attracted me to the Bentley was, believe it or not, the advertising for the Rolls Royce years ago when it was the same car, the only difference being the grille. The ad extolled the virtues of the Rolls Royce and, almost as an afterthought, said the Bentley was available for a couple hundred less for us discriminating and discerning patrons with a touch of diffidence—

Well, that was me, diffidence to the tip of my toes.

But I gotta tell you something, Reid. Until this very moment, when I looked up the word "diffidence," I thought it meant modesty. Not wanting to show off. Well, the *Oxford English* from guess where? says it is "Want of confidence, distrust of one's self." "Shyness of disposition" is buried in a morass of "Want of confidence in one's own ability."

A fine kettle of fish. Almost enough to put you off the Bentley. But I think, finally, that anyone who knows me knows that my driving a Bentley will be in keeping with my innate modesty and shyness of disposition. People who will at the same time understand that I am not wanting in confidence. Well, actually, maybe there is a time when I am wanting in confidence, and that is when I set out to buy a new car.

My first new car was a Fiat, bought with the soundest of reasoning: It was the cheapest car, bar none, available in the U.S. One trip across that same U.S. and some twenty thousand more miles, and pft—no more Fiat.

Reliability was my next quest. It led me to the Volkswagen Beetle. How could anyone resist those cute ads?—"How does the snowplow driver get to work?" Or "How to make a '54 VW look like a '64. Paint it." Or the pictures of the VW floating then sinking. "Because VW's definitely float, but not indefinitely. So drive around the big puddles, especially if they're big enough to have a name." Or the ad that headlined "LEMON," because the chrome strip on the glove compartment is blemished. "We pluck the lemons; you get the plums."

How long would a Bentley float? Selling that VW Bug may be the biggest mistake I ever made. Too bad they are no longer available. I wouldn't think twice about a Bentley. Except if my wife makes it in the Colonial Dames, I can't be seen driving her around in an old heap.

But holy smoke, Reid, you may have to get me quite a little increase. I just read that a new Bentley costs $250,000.

It certainly puts a strain on the old diffidence. Do you think they have 100-year mortgages? I still think my reasons for wanting the Bentley are sound. Can you help me out?

Ted

Dear Ted:

Used Bentleys are cheaper. I'll sell you mine.

Reid

Nudists Fuss Over Nothing

One of those heavy down-town newspapers is at it again, fomenting discord between the sexes.

John F. Lawrence, writing in a paper whose mega-circulation is built on tele-phone solicitation, claims sex bias still lives. He points his fin-ger at dry cleaners—and, parenthetically, at clothing manu-facturers.

Why should a woman pay more to clean a shirt than a man, and why more to buy one? The shirts are virtually the same.

Okay—why does a bikini, with its hardly-visible fab-ric, cost more than a tent for a healthy woman?

Whomsoever could conquer this dilemma would endear himself to the downtrodden women of the world, and make himself a tidy sum in the process.

I was man enough for the job, my wife insisted.

Peter Drucker, the widely-respected business manage-ment sage, says a businessman must analyze all the data and settle on his goal before he acts.

My goal was to find some garments for women that would be inexpensive to buy and cost less to dry-clean.

It seems the less fabric there is in a garment, the more expensive it is. From this hypothesis I deduced a theorem— "The Inverse Relationship Between the Cost of Yard Goods and the Yards the Goods Cover—or: You Can Afford to Have Less if You Are Only Willing to Pay More."

The natural extension of this theorem is, naturally, a natural line of apparel where the amount of fabric used in the designer's creations would be nil, thereby commanding the highest prices, as well as the highest visibility for the product, or lack of it.

After years of research, I have solved this dilemma for the women of the world with a completely dry cleaning-free apparel line of my own devising.

Nothing.

There is nothing less expensive to buy that needs less dry cleaning than Nothing.

Nothing should not be confused with NON—the National Organization of Nudists—which has peripherally benefitted from our campaign.

Nothing had all the earmarks of a profitable enterprise. Our start-up costs were very low—our material bills were nonexistent, labor was cheap and inventory warehousing presented no problem at all. Our overhead was next to nothing.

In all modesty, I think I had a natural flair for Nothing.

The promotion and marketing of natural apparel was a natural.

Nothing was a small company. Just the janitor, me and the two models who showed our line—Nothing.

They wore Nothing wherever they went, and created quite a stir.

And, of course, their dry cleaning bills were nil—and since they were employees of the company, as a fringe benefit we gave them a complete wardrobe of Nothing so they didn't have to pay more for clothing than men did.

We got a lot of free advertising with models wearing our line in magazines published by Messrs. Hefner, Guccione and Flynt, those eminent men of letters (usually 4 per word).

We bought some television time and turned out a cute dance routine to "I've Got Plenty of Nothing," but a few narrow-minded censors said we couldn't show the line without some serious cover-up editing that would not have shown the lines to their best advantage.

In periodicals, we advertised with nothing but a picture of a nude woman carrying a bag that had "Nothing" written on it. Above the woman were the words: "Nothing looks better than Nothing."

(Then the nude.)

Then at the bottom (of the page)

—"except Nothing."

It was a sensational campaign, but our message was lost somehow. The good news was that the campaign did coincide with an increase in nudity, so we know some people got some message.

It was a little rough on the apparel and dry cleaning industries, though.

I still think our reasoning was sound. If less is, in fact, more—and less demonstrably costs more—what would cost as much as Nothing?

Nothing.

Nothing would be more expensive than Nothing. Our fortunes should have been guaranteed. What was good for Nothing was good for the country.

But Nothing fails like success.

When my empire crumbled, a few people blamed me personally, but those who knew my work best admitted I was good for Nothing.

Our final tragedy was a class-action suit brought against us by a couple namby-pamby boys who claimed the Nothing line only looked good on women. Men were paying higher dry cleaning bills than women who wore Nothing. The fellas charged sex discrimination.

The plaintiffs won the suit (a rather loud racetrack gabardine, as I recall) and our models got Nothing.

But after all, when it comes to clothing, what is better than Nothing?

Nothing.

Pee-Wee, Gorby And Nurse Nancy

"Gorby?"

"*Da.*"

"Pee-wee."

"*Da!* Pee-wee Herman! Just what I need now, a couple laughs. I am here like the Volga boatman without, how you say? a paddle."

"Yeah, but, Gorby, I'm not laughing much these days—did you hear what the cops did to me in Sarasota?"

"Where is this Sarasota? On our Crimean?"

"No. It's in Florida."

"Black Sea? No matter, Pee-wee; I gotta tell you, at the moment I don't got too much, how you say? clout with the cops."

"I hear they got you locked up."

"*Da.* House arrest. You should see the goons they got guarding me. Apes!"

"From apes I can tell you, Gorby. Let me tell you what happened to me…I am sitting in this theater in Sarasota…"

"I got no clout, Pee-wee."

"No, no, Gorby, I'm not calling for clout—"

"Good! Commiseration I got plenty."

"So it's not your ordinary movie fare, Gorby. It is what you might say appealing to the more, how you say? prurient interests."

"*Da.*"

"Girls, you know. And boys—together. You know what they do together, Gorby?"

"*Da.*"

"Not a lot of wearing apparel. You know, Gorby?"

"*Da. Da.*"

"I don't have a girl at the moment. So I'm down here with mummy and daddy and, you know, Gorby, I'm a grown guy. Some people who've caught my kiddie shows will understand: a guy needs a break once and a while from his mummy and daddy."

"*Da.*"

"'Course, a lot of people think I'm just a kid 'cause of the way I carry on on the TV. But underneath, there beats a heart..."

"*Da*, of a horny adult. Ha ha ha, is a good joke, *nyet*?"

"Not today, Gorby."

"Sorry."

"The cops have time on their hands now, Gorby—they aren't looking for Communists anymore—you pretty much kiboshed that. Chasing drug dealers is way too dangerous—so three big fellas are on the X-movie theater circuit. A guy with his pants down is not liable to run very fast."

"They took my pants from me here. Extra precaution, they say."

"So this theater is showing *Nurse Nancy* and a couple other hot flicks—capisce?"

"*Da*."

"Not like Disneyland."

"*Nyet, nyet*. Disneyland was Khrushchev—*Nurse Nancy* I have seen when Raisa visit her mummy and daddy. Hot stuff!"

"They letting you watch flicks, Gorby?"

"*Nyet*. I have nothing. They say I am sick."

"Me too."

"I feel fine."

"Me too."

"So what the cops want with you, Pee-wee?"

"Ah, they say I am exposing my, you know, how you say...?"

"*Da*, Pee-wee."

"Yeah. So here I am, *alone* in the theater—nobody anywhere near me, and sure, maybe I'm scratching. The details are fading, Gorby."

"*Da*."

"Three goons, Gorby, you should have seen them—with flashlights. One minute Nurse Nancy is giving massage therapy to some poor stiff in the hospital, and the next minute, wham! the spotlight is on me."

"*Nyet*!"

"*Da*. So they haul me in. The papers have a field day and I'm off all my shows."

"Exactly what happened to me here, Pee-wee. Oh, oh, they are coming at me with the big syringe. They say I need medicine."

"Don't let them do it, Gorby! Don't take any injections—"

"No, wait, the injection is not for me. They want me back, Pee-wee, they want me *back*. I gotta, how you say? run, Pee-wee. I hope they take you back too."

"No chance, Gorby, this is a democracy."

Russell Baker Here I Come

I imagine certain editors and publishers very close to home are getting mighty nervous about losing a certain Saturday Observer to the Big Apple.

I speak, of course, of Russell Baker's announcement that he will no longer write his Sunday Observer column in the *New York Times Sunday Magazine*.

New York City, also known as the Big Bagel, the Big Tortilla, the Big Grits, the Big Mostaccioli, the Big Moussaka, and the Big Borscht, is a cosmopolitan city that might well be ripe for my talents.

It's no secret I have been compared countless times to Russell Baker (no relation to Mary, Jim, Tammy or Seth)—well, perhaps not always so favorably, but the important thing is, the one who leaps to so many minds when you mention Russell Baker, is me.

I would be a natural. Some may say there is some difference in the size of the papers we write for. While there may be some truth in that, scads of people are after me to apply for the job. At first I argued, thinking it more appropriate for the New York *Times* to make the first move.

Because of the prolonged, mysterious silence from

that quarter, I have been compelled to state my case.

I posted, posthaste, the following irresistible inquiry the moment I realized some unmentionable someone at the Peninsula *News* probably refused to give the New York *Times* my number when they called to check my availability.

Dear Editor or Editress as the case may be:

It has come to my immediate attention that you might be in the market for a replacement personage for Russell Baker and his Sunday Observer column.

For some time now, my close friends here have taken to calling me the Saturday Observer, in reference to my wonderful Saturday column in one of Southern California's larger newspapers, which you formerly owned.

Moreover, a lot of my family and friends say I am the obvious choice to fulfill this void in your Sunday tabloid because of my succinct and fascinating style and the distinctive character of my work, generally speaking, and I can't argue with them less.

I am famous through my work for my competent badinage, repartee, ripostes, and sundry parries, thrusts and circumlocutions, and, as you can see, I am at home with the gamut of big words, two dollars and above that are guaranteed to delight your diverse and dense readership, and I can use very swift and punchy sentences or good, intricate, often daringly-convoluted ones, like William Faulkner of old Mississippi used to use before he won the Nobel Prize for literary peaces and gave that memorable speech about blood and sweat and stuff before he passed on to his eternal reward that shut him up for good.

And you want short sentences. I'm your man. Like nobody's business. I am. I do it. All.

Though a complete résumé of my skills and activities would be far too long for your Sunday edition, let alone to fit in this envelope, I am enclosing a sheet that hits the highlights. I am, you will notice, instantly available, should that fit your special requirements.

RÉSUMÉ
TED GARDNER
AUTEUR

CAREER OBJECTIVES: To utilize my education, expertise, skills, talents, training (in alphabetical order; as alphabetizing also an added adjunct attainment. Attention also at an awesome aptitude at alliteration) to fulfill my manifest destiny with the New York *Times*.

EDUCATION: Definitely! In spite of the rumors.

RELATIVE EXPERIENCE: Various aunts, uncles, cousins; a brother, sister, mother, father; three wives and children.

REFERENCES: Reid Bundy and Seth Baker at the Peninsula *News* might tend to the negative side of things because they would naturally have unnatural fears of losing me. But feel free to call my mother anytime. You could call Bundy and Baker if you were willing to sign me to a nonexclusive contract. If you need me exclusively, it would give them the shakes, so I'd suggest sticking with Mom as the better part of valor.

AVAILABILITY: Instantaneous. A smooth transition could be made where you could continue to use Russell Baker's name until your readers got used to my succinct, sophisticated style, then we could switch the masthead from "Russell Baker" to "Ted Gardner" and probably nobody would notice old Russell was gone.

Dear Mr. Gardner:

Thank you for your interest in our Sunday Observer column.

I am pleased to offer you the daily New York Times *as well for only a few pennies more per week. I have taken the liberty to request the Subscription Department send you the complete information.*

We look forward to adding you to our rolls of satisfied daily subscribers, and I remain,

Sincerely yours,

Boots

I have just purchased a pair of boots. They cost me ten of these columns (before taxes), so they weren't too expensive, but I thought, with my last legitimate child through college, it was high time I threw caution to the wind and bought my first pair of boots.

At this time of life, men may sense a spirit of abandon. If so, they have several options:

1. Throw it all over and move to Big Sky, Montana.
2. Buy a red sports car.
3. Have their ears pierced.
4. Buy a pair of boots.

I bought boots.

You are probably dying to know how the boots changed my life. In a minute. First you should know I never coveted a red sports car. The color red may be all right on fire engines and real estate franchise blazers, but on cars? Not for me.

As for the Big Sky Country, it gets bitter cold.

Piercing the ears is another temptation entirely. I know a gray-haired burly electrician with a pierced ear stopped up with a turquoise ear plug, so delicate any woman would be proud to wear it. I know the linebackers have pierced ears, but I finally decided against it as being, well, *too* macho. If I was going to pierce anything, I decided, it should be my nose. It would be an act of fierce individualism. You don't even see many *women* with their noses pierced.

So I settled on boots. Hadn't I just seen a big-time movie star (Batman) clumping around in boots? Weren't boots meant to be man's answer to females' high heels? Sexy at the expense of ease of ambulation?

Because of my diffidence (see column on buying a Bentley motorcar), I took Henry Ford's advice and bought the basic black. Besides being able to wear black with just about anything, black is a slimming color. And there is nothing worse than fat feet.

I didn't want the cowboy look because I am not a cowboy and there is no use pretending. I mean, if I couldn't bring myself to buy a red sports car, cowboy boots were definitely out. Cowboy boots are for fellas with pierced ears.

I am sitting this very moment in my new boots. One must break them in, of course. I read a William Hamilton novel years ago, in which the main man had his chauffeur walk around breaking in his shoes. I don't have a chauffeur—I don't need one—Bentleys are cars for those diffident souls who want to drive themselves.

The boots give me a macho feeling at a time of life when macho is melting into wimpdom. Of course, I still have a little trouble *walking* in them, but sitting in them is fine.

I am sitting and imagining what it will be like when I can walk as naturally in my new boots as, well, walking.

Now the action is a little stiff and I look something like a storm trooper in his first parade.

But when I get going! Envision the eyes of the women, young as well as gray-haired Colonial Dames, following my every step. Their hearts and minds throbbing in cadence with these rakish, irresistible black boots. Dinner invitations cannot be far behind. I will get marriage proposals by the dozens. (It should be noted that I have no strong feelings against bigamy.)

I wouldn't be a bit surprised to witness more than one physical altercation between two or more females brought about by my black boots. Of course I would attempt to stop any fight over me in my presence, assuming I had by that time conquered the immobilizing effect of the new boots.

Walking in new boots is something like having your feet in concrete blocks (with apologies to Jimmy Hoffa, his friends and enemies). They aren't heavy, just stiff. The tops of them bang against your shins, the feet flop up and down inside the boot like a woman in strapless flats. The sole doesn't bend, so it is like you are walking with plywood strapped to your feet. You have to lift your feet and put them down flat, like climbing stairs without ever getting to the first step.

Cal Coolidge said, "Persistence pays," and I have no

intention of giving up. My wife, Ginny, has just come in. She is, you may recall, Colonial Dame material. Ginny has not seen me walk in my boots because I have frankly hoped to master the casual stride befitting a seasoned wearer of boots before I strutted my stuff in front of her.

She has her arms loaded and seems to be having trouble opening the front door.

Gallantly, I leap to the rescue. I bend, but the boots do not. I fall on my face and Ginny has a good laugh.

Contributing something original to the universal fund of knowledge, she says: "You must remember to take your boots off when you want to walk."

No good deed goes unpunished.

Don't Wait For Lefty

I just read something that has changed my life.

It is from a New York *Times* review of a book called *The Left-Hander Syndrome.*

"At age 10, 15 percent of the population is left-handed...But by age 50, the percentage...drops down to 6 and by age 80, there are virtually no left-handers left. None.

...It is not because 80 years ago left-handers were forced to become right-handed whereas today's left-handers are accepted. No. Left-handers disappear because they die earlier."

The piece is entitled "Don't Wait for Lefty, He's Dead." A cute bastardization of the title of a play by that incorrigible left-winger Clifford Odets.

You-know-who is left-handed. And you-know-who is within shouting distance of 79 (the last year that can be hoped for). "Geez," I lamented to my long-suffering spouse, "things are looking bleak. Says here there are no left-handers who live to be even 80."

"Oh, your parents are 88 already," she said, missing the point.

"They're not left-handed," I said. "Do you know anyone over 80 who is left-handed?"

"Not offhand."

"You see."

"Ah, maybe you are really right-handed—but you switched to be different," she said, with an engaging naivete.

Within a half-hour I had experienced a mild heart attack as well as a brain tumor.

Spousal support? Spousal sympathy? None existent. She actually had the temerity to laugh off these serious life-threatening maladies. Frankly, I should have expected, under the circumstances, an outpouring of sympathy, deference, consolation and accommodation from the distaff, whose real name is getting harder and harder for me to remember. It is something like Veronica, but that will have to do for the nonce, as those pretentious writers are wont to say. Under the circumstances I think it best to save her the embarrassment of disclosing her shocking treatment of her husband, whose days, as they say, are numbered.

For example—a helpful suggestion made without any expectation of reward about her driving, was met with scornful physical force which caused, I'm sure, the beginnings of cancer in the subject.

She has also taken (indignity of indignities) to calling me "Lefty." My subsequent reactions became more self-indulgent. I ate some of Veronica's hamburger. Had a lead-solid chocolate cake for dessert.

Joseph Epstein, raconteur editor of *The American Scholar,* gave up smoking when the health nuts scared him out of his wits. He misses it. He has vowed if he lives to be 85 (he's right-handed, so he has a chance), he will take it up again.

I don't covet cigarettes, but what would you say to a motorcycle? They have some really sleek-looking ones these days and they get lots better mileage than a Bentley. Though, coming to think of it, who am I saving gas for? The supply should certainly last my left-handed lifetime.

I would be curious to see at just what age lefties zero out. There seems a gap in this research between 50 and 80, a range where I just happen to fall. But how about 75? Any lefties left? Or, should I say, any remaining? 66? 58? He doesn't tell us where the drop comes. The precipitous drop into the void. Coming to think of it, all the left-handers I notice are young.

Why would I want to know? Well, it will help me negotiate the price on the motorcycle. Help me gauge how hard a bargain to drive.

This motorcycle yen is not a mid-life macho thing. I took care of that when I bought my boots.

It is said there are only two kinds of motorcyclists: Those who have had accidents, and those who are going to. But, heck, I might not live long enough to have an accident.

Seriously, what age is the oldest surviving left-hander you know? Let me know, I'd be so relieved.

It was little comfort to see Veronica reading bank statements for the first time in her life. I tell her not to worry until the bank does.

"You know, I must say, you seem so blissfully unconcerned about the fate of your husband, who, according to statistics, is on his last legs."

"I never think about death, Lefty," she says in that way you can just tell she feels superior.

"Why should you?" I ask. "You're right-handed."

Dr. Gotrocks

On these PV *News* pages I read a new investment advice column under the heading "Investment Decisions."

Funny that in the late '50s I too had an investment column. I was known in those days as Dr. Gotrocks. Oh, maybe we were dealing with more modest amounts, but the advice was just as sound.

Luckily, I saved a few of the Gotrocks columns that might be savored today.

Dear Dr. Gotrocks:

I am a single woman, and, frankly, some people have told me I'm not terribly attractive. I might make an argument I wear my pounds well, but, I am told, if a young woman isn't as cute as a bug in a rug and wants to compete on today's marriage market, she has to have a little gelt on her bones. And let us face it, at forty-one-and-a-half I am not what you would call young anymore. So my question concerns how to get the gelt—that is, how do I go about building that all-important nest egg dowry on a salary of $80 a week?

Strapped

Dear Strapped:

Well, the old adage "A penny saved is a penny earned" sure holds true today, just as it did centuries ago when it was first uttered.

I have done some quick calculations and I estimate, with deductions, you must be taking home better than $50 a week. With normal expenses (no extravagances like a dinner out or the movies), I figure you should be able to salt away two, three dollars a week. At that rate, I don't see any reason why after thirty years or so you wouldn't have a nest egg that would attract the eye of any number of eligible bachelors.

And, if you are a little old at that time and the sexist pigs only have eyes for younger models, you can blow your dowry on yourself. There is a widely-held opinion that marriage might be overrated.

*   *   *

Dear Dr. Gotrocks:

My broker is recommending zero-coupon Treasury bonds. I don't understand why these securities don't pay any interest.

Perplexed,
Twenty-two years old and single

Dear Perplexed:

You have raised an interesting point. Zero-coupons pay zero until maturity. From the look of your letter, you are a long way from maturity and should probably steer clear of those little gems.

*   *   *

Dear Gotrocks:

I am in need of divesting myself of some investments to meet increasing personal expenses and wonder if you could tell me what to hang on to for the long haul to maximize my appreciation. I have Series E War Bonds and an ugly Van Gogh oil painting.

Sign me,
Confused

Dear Confused:

Series E War Bonds are backed by the full faith and credit of the U.S. Government, and safety of capital is a prime consideration in this market.

The Van Gogh oil is another matter. I must confess the name didn't mean anything to me, so I went to the library and looked him up. He is not an old master, so the value of his stuff is problematical. I did discover that he never sold one painting in his lifetime. That should tell you something! Who knows, you may have bought the first one. I wouldn't expect it to keep pace with inflation, and since you characterize it as "ugly" anyway, I don't see any sense in hanging on.

* * *

Dr. Gotrocks:

I have been married to the same man going on sixty years. And he's so darn tight, he squeaks. I know he's got some cash stashed somewhere, but darned if I can find it. He's such a light sleeper I don't dare go traipsing around at night. I have two questions:

1. How do I find the dough?
2. What shall I put it in if I find it? CDs, or what?

Sneaky

Dear Sneaky:

First, knock him out with sleeping pills in his warm milk, or use a baseball bat. It is essential you render him unconscious or you just won't be able to locate the stash. When you find it, consider several things:

1. How much you find. If it is only seven dollars and change, I say buy a hamburger and fries and forget it. If you find real money, you've got to

2. Consider your age. Married going on sixty years, you aren't spring chickens. Most counselors would have you seek stability and income. *"Au contraire,"* I say. At your age it's time to have a blast.

I'm saying put half of the cash in pork bellies futures. Take the other half to Vegas and put it on thirty-six on the roulette table. You'll have as good a chance with that as anything else I could recommend. And if the pork bellies belly-up, at least you'll have something to eat.

Birds Of A Feather

It is a mystery to me why I was not consulted on the peafowl controversy. My credentials are impeccable.

One local faction thinks peacocks are lovely, another says they make too much noise. There is even the suggestion of some poisoning. These drastic measures are not necessary. I have a solution.

The front page lead article by PV *News* staffer Chris Fortain makes several delightful points.

Espinosa Circle is the target area for peacock removal. A recent census indicates there are 23 males to 15 females there. That is, I suppose, if all the peacocks answered the census questions honestly.

There are a lot of similarities between peafowl and people, as we shall see. Fudging to the census taker is only one of them.

Dr. Martin Rigby, the expert hired by Palos Verdes Estates to study the birds, addresses this chicanery with refreshing candor:

"The problem is you have to start early in the morning to count the birds and do it quickly so they don't get ahead of you and make you accidentally recount them."

Indeed. Tricky as any Homo sapiens trying to outwit the tax gatherers.

The *piece de résistance* of the PV *News* opus is:

"Rigby explained that historical data shows that peafowl follow a one-third, one-third, one-third reproduction personality. That is, one-third are too young to mate, one-third is interested in mating and one-third is less interested in mating."

Precisely like people.

It is the later third, the old peacocks, that squawk the loudest. With 23 males to 15 females in Espinosa Circle alone, who can blame them?

It is the Homo sapiens male in his declining third of the mating cycle (still interested, but hopelessly inept) who is most affected by the noise.

This striking similarity was first brought to light in my fowl doctoral thesis, entitled:

"The Musicality of the Male Post-Menopausal Peafowl and its Effect on the Audio Responses of the Human Male in the Same Predicament."

Another example of Dr. Rigby's inexplicable obtuseness is the quote in the PV *News*: "In an urbanized environment there have probably been very few studies on peafowl population. This study here in Palos Verdes Estates will make its own history."

The fact is, he is just plain unfamiliar with my work.

I am not jealous of Dr. Rigby, as some fowl experts would have it—just because he got his doctorate and I missed mine by a hair's-breadth because of fowl academic politics.

I don't see why he should be jealous of me.

Dr. Rigby recommends trapping and deporting elder male peafowl to make the remaining males equal in number to the females. This is blatant sex discrimination, and ineffective.

Any fowl expert familiar with my work will realize the futility of this ploy.

My solution is not to deport the old males but to import young females. Like Homo sapiens, the females of any species have a calming influence.

The idea goes way back in this country. In the early days the males were raucous and unruly. There weren't enough women to go around. The females were imported by the boatload to quiet the nerves of the unruly men. It worked.

It can work for an old peacock too.

Instead of trapping the old males to correct the imbalance between the sexes, they should import some young chicks. The squawks will turn to coos.

What the "experts" don't realize is that the older males are squawking because there are not enough females to go around. If you indiscriminately take away the squawking old males, the old females will suddenly feel ignored and start squawking themselves.

So the solution is to add females—young ones—to soothe those crusty birds in the declining third of their lives.

This plan is the triple-edged sword.

1. The new young females will keep the harmless old males happy—and quiet.

2. The old females will be content. They know the old males will sooner or later wise up and settle for an old bird.

3. The true balance of nature will be restored. The old-third males, those on the mating wane, have hopes of re-entering the second third of the mating game with a young pea chick from the first third.

It will seldom happen, but hope springs eternal in the peacock's breast.

Peace will be restored between peacock and man.

Neither will squawk.

Play It Anew, Sam

With all the fuss over the re-release of a film called *Casablanca*, I was suckered into seeing it. Though I had a potful of film classes at the institute of higher learning in South-Central Los Angeles, I don't remember seeing *Casablanca*. Of course, my memory may not be what it used to be—I couldn't say, because I don't remember what it used to be.

Anyway, if you haven't seen *Casablanca*, save your money. The thing is about fifty years old and believe me, if this is any indication, they had no clue about making movies then.

First of all it wasn't even in color. How much better this might have been if we could have seen Ingrid Bergman's rosy cheeks. But what am I talking about? We hardly saw anything of Ingrid Bergman. There wasn't one nude scene in the entire picture.

Sure, there were a couple of bright lines, but this is the *movies* not radio. Not one of the women even held a gun in her hand. Car chases were nonexistent. No one ran through the city sewer system. Nobody was built like Schwarzenegger, nobody climbed walls or walked through them. A rain scene was as dangerous as it ever got.

A good movie today will give you a smack of violence every three minutes. Not here. There wasn't even one of my favorite scenes where the lead goes into a room and tears it apart, pulling things from the shelves, smashing glass, you know the bit. It gets more deliciously exciting every time you see it. Why, there's more excitement in the average modern preview than in all of *Casablanca*.

Movies sure have come a long way in 50 years. And as movies get older, the protagonists get younger. Ask any Hollywood producer today and he'll tell you if you don't appeal to the kids, you're dead in the water.

The only hope for *Casablanca* is a remake. Humphrey Bogart is no longer of this world, so you get Sylvester Stallone, the Italian Stallion, for his part. For Bergman's part, Julia Roberts and her body double for the nude stuff.

You get Spielberg or somebody with some special effects savvy to direct it, and you blow the saloon sky-high with Nazi bombs. Have the Gestapo chasing Stallone through the streets (Julia Roberts under his left arm, his right hand on a nonstop blazing Uzi, while Julia shoots an automatic pistol that never runs out of bullets). And just at the crucial moment, a sixteen-year-old boy and his fourteen-year-old girl friend (who are fleeing the Nazis and hope to hop a boat in Casablanca for the U.S.A.) step out and cause the Nazis (who really have hearts of gold) to swerve to avoid killing them; and in the most spectacular car crash ever filmed, they careen off each other into and out of shop windows, tearing through hanging salami, provolone, pickled cabbage and plucked chickens. Meanwhile, the teenagers slink off to an alley where they engage in a torrid "love" scene (obligatory). Meanwhile, the Nazis have got their cars under control and, infuriated that they lost Stallone and Julia Roberts by their humanitarian act, start hunting the teenagers, without whom, moviewise, you are dead in the water. Revenge in their hearts of now-tarnished gold, the Nazis turn into the alley where the aforementioned teens are in the throes of you-know-what, which they had heretofore been accomplishing in semi-darkness. But now the Nazis' headlights flash on their gleaming young skin as the Mercedes touring car heads for the romantic kids.

The teens are on the horns of a dilemma. Make no mistake about that. Will true love triumph, or will it be compromised by evil forces? And if the kids stop what they are doing, what chance would they have, half-dressed (the wrong half), against a speeding Mercedes hell-bent on destruction and mayhem? In that split second, love triumphs as the couple decides to die happy.

Fortunately, on the roof of the building above is Sly Stallone, the Italian Stallion, in a Batman costume. He leaps off the roof, his Uzi blazing, lands on the neck of the Nazi driving the Mercedes, swerves the wheel at the last possible moment, avoids hitting the blushing teenagers, crashing instead into a fire hydrant, sending water gushing three stories high to drench Julia Roberts (or her body double, as the case may be).

Julia has the best of intentions about jumping off the roof with the Italian Stallion, but her pants are so tight she can't move. Now, drenched as she is in water, it is completely out of the question.

The kids decide to marry, even if she isn't pregnant. Sly Stallone retraces his steps to the roof where he is surprised to see the girl he fell in love with was not Julia Roberts, but her body double. "No skin off my rear," Julia says, and as soon as her pants dry she proves it.

Now there's a *real* film.

Wooden Ships And Iron Men

They decided it would be best if I didn't speak at my father's funeral. The fear, not unfounded, was that I might tell some jokes as I have been known to do at the most awkward moments, and in that neck of the Pennsylvania woods people take their funerals seriously.

He would have been relieved. There is in the family an eye for propriety. While my father had a sense of humor, he also had a public face, and the twain seldom met. He was always uncomfortable at my outrageous roasts of him at the many celebrations in his honor.

He was, for a short period of his legal career, a judge. He was appointed by the governor of Pennsylvania to fill the unexpired 12-month term of a guy who died with his boots on.

He stood for reelection facing a Sunday school teacher who would have been lucky to boast half my father's legal acumen. Though my father was a believer and a faithful churchgoer, he had his share of human frailties. Some characterized the contest as a race between a mediocre saint and a dazzling sinner. The saint won, don't they always?

"No matter," my father espoused on the bright side, "I can still be called 'Judge,' and that's the important thing. That title is for life."

And no one got more mileage out of a title since the Kentucky colonel. But it should not be surprising the title was important to him. He was the quintessential bootstrapper.

My father was born in the latter third of a family of nine children in a small row house on a narrow street in Allentown, Pa., which the indelicate might call an alley. They slept four to a room, two to a bed.

At 15, he forged a new birth certificate and ran away from home to help make the world safe for democracy. He liked to say he was in the Navy when they had wooden ships and iron men.

He finished high school at night, and, hearing there was money to be had for ministerial students, he signed up for the ministry. When that didn't pan out, he got a job as a chauffeur for the athletic director. He worked the angles. You had to to get out of the alley.

He was the only one of the nine siblings to go to college, not to mention law school which he attended on a senatorial scholarship provided him by the undertaker's grandfather. It is difficult to imagine our father as a minister, though I expect he could have met the challenge.

His father never owned a car. None of his five sisters ever drove a car. Other than my father, I don't believe any of the nine children were ever on an airplane, or ventured over fifty miles from their birthplace.

He sent all of his children to college, and two thirds of the brood to law school. The guy from the alley made it easier on the offspring.

Of all the euphemisms for death, my father loved "He cashed in his beer checks." It was a saying born of the Depression, when he began his practice of law. Barter was the mode of survival. Many brewers and bar owners gave beer checks in exchange for goods and services. When a man died, his widow cashed in the beer checks.

The Judge, as we called our father, was a creature of ceremony. He wanted an open casket so people could look at him dead. This practice I find a little barbaric. But I was given more advantages.

Twenty-some years ago I asked him how long he wanted to live. He said he wanted to live to see his first grandchild (my oldest daughter) married.

He made it with a year and a half to spare.

My brother, a judge; and nephew, a district attorney, gave superb talks at the memorial service to the assembled seven judges and numerous friends. The night before, over three hundred people stood in the snow in a line around the block to pay their respects. You would have thought Lenin was in his tomb. He would have been pleased.

On the death certificate there is a square headed

"Occupation for major part of life." In it is typed "Judge." He would have been pleased.

He was buried next to the Rodales of the Rodale Press. The health nuts who died younger than he did. The Judge would not have known a bean sprout if he fell on it.

I noticed the marble headstone for the Rodales was the largest in the cemetery, prompting me to suggest we get one larger.

"Will you pay for it?" I am asked.

"I'll pay the difference," I said, "if I may have editorial control of the epitaph." My idea was:

Here lies
Judge Theodore Roosevelt Gardner
Born August 14, 1904
Cashed in his beer checks
March 15, 1992
He served his country
when they had wooden ships
and iron men.
The wooden ships have
long since splintered and decayed
And now he lies here
getting rusty.

The other survivors nixed the sentiment.

He would have been pleased.

INDEX

Off The Wall

Order your extra copies of *Off The Wall* at $17.95 each.

Also by Ted Gardner:

The Paper Dynasty

The Paper Dynasty is a fictional account of the most remarkable 4 generation family in the country. It is the story of how the Los Angeles Times newspaper family triumphed over all their rivals spanning 100 years and how they made the sleepy cowtown on the western edge of nowhere into a leading metropolis. What they kept out of the paper, Gardner put in his book.

"Spellbinding ...rooted in History." --Robert Lindsey, author of A Gathering of Saints, and The Falcon & the Snowman

"A damn good read." Vint Lawrence, The New Republic

"Crackling entertainment" --Publishers Weekly   **$23.45**

. . . .

Please send me ______ hardcover copies of **Off The Wall** ISBN 9637297-7-9 at $17.95 each/U.S. and Canada. (Please add $1.95 per order to cover postage and handling.)

Please send me_______hardcover copies of **The Paper Dynasty** ISBN 0-9627297-0-1at $23.45 each/U.S. and Canada. (Please add $1.95 per order to cover postage and handling.)

I enclose:

☐ check ☐ money order (no cash or C.O.D.s) or charge my ☐ Master Card ☐ Visa.

Card#__________________________   Exp. Date_____________

Signature____

Name of Business_____________________________________

Name____

City_____________________State_____Zip Code_____________

Telephone number(s)___________________________________

Mail to: Allen A. Knoll, Publishers, 625 East Victoria
Santa Barbara, CA 93103   1-800-777-7623